The Next Crash

Lessons from 1929 and Warning Signs for Today's Markets

J.F. Sachs

Copyright and Legal Disclaimer

Copyright Notice

Legal Disclaimer and Important Information

PLEASE READ THIS DISCLAIMER CAREFULLY BEFORE READING THIS BOOK

Investment Advice Disclaimer

This book is presented solely for educational and informational purposes. The author and publisher are not offering it as legal, accounting, investment, financial, or other professional services advice. While best efforts have been used in preparing this book, the author and publisher make no representations or warranties of any kind and assume no liabilities of any kind with respect to the accuracy or completeness of the contents. Neither the author nor the publisher shall be held liable or responsible to any person or entity with respect to any loss or incidental or consequential damages caused, or alleged to have been caused, directly or indirectly, by the information or advice contained herein.

The content of this book should not be construed as financial advice, investment advice, trading advice, or any other sort of advice. Nothing in this book constitutes a solicitation, recommendation, endorsement, or offer by the author, publisher, or any third party to buy or sell any securities or other financial instruments.

All investment strategies and investments involve risk of loss. No information contained in this book should be construed as investment advice. Any reference to an investment's past or potential performance is not, and should not be construed as, a recommendation or as a guarantee of any specific outcome or profit.

No Guarantee of Results

Past performance is not indicative of future results. The historical examples and case studies presented in this book are provided for illustrative purposes only. They do not guarantee that similar results can or will be achieved in the future. Market conditions change, and strategies that worked in the past may not work in the future.

The author makes no representations, warranties, or guarantees, expressed or implied, that following the strategies, advice, or recommendations presented in this book will result in profitable trading or investing, will not result in losses, or will improve your financial situation. Investment results will vary, and losses are possible.

Personal Responsibility

You are solely responsible for your own investment and financial decisions. Before making any investment decision, you should conduct your own research and due diligence, and consult with qualified financial, legal, tax, and other professional advisors as appropriate to your personal circumstances.

The author and publisher strongly recommend that readers consult with their own investment advisors, attorneys, accountants, and other professionals before making any investment or financial decisions. Every reader's financial situation is unique, and the strategies discussed in this book may not be suitable for all individuals.

Forward-Looking Statements

This book contains forward-looking statements, opinions, and predictions about future market conditions, economic trends, and potential investment outcomes. These statements are based on current expectations, estimates, and projections about future events and are subject to inherent uncertainties and risks.

Forward-looking statements are not guarantees of future performance. Actual results may differ materially from those expressed or implied in forward-looking statements due to various factors including, but not limited to:

- Changes in economic conditions
- Market volatility and fluctuations
- Changes in laws, regulations, and tax policies
- Geopolitical events and international developments
- Natural disasters and pandemics
- Changes in investor sentiment and behavior
- Technological disruptions
- Other risks and uncertainties that cannot be predicted or quantified

The author and publisher undertake no obligation to update or revise any forward-looking statements, whether as a result of new information, future events, or otherwise.

Market Risk and Volatility Disclosure

All investments involve risk, including the potential loss of principal. The securities markets can be volatile, and the value of investments can fluctuate significantly. There is no guarantee that any investment strategy will achieve its objectives or avoid losses.

Different types of investments involve varying degrees of risk, and there can be no assurance that any specific investment or investment strategy will be profitable or suitable for a particular investor's financial situation or risk tolerance.

Leverage, derivatives, options, and other complex financial instruments involve additional risks and may not be suitable for all investors. These instruments can magnify both gains and losses and may result in the loss of more than your initial investment.

No Client Relationship

The content of this book does not create a client relationship, advisory relationship, or fiduciary duty between the reader and the author or publisher. The author is not acting as your financial advisor, investment advisor, broker, or agent.

If you need personalized investment advice, you should seek the services of a qualified professional who can evaluate your specific circumstances and objectives.

Information Sources and Accuracy

While the author has made every effort to ensure the accuracy of information presented in this book, information is provided "as is" without warranty of any kind. The author and publisher make no guarantees about the completeness, reliability, or accuracy of this information.

Information about companies, securities, markets, and economic conditions is subject to change. Historical data and statistics are derived from sources believed to be reliable but have not been independently verified. The author and publisher assume no responsibility for errors or omissions in the content of this book.

Third-Party References

This book may contain references to third-party websites, products, services, or publications. These references are provided for convenience only and do not constitute an endorsement or recommendation by the author or publisher. The author and publisher have no control over, and assume no responsibility for, the content, privacy policies, or practices of any third-party sites or services.

Hypothetical Performance

Any hypothetical performance results or back-tested data presented in this book have inherent limitations. Unlike actual performance records, hypothetical results do not represent actual trading and may not reflect the impact of market factors such as liquidity constraints, slippage, fees, and commissions.

Hypothetical or simulated performance results have certain limitations. Unlike an actual performance record, simulated results do not represent actual trading. Since trades have not actually been executed, results may have under- or over-compensated for the impact of certain market factors. No representation is being made that any account will or is likely to achieve profits or losses similar to those shown.

Tax Considerations

The tax treatment of investments discussed in this book may vary depending on your individual circumstances and jurisdiction. Tax laws are complex and subject to change. The information provided in this book should not be construed as tax advice.

You should consult with a qualified tax professional regarding the tax implications of any investment or financial strategy before implementation. The author and publisher are not responsible for any tax consequences resulting from actions taken based on information in this book.

Indemnification

By reading and using this book, you agree to indemnify, defend, and hold harmless the author, publisher, and their respective officers, directors, employees, agents, licensors, and suppliers from and against all losses, expenses, damages, and costs, including reasonable attorneys' fees, resulting from any violation of these disclaimers or any activity related to your use of this book, including negligent or wrongful conduct.

Changes and Updates

The author and publisher reserve the right to make changes, corrections, and updates to the content of this book at any time without prior notice. Information in this book may become outdated, and the author and publisher have no obligation to update such information.

Financial markets, economic conditions, regulations, tax laws, and investment products change frequently. Readers are responsible for staying informed about current conditions and should not rely solely on information that may be outdated.

Acknowledgment

BY READING THIS BOOK, YOU ACKNOWLEDGE THAT YOU HAVE READ THIS DISCLAIMER, UNDERSTAND IT, AND AGREE TO BE BOUND BY ITS TERMS. If you do not agree with any part of this disclaimer, you should not read or use this book.

Author's Note

While the legal language above is necessary to protect all parties, the spirit of this book is to educate and empower you as an investor. The strategies and frameworks presented here are based on extensive research and historical analysis, but they are not substitutes for personalized professional advice.

Investing is personal. Your risk tolerance, time horizon, financial situation, and goals are unique. Use this book as a foundation for your own thinking and decision-making, but always remember that you are ultimately responsible for your own financial future.

The goal of this book is to help you navigate uncertain markets with greater confidence and understanding, not to guarantee specific outcomes or eliminate all risks. Markets will always involve uncertainty and risk. The question is whether you'll face that uncertainty with knowledge and preparation or without them.

I wish you wisdom, discipline, and success in your investing journey.

J.F. Sachs

Table of Contents

Introduction

On September 3, 1929, the Dow Jones Industrial Average reached 381.17, a record that would stand for a quarter century. Investors celebrated what seemed like the beginning of a new era of permanent prosperity. The market had risen relentlessly for years, driven by technological revolution, easy credit, and the widespread conviction that the old rules no longer applied. Anyone suggesting caution was dismissed as hopelessly out of touch with the modern world.

Seven weeks later, on October 29, 1929, Black Tuesday the market collapsed. By mid-November, nearly forty percent of the peak value had evaporated. Fortunes built over years disappeared in days. Investors who'd bought on margin faced total ruin. Banks failed. Companies collapsed. What followed was not a quick recovery but the Great Depression, a decade-long economic catastrophe that fundamentally reshaped American society.

The crash didn't come from nowhere. The warning signs were visible to those willing to see them: extreme valuations disconnected from earnings, rampant speculation by inexperienced investors, dangerous levels of leverage, growing wealth inequality, stagnant wages even as asset prices soared, and the persistent belief that "this time is different." A few clear-eyed observers recognized the danger and warned of disaster. Most were ignored.

Nearly a century later, I'm writing this book because those same warning signs are flashing again.

Why This Book, Why Now

I need to be clear from the start, I don't know when the next major crash will occur. It might happen before this book reaches publication. It might not happen for another decade. Anyone claiming to predict the exact timing of market crashes is either delusional or dishonest.

But I do know with certainty that another crash is coming. Not because I possess mystical insight into the future, but because crashes are inherent features of financial markets. They've occurred throughout history, the Tulip Mania of 1637, the South Sea Bubble of 1720, the Panic of 1907, the crash of 1929, the bear market of 1973-1974, the 1987 Black Monday, the tech bubble of 2000, the housing crisis of 2008, and countless others across centuries and continents.

Crashes happen because human psychology interacting with financial systems creates recurring patterns of euphoria, speculation, excess, and eventual collapse. The specific catalysts change from tulips, railroads, technology stocks to subprime mortgages but the underlying dynamics remain remarkably consistent. We convince ourselves that new technologies or policies have ushered in a "new era" where old limitations no longer apply. We leverage ourselves to amplify returns. We dismiss warnings as outdated thinking. And then, inevitably, reality reasserts itself.

What makes this moment particularly concerning isn't any single indicator, it's the confluence of factors that echo previous market peaks. The parallels between the 1920s and today are striking enough to warrant serious attention:

Then: The Federal Reserve maintained easy money policies through most of the 1920s, fueling credit expansion and asset speculation. **Now**: Zero interest rate policies and quantitative easing from 2008-2021 created an unprecedented flood of liquidity that inflated asset prices across every category.

Then: Margin buying allowed investors to purchase stocks with just ten percent down, amplifying both gains and losses. **Now:** Retail options trading, especially zero-days-to-expiration (0DTE) contracts, provides similar leverage. Private equity and venture capital deploy record amounts of borrowed money. Corporate debt levels have reached historic highs.

Then: Investment trusts, essentially unregulated funds that used leverage to buy other investment trusts created dangerous pyramids of speculation. **Now:** SPACs, private credit markets, structured products, and complex derivatives create similar layering of risk and opacity.

Then: Stock ownership became democratized as ordinary Americans poured money into markets, often borrowing to do so. **Now:** Commission-free trading apps and social media have created an army of retail investors trading options, meme stocks, and cryptocurrencies with little understanding of the risks.

Then: A widening gap between soaring asset prices and stagnant wages for most Americans created instability. **Now:** Wealth inequality has reached levels not seen since the 1920s, with asset owners prospering while wage earners struggle.

Then: Faith in new technologies such as electricity, radio and automobiles convinced investors that traditional valuation metrics no longer mattered. **Now:** Enthusiasm for artificial intelligence, blockchain, and other innovations justifies valuations that would have seemed absurd by historical standards.

Then: Respected voices warning about overvaluation were dismissed as dinosaurs who didn't understand the modern economy. **Now:** Well... some things never change.

These parallels don't guarantee an imminent crash, history doesn't repeat precisely. But they suggest we're in a period of elevated risk that demands serious preparation.

What This Book Is and Isn't

This book is not a prediction that markets will crash tomorrow, next month, or even next year. I'm not going to tell you to sell everything and hide in a bunker. I'm not a permabear who has been predicting crashes for decades while markets rose (though we'll examine why such voices, while often wrong on timing, sometimes serve a valuable purpose).

What this book provides is a framework for understanding crash dynamics, recognizing warning signs, and positioning yourself to survive and potentially profit from the next major market dislocation whenever it arrives.

We'll start by examining the 1929 crash in detail, understanding not just what happened but why it happened. The Roaring Twenties weren't simply a period of irrational exuberance, they were a complex interplay of monetary policy, technological change, financial innovation, psychological factors, and structural economic imbalances. Understanding these dynamics provides invaluable context for today.

Then we'll systematically examine today's markets through the same lens, looking at leverage, speculation, valuation metrics, behavioral indicators, and structural risks. Not to create a laundry list of doom, but to develop a clear-eyed assessment of where risks are concentrated and how elevated they are relative to history.

We'll explore the experiences of investors who successfully navigated previous crashes and those who didn't. Jesse Livermore made a fortune shorting the 1929 crash but died broke and broken. Michael Burry correctly predicted the 2008 housing collapse but nearly lost his fund while being early. Paul Tudor Jones profited enormously from the 1987 crash but built his lasting success on risk management principles, not crash predictions. Their stories contain crucial lessons about the difference between being right and staying solvent.

Perhaps most importantly, we'll examine what happens after crashes, the false rallies, the second legs down, the grinding bear markets that destroy hope more thoroughly than any single day of panic. Understanding these patterns won't let you time the market perfectly, but it can prevent the catastrophic mistakes that turn temporary losses into permanent capital destruction.

Finally, we'll discuss practical strategies for navigating uncertain times. Not market timing systems or get-rich-quick schemes, but frameworks for building portfolios that can handle extreme volatility while still participating in long-term wealth creation. The goal isn't predicting crashes, it's surviving them with your capital and confidence intact.

Who Should Read This Book

This book is for investors who recognize that markets are expensive and fragile but aren't sure what to do about it. You don't want to miss continued gains if markets keep rising, but you're worried about catastrophic losses if they crash. You're looking for the middle path between complacency and paralysis.

It's for anyone who wants to understand market history and cycles without becoming a professional economist or trader. The concepts here are sophisticated but the explanations are accessible. You don't need a PhD in finance to benefit from this analysis.

It's for professional investors and portfolio managers who feel pressure to stay fully invested despite private concerns about valuations. You'll find both intellectual frameworks and practical ammunition for more defensive positioning.

It's for anyone still haunted by losses from 2008 (or 2000, or any previous crash) who wants to be better prepared next time. The psychological scars from previous crashes often prevent investors from building wealth in subsequent bull markets, understanding the full cycle can help break that pattern.

It's for young investors who've only known bull markets and haven't experienced a genuine bear market. Your biggest risk isn't the next crash, it's your reaction to it. Building mental frameworks now, while markets are calm, can prevent catastrophic decisions later.

This book is not for day traders looking for timing signals or get-rich-quick strategies. It's not for permabears seeking confirmation that everything is terrible (though you'll find plenty of concerning data). And it's not for those who want simple, definitive answers, the reality of markets is complex and uncertain, and this book respects that complexity.

A Note on Predictions and Humility

I've spent thousands of hours studying market history, crash dynamics, valuation frameworks, and behavioral finance. I've analyzed the 1929 crash, the 1973-1974 bear market, the 1987 Black Monday, the 2000 tech bubble, and the 2008 financial crisis. I understand the warning signs and the patterns that typically precede major dislocations.

And yet I cannot tell you with certainty when the next crash will occur.

This isn't false modesty, it's intellectual honesty. The timing of crashes is inherently unpredictable because it depends on catalysts we can't foresee and psychological tipping points we can't measure with precision. Markets can remain overvalued for years. Warning signs can flash red for a decade.

The specific trigger that finally breaks the camel's back is usually something that seems minor at the time.

What I can tell you is that risk is elevated. Valuations are extreme by historical standards. Leverage is widespread. Speculation is rampant. These conditions have preceded every major crash in history. They don't guarantee a crash tomorrow, but they should inform you how you position your portfolio today.

This book embraces uncertainty rather than pretending it doesn't exist. I'll show you frameworks for assessing risk, but I won't promise perfect foresight. I'll provide strategies for defensive positioning, but I won't claim they'll let you avoid all losses. I'll examine warning signs in depth, but I'll acknowledge their limitations for precise timing.

The goal is to help you navigate an uncertain future skillfully, not to pretend we can eliminate uncertainty entirely. Because the investors who survive crashes aren't those who predict them perfectly, they're those who build enough resilience to weather them whenever they arrive.

The Road Ahead

The structure of this book follows a logical progression. We'll start with history, understanding the 1929 crash and its aftermath in detail. Then we'll examine today's markets systematically, looking at parallels and differences. We'll explore the psychology of crashes and the experiences of those who navigated them successfully (and those who didn't). We'll discuss what happens after crashes, the often-overlooked period that's more dangerous than the initial plunge. Finally, we'll turn to practical strategies and action steps.

Each section builds on the previous ones, creating a comprehensive framework for understanding crashes and positioning yourself appropriately. You can read straight through or jump to sections most relevant to your concerns, though I'd recommend reading Part I (the 1929 crash) even if you're tempted to skip to current markets, as the historical foundation provides crucial context for everything that follows.

Throughout, I've tried to balance intellectual rigor with readability, detailed analysis with big-picture thinking, historical lessons with contemporary applications. My goal is to provide a book that's both informative enough for sophisticated investors and accessible enough for anyone willing to engage seriously with the material.

One Final Point

If you're reading this hoping for reassurance that everything is fine and you should ignore the permabears, this isn't that book. The warning signs are real. The risks are elevated. The parallels to previous market peaks are too striking to dismiss.

But if you're reading this hoping for permission to liquidate everything and hide in cash until the crash passes, this isn't that book either. That strategy has destroyed more wealth through opportunity cost than most crashes destroy through direct losses.

What I'm offering is a third path: eyes wide open about risks, but still engaged and building wealth. Defensive without being paralyzed. Cautious without being dogmatic. Prepared for crashes while hoping they don't happen soon.

Because here's the truth that underpins everything in this book: crashes are inevitable, but so is long-term wealth creation through markets. The goal isn't choosing between these realities, it's learning to live with both simultaneously.

The next crash is coming. But so is the recovery that follows it, and the bull market after that, and eventually another crash, and another recovery, on and on for as long as markets exist. Success doesn't come from avoiding this cycle, it comes from navigating it skillfully enough to survive the downs and participate in the ups.

That's what this book will teach you to do.

Now, let's begin with a journey back to 1929, not as ancient history but as a mirror showing us what we're becoming.

Part I: The Roaring Twenties - Origins of the 1929 Crash

Chapter 1

The Post-War Boom

The morning of November 12, 1918, dawned on a world transformed. The previous day, at the eleventh hour of the eleventh day of the eleventh month, the guns had finally fallen silent across the Western Front. After four years of mechanized slaughter that had consumed ten million lives and left Europe's economic infrastructure in ruins, the Great War was over. Americans, who had entered the conflict relatively late but with decisive effect, returned home to a nation that stood alone among the great powers, physically untouched by war, its factories humming, its fields abundant, and its coffers swelling with gold as European nations paid for American supplies.

Yet the immediate post-war period brought not celebration but crisis. The transition from wartime to peacetime production proved chaotic. Factories that had churned out artillery shells and military uniforms suddenly found their government contracts canceled. Soldiers flooded back into a labor market unprepared to absorb them. In 1919, inflation surged as pent-up consumer demand collided with supply constraints. Workers, watching their wages lose purchasing power, launched a wave of strikes that swept through industries from steel to coal to even the police forces of major cities. The Red Scare gripped the nation as authorities, watching the Bolshevik Revolution in Russia with alarm, saw communist agitation behind every labor disturbance.

The sharp recession of 1920-1921 seemed to confirm the pessimists' worst fears. Unemployment spiked, prices collapsed, and banks failed by the hundreds. Agricultural prices, which had soared during the war years as American farmers fed not only their own nation but much of Europe, crashed spectacularly. Wheat that had sold for $2.50 per bushel in 1919 fetched less than a dollar by late 1921. Farmers who had borrowed heavily to expand their acreage during the boom years found themselves underwater, unable to service debts that now exceeded the value of their land.

But something remarkable happened next. By late 1921, the economy began to recover, and unlike previous post-war adjustments, this recovery accelerated into something unprecedented in American history. The decade that followed would be marked by such sustained prosperity, such spectacular technological transformation, and such infectious optimism that it would earn a name reflecting its exuberant spirit: the Roaring Twenties. This boom would create the preconditions for the greatest financial crash in American history, but in the early 1920s, such concerns seemed absurd. America was entering a New Era, and the old rules no longer applied.

The Engine of Transformation

At the heart of the 1920s boom lay a technological revolution as profound as any the world had witnessed. Three transformative technologies, the automobile, the radio, and electrification reshaped not just the economy but the very fabric of American life.

The automobile led the charge. When Henry Ford introduced the Model T in 1908, automobiles were luxury playthings for the wealthy, hand-crafted machines that cost several years' wages for the average worker. Ford's innovation of the moving assembly line, perfected at his Highland Park plant in 1913, changed everything. By breaking down the complex task of building a car into simple, repetitive motions that could be performed by relatively unskilled workers, Ford slashed production time from twelve hours to ninety minutes. The efficiency gains were passed along in lower prices. A Model T that cost $850 in 1908 sold for just $260 by 1925.

The impact rippled through the entire economy. In 1919, there were roughly 6.7 million registered automobiles in America. By 1929, that number had exploded to more than 23 million, nearly one car for every five Americans, a level of automobile ownership that wouldn't be matched in Europe for another forty years. The automobile industry alone came to account for one in every nine manufacturing jobs. But the indirect effects dwarfed even this massive direct impact.

The demand for automobiles created voracious appetites for steel, glass, rubber, and petroleum. The steel industry boomed, developing new alloys and production techniques. The rubber industry transformed from producing primarily industrial belting and bicycle tires to an enormous enterprise dependent on vast plantations in Southeast Asia and Africa. The petroleum industry, which had previously focused largely on kerosene for lighting, found a far larger market in gasoline and launched a frenzied search for new oil fields. Discoveries in Texas, Oklahoma, and California made America the world's dominant oil producer.

The automobile reshaped the physical landscape. America in 1920 had perhaps 369,000 miles of paved roads, most of them in or near cities. By 1929, aggressive road-building programs had created more than 662,000 miles of paved highways, with hundreds of thousands more miles graveled or improved. This infrastructure boom employed hundreds of thousands of workers and consumed mountains of concrete, asphalt, and steel. The Federal Highway Act of 1921 established federal aid for highway construction, marking a new level of government involvement in economic development.

Beyond the roads, the automobile enabled the birth of entirely new industries and reshaped existing ones. Gas stations sprouted on street corners. Motels appeared along highways. Tourist cabins, diners, and roadside attractions catered to a newly mobile population. The automobile freed factories from needing to locate near railroad lines, enabling industrial dispersion. It allowed workers to live farther from their jobs, accelerating suburban development around major cities. Saturday afternoon drives became a national pastime. The automobile court replaced the front porch as a center of social life for young people, with consequences that alarmed moralists of the era.

While the automobile revolutionized ground transportation, the radio created a revolution in communication and entertainment. When Pittsburgh's KDKA broadcast the results of the 1920 presidential election, only a handful of amateur enthusiasts heard the transmission. Yet within just a few years, radio transformed from a hobbyist pursuit into a mass medium that united the nation as never before.

The growth was explosive. In 1922, there were perhaps 60,000 households with radio receivers. By 1929, more than 10 million American homes, roughly 40% of all households owned radios. Early radios were finicky crystal sets requiring headphones and considerable technical skill to operate. By the late 1920s, plug-in models with loudspeakers made radio accessible to anyone who could afford the purchase price, which fell steadily as production scaled up.

Radio created shared national experiences. For the first time, Americans in Maine and California could listen to the same news broadcast, the same baseball game, the same musical performance. The 1927 heavyweight boxing match between Jack Dempsey and Gene Tunney drew an estimated radio audience of 50 million people, nearly half the nation listening simultaneously to a single event. When Charles Lindbergh completed his solo flight across the Atlantic that same year, radio brought the news to the nation within minutes, creating an instant national hero.

The commercial implications proved enormous. Radio drove demand for electronic components, creating a substantial manufacturing sector. Companies like RCA, Westinghouse, and General Electric became household names. Radio advertising, initially controversial, became an accepted and then dominant form of marketing, creating the foundation for consumer culture. National brands could speak directly into people's homes, creating demand for products that local retailers had no choice but to stock. The economic power of radio networks became so significant that they shaped everything from popular music to political campaigns.

But perhaps no development was more fundamentally transformative than the spread of electrical power. In 1912, only 16% of American manufacturing establishments used electric power. By 1929, that figure had soared to 70%. The implications extended far beyond simple statistics.

Electric power liberated factories from the constraints of steam power and belt-driven machinery. Older factories had clustered machines around a central power source, with leather belts transferring power from overhead drive shafts. This arrangement was inflexible, dangerous, and inefficient. Electric motors allowed each machine to have its own power source, enabling rational factory layouts designed around production flow rather than power transmission. Factories could spread horizontally rather than stacking vertically. Production lines became possible. The efficiency gains were spectacular, manufacturing productivity soared.

Electrification reached beyond factories into homes and businesses. In 1912, only 16% of American homes had electricity. By 1927, that figure had risen to 63%, and in urban areas, electrification was nearly universal. Electric lighting replaced gas and kerosene lamps, reducing fire hazards and improving quality of life. But electricity's impact went far deeper.

Electric power enabled a revolution in household appliances that began to free women from the grinding labor of housework. Electric irons replaced sad irons that had to be heated on stoves. Vacuum cleaners replaced carpet sweepers and rugs that had to be beaten. Electric washing machines began to displace the washboard and tub. Refrigerators started to replace iceboxes, eliminating the need for daily deliveries from the iceman and reducing food spoilage. Each of these innovations represented a substantial purchase, driving consumer spending and manufacturing employment.

The electric power industry itself became a major economic force. Utility companies invested billions in generation plants, transmission lines, and distribution networks. Entrepreneurs like Samuel Insull built vast utility empires spanning multiple states. The demand for electricity seemed insatiable, doubling between 1920 and 1929, and the industry's growth appeared to validate the era's faith in perpetual progress.

The New Industrial Order

These technological revolutions reshaped not just what Americans produced but how they produced it. The 1920s saw the triumph of scientific management, mass production, and industrial standardization.

Frederick Winslow Taylor's principles of scientific management, first articulated before World War I, found their fullest application in the 1920s. Taylor's time-and-motion studies broke down every task into its component movements, identifying and eliminating wasted effort. His principles emphasized planning, standardization, and the systematic training of workers to perform tasks in the most efficient manner. Critics attacked Taylorism as dehumanizing, reducing workers to mere cogs in an industrial machine, but employers embraced it enthusiastically for its ability to boost output per worker.

Henry Ford took these principles further, combining them with the moving assembly line and high wages to create a new industrial model. Ford's famous $5 day, introduced in 1914, nearly doubled prevailing wages and attracted worldwide attention. Ford understood that high wages created a virtuous cycle: well-paid workers could afford to buy the products they made, creating consumer demand that justified further expansion. Moreover, high wages reduced turnover, allowing workers to develop skills that boosted productivity even in supposedly unskilled jobs.

The Ford model influenced industries far beyond automobiles. Manufacturers across sectors adopted assembly-line production, breaking complex products into simple components that could be assembled by semi-skilled workers using standardized parts. The result was spectacular productivity growth. Manufacturing output per worker-hour rose by roughly 40% during the 1920s, one of the most rapid gains in American history.

This productivity revolution had profound implications. Rising productivity meant that fewer workers could produce more goods. Some economists warned that technological unemployment would become a crisis as machines displaced workers. But the 1920s seemed to prove these worries unfounded. While employment in some sectors declined, coal mining for instance shed workers as oil replaced coal, the overall economy created millions of new jobs in growing industries. Automobile factories, radio plants, and electrical equipment manufacturers hired enthusiastically. The service sector expanded rapidly. And new industries emerged seemingly overnight.

The benefits of productivity growth, however, were distributed unevenly. Corporate profits soared, rising from about $4 billion in 1921 to more than $10 billion by 1929. Stockholders reaped enormous gains. Top executives saw their compensation packages balloon. But ordinary workers' wages, while rising, grew far more slowly. Real wages for manufacturing workers increased by perhaps 20% during the decade, a respectable gain but a fraction of the increase in productivity and profits.

This divergence had consequences that would only become apparent later. Consumer spending drove the economy, but consumers' ability to spend ultimately depended on their incomes. As wealth concentrated at the top, the broad mass of Americans found their purchasing power growing more slowly than the economy's capacity to produce goods. Credit would bridge this gap temporarily, but the underlying tension would eventually help bring the boom to a catastrophic end.

The Birth of Consumer Culture

The 1920s marked the decisive shift from a production-oriented economy to a consumption-oriented one. For most of American history, the economic problem had been how to produce enough goods to meet basic needs. By the 1920s, for the first time, American industry could produce more than consumers needed for mere subsistence. The challenge became convincing people to buy beyond their immediate needs to embrace consumption as a value in itself.

Advertising became the handmaiden of this cultural transformation. The industry exploded during the 1920s, with expenditures rising from $1.4 billion in 1919 to more than $3 billion by 1929. Advertising evolved from simple product announcements into sophisticated psychological manipulation. Practitioners like Edward Bernays, nephew of Sigmund Freud, applied insights from psychology to make advertising more effective. Bernays and his contemporaries understood that effective advertising sold not just products but lifestyles, aspirations, and identities.

Advertisers created anxieties to sell solutions. Bad breath, previously not recognized as a social problem, became a source of embarrassment that Listerine could cure. Body odor became "B.O.," a shameful condition that demanded Lifebuoy soap. Halitosis, that dreaded condition, required specialized products. Women learned they needed different products for each body part and each time of day. Men discovered that only certain brands conveyed the image of success. The implicit message was clear: you could buy your way to social acceptance, romantic success, and personal fulfillment.

National brands dominated as never before. Coca-Cola, Lucky Strike cigarettes, Palmolive soap, and dozens of other brands became household names coast to coast, their ubiquity established by massive advertising campaigns. Chain stores like A&P, Woolworth's, and later grocery chains displaced local merchants, offering lower prices through volume purchasing but also homogenizing the retail landscape.

Consumer credit made the transformation possible. Before the 1920s, credit for consumer purchases was generally limited to running tabs at local stores. Middle-class people paid cash or saved until they could afford major purchases. Going into debt for consumption was considered improvident, even immoral. The 1920s overturned this moral framework.

Installment buying became respectable, then commonplace. By 1929, roughly 60% of automobiles, 70% of furniture, 75% of radios, and 80% of phonographs were purchased on credit. The typical arrangement required 20-30% down and monthly payments spread over one to two years. Finance charges added significantly to the total cost, but the allure of immediate possession overcame older habits of thrift.

Credit democratized consumption while creating new vulnerabilities. Families could enjoy automobiles, appliances, and entertainment without waiting years to save. But they also became dependent on continued income to service debts. If income faltered, the entire structure could collapse. During the boom years, however, such concerns seemed unduly pessimistic. Incomes were rising, jobs were plentiful, and the future looked bright.

The "New Era" Psychology

By the mid-1920s, a powerful belief had taken hold: America had entered a New Era in which the old rules no longer applied. Economic cycles, those alternations of boom and bust that had characterized capitalism since its inception, were thought to be things of the past. Science, technology, and enlightened management had conquered economic instability.

This confidence had multiple sources. The Federal Reserve System, established in 1913, was believed to have created a mechanism for stabilizing the economy. By adjusting interest rates and managing the money supply, the Fed could smooth out economic fluctuations, preventing both inflation and deflation. The severe recession of 1920-1921 had been followed by rapid recovery, which some attributed to wise Federal Reserve policy. When the economy expanded steadily through the mid-1920s with low inflation, faith in the Fed grew.

The unprecedented productivity gains reinforced New Era thinking. If productivity rose perpetually, prosperity could continue indefinitely. Corporations would generate ever-larger profits, stock prices would rise to reflect those profits, and everyone would grow wealthy. Some economists and business leaders proclaimed that America had discovered the secret to permanent prosperity.

President Calvin Coolidge embodied this optimism. His famous declaration that "the business of America is business" captured the era's faith in free enterprise. Coolidge believed that the best government policy was to let business operate with minimal interference. Tax cuts, particularly on high incomes and corporate profits, would encourage investment and growth. Regulation should be light. The market, given freedom, would generate prosperity.

For most of the decade, events seemed to vindicate this philosophy. The economy expanded, unemployment remained low, and the stock market climbed steadily. Coolidge's Treasury Secretary, Andrew Mellon, one of the wealthiest men in America, implemented tax cuts that reduced the top rate from 73% to 25%. Corporate taxes fell as well. The wealthy saved enormous sums, which they invested heavily in the stock market and other assets.

The New Era psychology created a self-reinforcing cycle. Optimism about the future encouraged investment and consumption. Investment and consumption drove economic growth. Economic growth validated the optimism, encouraging further investment and consumption. Rising stock prices created a wealth effect, making stockholders feel richer and more willing to spend. The system seemed perfect, a perpetual motion machine of prosperity.

Dissenting voices were few and largely ignored. A handful of economists and observers questioned whether the boom was sustainable. They pointed to warning signs: agriculture remained depressed throughout the decade, industrial production showed signs of plateauing by late 1928, and stock prices had clearly detached from underlying business fundamentals. But such pessimism was dismissed as the carping of old-fashioned thinkers who failed to understand the New Era.

The mood of the times was captured in a thousand ways: the frenetic energy of jazz, the defiant hedonism of flappers, the architectural ambition of skyscrapers racing higher, the literary celebration of wealth in Fitzgerald's novels. America was young, rich, and modern. The future belonged to those bold enough to seize it. The generation that had survived a world war and a pandemic was determined to enjoy its prosperity. And enjoy it they did, right up until the moment the music stopped and the lights went out, and they discovered that the New Era was as subject to the old laws of gravity as every era before it.

But that reckoning still lay ahead. In the mid-1920s, as production soared and stock prices climbed and the cash registers rang, America believed it had found the formula for permanent prosperity. The crash, when it came, would be proportional to that confidence, devastating precisely because it had seemed impossible.

Chapter 2

Easy Money and Speculation

In the spring of 1928, a Chicago housewife named Mrs. Martha Nelson made a decision that would have been unthinkable just a few years earlier. Using $500 she had saved from her household budget, she opened an account with a local brokerage firm and purchased shares in Radio Corporation of America. Within six months, her investment had doubled. She borrowed against those shares to buy more stock. By the following spring, her portfolio was worth $3,000. Mrs. Nelson was hardly unique. Across America, millions of ordinary citizens, teachers, doctors, shopkeepers and secretaries were playing the stock market with borrowed money, convinced they had discovered a path to easy wealth.

The great bull market of the 1920s stands as one of history's most spectacular episodes of financial mania. Between 1924 and September 1929, the Dow Jones Industrial Average rose from 95 to 381, a gain of more than 300% in just five years. But the raw numbers only hint at the frenzy that gripped the nation. The stock market became a national obsession, a topic of discussion in barbershops and beauty parlors, at dinner parties and factory lunch breaks. Shoe shine boys offered stock tips. Taxi drivers discussed the latest movements in General Motors or U.S. Steel. The market seemed to offer a democratic path to prosperity, open to anyone with a few dollars and enough daring to take the plunge.

What transformed the stock market from a mechanism for capital formation into a casino for mass speculation? The answer lies in a toxic combination of easy credit, financial innovation, lax regulation, and the psychological momentum of rising prices. Understanding this alchemy is crucial, for its essential elements would reappear in later bubbles, each time dressed in contemporary garb but driven by the same fundamental forces.

The Federal Reserve and the Flow of Money

At the heart of the 1920s boom lay the policies of the Federal Reserve System. Created in 1913 in response to the banking panics that had periodically paralyzed the economy, the Fed was designed to provide an "elastic currency", the ability to expand and contract the money supply to meet the economy's needs. In practice, however, the Fed's actions during the 1920s fueled the speculative fires that would eventually consume the economy.

The Fed's primary tool was the discount rate, the interest rate at which it would lend to member banks. By lowering this rate, the Fed made it cheaper for banks to borrow, encouraging them to extend more loans. By raising the rate, the Fed could tighten credit and slow economic activity. Through much of the 1920s, the Fed kept rates relatively low, particularly during crucial periods when a more restrictive policy might have cooled speculative enthusiasm.

The most consequential decision came in the summer of 1927. The American economy was slowing slightly, and European central banks, struggling with gold outflows and economic weakness, pleaded with the Fed to lower rates. The goal was to make dollar-denominated investments less attractive, reducing capital flows from Europe to America. In July 1927, the Federal Reserve Bank of New York, led by the influential Benjamin Strong, cut its discount rate from 4% to 3.5%.

The rate cut worked too well. Instead of merely stabilizing international capital flows, it unleashed a wave of speculation that dwarfed anything seen before. Stock prices, which had already been rising steadily, began a parabolic ascent. The Dow Jones Industrial Average, which stood at 152 in July 1927, would reach 300 by the end of 1928 and peak above 380 in September 1929. The cut has been called "the beginning of the end," the moment when the Federal Reserve, in attempting to help European central bankers, lit the fuse that would eventually detonate the American economy.

But the Fed's culpability extended beyond any single rate decision. Throughout the mid-1920s, the Fed maintained policies that kept money relatively easy even as speculation intensified. The reasoning seemed sound at the time: consumer prices remained stable, showing little inflation. Traditional economic theory suggested that if prices weren't rising, monetary policy wasn't too loose. What the Fed failed to recognize, or chose to ignore, was that easy money was flowing not into consumer goods but into assets such as stocks, real estate, and other investments whose rising prices didn't show up in the consumer price index.

This analytical blind spot would have enormous consequences. The Fed was fighting the last war, focused on preventing the inflation that had plagued the immediate post-World War I period. It missed the asset bubble forming under its nose, or when members did notice, they convinced themselves that rising stock prices reflected genuine improvements in business prospects rather than speculation. After all, corporate earnings were growing. Productivity was rising. Perhaps stocks deserved higher valuations.

Some Federal Reserve officials recognized the danger. Adolph Miller, a member of the Federal Reserve Board in Washington, warned repeatedly about the speculative excess and urged tighter policy. But Miller and other skeptics faced determined opposition from Benjamin Strong and other regional Fed bank presidents who believed the economy could sustain both growth and rising stock prices. The institutional structure of the Federal Reserve, which divided power between the Board in Washington and twelve regional banks, made decisive action difficult. Consensus was elusive, and by the time consensus formed around the need for tighter policy, the situation had spiraled beyond control.

Margin Buying: Leverage for the Masses

While Federal Reserve policy set the monetary backdrop, it was the mechanics of stock market trading that transformed easy money into speculative mania. The key was margin buying was the ability to purchase stocks with borrowed money which democratized leverage and allowed small investors to make enormous bets.

The concept of buying on margin was not new. Sophisticated investors had long used borrowed money to amplify returns. But what changed in the 1920s was the scale and the participants. Margin buying became accessible to ordinary Americans, and the terms became progressively more generous as brokers competed for business.

Here's how it worked: An investor who wanted to buy $1,000 worth of stock didn't need $1,000 in cash. Instead, he might put up only $100, a 10% margin and borrow the remaining $900 from his broker. The stock itself served as collateral for the loan. If the stock rose to $1,200, the investor could sell, repay the $900 loan plus interest, and pocket a profit of perhaps $280 on his $100 investment, a 280% return. This leverage was intoxicating.

Of course, leverage worked both ways. If the stock fell to $900, the investor had lost his entire $100 stake. If it fell below $900, he would face a margin call, a demand to put up additional cash to maintain the required margin percentage. Failure to meet a margin call meant the broker would sell the stock, locking in the loss. But during the great bull market, such scenarios seemed remote. Stocks went up, and leverage magnified the gains.

Margin requirements, the percentage of a stock's price that had to be paid in cash varied but grew progressively lax as the boom intensified. In the early 1920s, 50% margins were common. By 1929, margins had fallen to 10% or even lower on some accounts. An investor could control $10,000 worth of stock with just $1,000 in cash. The rest was borrowed, either from the broker directly or through call loans, short-term loans from banks to brokers that could be called (demanded back) at any time.

The statistics are staggering. Margin debt, money borrowed to buy stocks rose from about $1 billion in early 1926 to $8.5 billion by October 1929. To put that in perspective, margin debt grew from roughly 2% of the value of all stocks on the New York Stock Exchange to nearly 20%. In a $40 billion stock market, $8.5 billion was borrowed money. This created enormous fragility. If stock prices fell, margin calls would force selling, which would push prices lower, triggering more margin calls in a potentially catastrophic cascade.

The lenders who provided call loans were attracted by the returns. Interest rates on call loans ranged from 6% to 12%, and sometimes spiked higher during periods of heavy demand. These were attractive rates compared to other safe investments, and the loans were supposedly secure, they were backed by stock collateral and could be called at any time. Banks began diverting resources from traditional commercial lending to call loans. Corporations discovered they could earn better returns lending to stock brokers than investing in their own businesses. Even money from overseas flowed into the call loan market, drawn by the combination of high returns and apparent safety.

This created a perverse situation: the more stock prices rose, the more money flowed into call loans, which funded further stock purchases, which pushed prices higher still. The system had become a self-reinforcing cycle, a feedback loop that amplified every upward movement. As economist John Kenneth Galbraith would later observe, the effect was "to substitute for the customary orderliness of a continuing process a kind of explosive culmination."

Ordinary Americans, observing their neighbors growing wealthy through stock market speculation, felt an overwhelming pressure to participate.

The fear of missing out, a psychological force as powerful in the 1920s as in any later era drove people to take risks they would never have considered in calmer times. The social pressure was intense. At parties, conversations turned inevitably to the market. Those who had profited were admired; those who had missed out were pitied. The few voices urging caution were dismissed as old-fashioned killjoys who didn't understand the New Era.

Investment Trusts: Leverage upon Leverage

If margin buying represented financial leverage for individual investors, investment trusts provided leverage for the system as a whole. These vehicles, the precursors to modern mutual funds but operating under far looser rules, proliferated wildly in the late 1920s and became perhaps the most dangerous innovation of the era.

The concept seemed sound enough. An investment trust would raise money from public investors and use that money to purchase a diversified portfolio of stocks. Small investors who couldn't afford to build diversified portfolios themselves could buy shares in the trust, gaining instant diversification and professional management. In theory, this made sense. In practice, investment trusts became vehicles for speculation, self-dealing, and leverage that magnified the eventual crash.

The growth was exponential. In 1926, there were perhaps 160 investment trusts with total assets of about $450 million. By 1929, there were nearly 750 trusts with assets exceeding $8 billion. New trusts were launched almost daily, often with great fanfare and immediate public enthusiasm. Some were sponsored by reputable financial institutions, but many were created by promoters whose primary goal was personal enrichment rather than investor welfare.

The problems were manifold. First, many investment trusts were grotesquely leveraged. They didn't merely use the money raised from shareholders to buy stocks; they borrowed additional money, sometimes doubling or tripling their purchasing power through debt. A trust might raise $10 million from shareholders, borrow another $10 million, and invest $20 million in stocks. If those stocks rose 20%, the trust's equity would increase 40% (before debt service costs). But if stocks fell 20%, the trust's equity would be wiped out, and shareholders would lose everything. This leverage magnified both gains and losses.

Second, many trusts engaged in pyramiding where investment trusts own shares in other investment trusts. A parent trust would create subsidiary trusts, buying shares in those subsidiaries with money raised from its own shareholders. The subsidiaries might create their own sub-subsidiaries in turn. The result was a towering structure of leverage upon leverage, with the same underlying stocks owned multiple times through different corporate layers. When the pyramid collapsed, the losses would cascade through every level.

Third, investment trusts often engaged in self-dealing that enriched insiders at shareholders' expense. Sponsors would sell stocks to their trusts at inflated prices, pocketing the difference. Management fees were often excessive, sometimes calculated on gross rather than net assets, rewarding managers even when investment performance was poor. Some trusts traded actively to generate brokerage commissions that flowed to affiliated firms. Conflicts of interest were rampant and largely undisclosed.

Fourth, many investment trusts made wildly speculative investments that bore little resemblance to their stated conservative objectives. Trusts that claimed to provide safe, diversified exposure to American industry would invest heavily in unproven ventures, foreign securities of dubious value, or concentrated positions in a few high-flying stocks. The diversification benefits that supposedly justified the trusts' existence often proved illusory.

The most famous example was the Goldman Sachs Trading Corporation, launched in December 1928 with great fanfare and initial capital of $100 million. Goldman Sachs, already a prestigious investment bank, lent its name and reputation to the venture. The initial public offering was oversubscribed, and shares quickly rose from their $104 issue price to $136. Goldman Sachs Trading Corporation then created the Shenandoah Corporation and the Blue Ridge Corporation, which in turn created their own subsidiaries. The complex structure involved layers of leverage and cross-ownership that few investors understood.

When stock prices peaked in September 1929, Goldman Sachs Trading Corporation shares traded around $326. By 1932, they would be worth $1.75, a loss of 99.5%. Investors who bought at the peak lost virtually everything. The Goldman Sachs name, once synonymous with financial probity, became associated with one of the era's most spectacular failures. The damage to the firm's reputation would take decades to repair.

Investment trusts were not the only financial innovations that amplified speculation. Holding companies, particularly in the utility sector, created similar pyramids of leverage. Holding companies would own operating companies, which generated actual revenues from selling electricity or gas. But the holding companies themselves would be owned by other holding companies, creating multiple layers of equity claims on the same underlying cash flows. Samuel Insull, the utility magnate, constructed a holding company empire so complex that even sophisticated analysts struggled to understand it. When the structure collapsed, it would take Insull and thousands of investors down with it.

The Democratization of Speculation

Perhaps the most striking feature of the late 1920s speculation was its democratic character. Previous financial manias had been largely confined to professional investors and the wealthy. The 1920s stock boom reached deep into the middle class and even the working class.

Brokerage firms opened branch offices in cities and towns across America, making it easy for ordinary citizens to open accounts. Some firms advertised aggressively, promising wealth through stock market participation. The messages were seductive: "Why work for a living when you can make money in the stock market?" or "Invest in American prosperity!" The firms made the process simple, offering to handle all the details while the customer merely approved trades.

Stock market tickers became fixtures in public spaces. Brokerage offices installed large boards where crowds could watch stock prices update throughout the trading day. It became a form of entertainment, a spectator sport where anyone could participate. The crowds watching ticker tapes were as absorbed as sports fans following a baseball game, cheering rallies and groaning at setbacks.

The financial press, which expanded dramatically during the 1920s, fed the obsession. Multiple daily newspapers in major cities carried extensive stock tables and market commentary. Weekly magazines like The Saturday Evening Post and Collier's ran articles about investing, often written with breathless enthusiasm about the opportunities available. Books promising to unlock the secrets of stock market success became bestsellers. Jesse Livermore, the most famous speculator of the era, was profiled endlessly, his methods analyzed and his success envied.

Financial tipsters and advisors proliferated. Some were legitimate analysts attempting to evaluate stocks based on financial fundamentals. But many were charlatans who made money from selling advice rather than following it themselves. Newsletters promised inside information or secret systems for beating the market. Market "services" claimed to have discovered patterns in stock prices that could predict future movements. The advisory business was essentially unregulated, allowing anyone to hang out a shingle and claim expertise.

What's striking in retrospect is how few people questioned the sustainability of the boom. The warning signs were clear to anyone who looked. Stock prices had detached from any reasonable relationship to earnings or dividends. Price-earnings ratios, which historically averaged around 15, had climbed above 30 for many leading stocks. Dividend yields, which had traditionally provided much of stocks' total return, had fallen to negligible levels as investors focused entirely on price appreciation. Yet these fundamental metrics were dismissed as old-fashioned thinking, irrelevant in the New Era.

The rationalizations were creative. High price-earnings ratios were justified by expectations of future growth. Low dividend yields didn't matter because companies could reinvest retained earnings at high rates of return. The old relationships between stock prices and tangible metrics like book value were said to undervalue the worth of intangible assets like brand names and management quality. Every traditional valuation metric that suggested overvaluation was explained away.

Some observers did recognize the danger. Paul Warburg, a respected banker and one of the architects of the Federal Reserve System, warned in March 1929 that the speculative orgy would end badly. Roger Babson, a statistician and market analyst, repeatedly predicted a crash. Alexander Noyes, the financial editor of The New York Times, cautioned against speculation throughout 1928 and 1929. But these voices were drowned out by the chorus of optimism, and those who heeded them missed the final months of spectacular gains that preceded the crash.

The Psychology of Mania

Understanding the mechanics of easy money and leverage is essential, but it doesn't fully explain why millions of rational people convinced themselves that borrowed money invested in overvalued stocks represented a prudent course of action. The psychology of financial manias, which would be studied extensively by later economists and behavioral psychologists, was on full display in the late 1920s.

Several psychological forces converged. First was the recency bias, the tendency to extrapolate recent trends into the indefinite future. Stocks had risen for years. Everyone who had bought stocks had made money. It seemed obvious that stocks would continue rising, making it foolish not to participate. The longer the boom lasted, the more firmly people believed it would continue. Each passing month without a crash reinforced the conviction that no crash was coming.

Second was social proof, the tendency to look to others' behavior when uncertain how to act. When neighbors, coworkers, and family members were all making money in the stock market, abstaining seemed perverse. If everyone else was doing it, it must be right. The fear of being left out overwhelmed natural caution. Nobody wanted to be the fool who stayed on the sidelines while everyone else got rich.

Third was the confirmation bias, the tendency to seek out information confirming what one wants to believe while dismissing contradictory evidence. Investors devoured bullish market commentary while dismissing bearish warnings as the carping of bitter pessimists. Every uptick in stock prices confirmed the wisdom of being invested. Every prediction of doom that proved premature discredited the doomsayers and validated the optimists.

Fourth was the illusion of control, the belief that one could get out before the top, that one would recognize when the party was ending and exit before the crash. Many investors understood intellectually that prices couldn't rise forever, but they believed they would be smart enough to sell before the inevitable reversal. This illusion was reinforced by the fact that there had been corrections during the bull market, brief periods when prices fell before resuming their rise. Those who had bought during dips and profited when prices resumed climbing felt they had mastered the art of market timing.

Fifth was the wealth effect, the feeling of being richer that comes from rising asset prices, even before those gains are realized. As stock portfolios swelled in value, investors felt wealthier and spent more freely. This spending boosted the economy, which seemed to validate the stock market gains, creating a self-reinforcing cycle. The wealth was largely on paper, dependent on continued price appreciation, but it felt real enough to change behavior.

Finally, there was the factor of trust in authority. When respected business leaders, economists, and even government officials proclaimed that the economy was fundamentally sound and stock prices were justified, ordinary people took comfort. Irving Fisher, one of the most prominent economists of the era, famously declared in October 1929 that "stock prices have reached what looks like a permanently high plateau." That statement, made just days before the crash, would haunt Fisher for the rest of his life, but at the time it reassured investors that their faith was warranted.

The psychology of speculation creates its own momentum. Rising prices attract attention, attention attracts new buyers, new buyers push prices higher, which attracts still more attention in an accelerating cycle. The momentum becomes self-sustaining until some shock disrupts the psychology, at which point the cycle reverses with equal or greater force. The descent can be far faster than the ascent, because fear is a more powerful emotion than greed, and the need to meet margin calls creates forced selling that accelerates the decline.

By the summer of 1929, the stock market had become unmoored from economic reality. Easy money from the Federal Reserve, amplified by margin debt and investment trust leverage, had created a speculative bubble of unprecedented magnitude. The democratic character of the speculation meant that millions of Americans had become financially vulnerable in ways they didn't fully comprehend. The stage was set for catastrophe. All that was needed was a trigger, some event that would puncture the collective delusion and start the terrible unraveling that would define the next decade of American history.

Chapter 3

Warning Signs Ignored

The greatest tragedies in financial history share a common characteristic: they were entirely preventable. The 1929 crash was no exception. In the months and years preceding Black Thursday, a chorus of warning signs echoed through the American economy, each one a flashing red light that went unheeded by a public drunk on unprecedented prosperity. The story of these ignored warnings is not merely historical curiosity, it is a psychological study in human nature's dangerous tendency to mistake a bull market for genius and to confuse the absence of immediate consequences with the absence of risk itself.

The Inequality Chasm

Perhaps no warning sign was more visible, yet more thoroughly rationalized away, than the growing chasm between America's wealthy elite and everyone else. The 1920s witnessed a concentration of wealth that would not be matched again until our own era. By 1929, the top 0.1 percent of Americans controlled a staggering portion of the nation's wealth, while the bottom 93 percent saw their share of the economic pie steadily shrink.

The numbers told a troubling story that few wanted to hear. Between 1920 and 1929, worker productivity increased by an impressive 43 percent. The fruits of this productivity revolution, however, flowed almost exclusively upward. Corporate profits soared by 62 percent during the same period, while average wages for workers increased by a mere 8 percent, barely keeping pace with inflation. Real wages for manufacturing workers actually stagnated throughout much of the decade.

This created a fundamental problem that economists at the time identified but the public ignored: who would buy all the goods American factories were now capable of producing? The wealthy could only purchase so many automobiles, refrigerators, and radios. A sustainable economy required a broad middle class with purchasing power, yet the middle class was being systematically hollowed out.

The Brookings Institution published a prescient study in 1929 showing that 60 percent of American families lived below what they calculated as the minimum comfort level income. These families were barely scraping by, yet the stock market soared on the assumption that consumer demand would continue indefinitely. The contradiction was stark: an economy supposedly built on mass consumption was concentrating wealth in the hands of those who could consume only so much.

Even more troubling was the source of middle-class consumption that did occur. Unable to afford goods from wages alone, Americans turned increasingly to credit. Installment buying exploded during the decade, allowing families to purchase automobiles, furniture, and appliances on payment plans. By 1929, 60 percent of automobiles and 80 percent of radios were purchased on credit. This debt-fueled consumption created an illusion of prosperity that masked the underlying weakness in wage growth.

The wealthy, meanwhile, faced a dilemma of their own: what to do with their accumulating capital? With limited profitable opportunities in an economy already producing more than consumers could afford, and with wages kept artificially low, the money flowed increasingly into financial speculation. The stock market became not a mechanism for capitalizing productive enterprises, but a casino where the wealthy placed increasingly leveraged bets with money that had nowhere else to go.

A few voices warned of the danger. Economists noted that such extreme inequality was inherently unstable, creating an economy built on sand. When the inevitable shock came, whether from overproduction, credit exhaustion, or simple market psychology there would be no cushion. The working class had no savings to fall back on, while the wealthy had their fortunes tied up in overvalued securities. But in the intoxicating atmosphere of the late 1920s, such warnings were dismissed as the pessimism of academic killjoys who simply didn't understand the "New Era."

The Forgotten Depression: Agriculture's Decade of Despair

While stockbrokers and urban professionals celebrated unprecedented prosperity, America's farmers endured a grinding depression throughout the entire decade of the 1920s. This agricultural crisis was not merely a sectoral problem, it was a warning sign that nearly one-quarter of the American population was already experiencing the hardship that would soon engulf everyone.

The roots of agricultural distress lay in World War I. European demand for American agricultural products had soared during the war, and farmers responded by expanding production, purchasing additional land, and taking on substantial debt to finance mechanization. When European agriculture recovered after the war, demand collapsed, but American farmers found themselves saddled with debt payments based on wartime prices and production levels that now generated chronic surpluses.

Farm prices went into free fall. Wheat that sold for $2.19 per bushel in 1919 dropped to $0.93 by 1922. Corn prices collapsed similarly. The agricultural price index, which stood at 205 in 1920, plummeted to 116 by 1921 and never recovered to pre-crash levels throughout the decade. Farmers found themselves in an impossible position: they couldn't afford not to plant, yet every harvest drove prices lower through oversupply.

The human cost was staggering. Farm foreclosures became epidemic. Rural banks, heavily exposed to agricultural loans, began failing at an alarming rate—more than 5,000 rural banks failed during the 1920s, long before the general banking crisis of the 1930s. Farmers who managed to hold onto their land often did so by reducing their standard of living to subsistence levels, unable to participate in the consumer boom celebrated in the cities.

This agricultural depression had profound implications for the broader economy that almost no one recognized. Farmers represented a massive market for manufactured goods such as tractors, automobiles, tools, clothing and household goods. As rural purchasing power collapsed, manufacturers lost a crucial customer base. The farm belt became an economic dead zone, a warning sign that consumption-driven prosperity had limits when entire sectors were excluded from participating.

Moreover, the agricultural crisis demonstrated a troubling reality: overproduction could be just as devastating as underproduction. The same technological advances that allowed American industry to produce unprecedented quantities of consumer goods could easily lead to the same glutted markets and price collapses that plagued agriculture. A few economists made this connection, warning that industrial overproduction might follow the agricultural pattern. They were ignored.

Politicians made token efforts to address the farm crisis, but fundamental solutions were blocked by an ideological commitment to free markets and minimal government intervention. President Coolidge vetoed the McNary-Haugen Farm Relief Bill twice, declaring that agriculture must adjust to market realities without government support. The irony would later become clear: while the government refused to intervene to prevent agricultural collapse, it would be forced into unprecedented intervention to clean up the wreckage of the industrial and financial collapse that followed.

The Industrial Peak and Hidden Decline

In the summer of 1929, with the stock market still climbing toward its September peak, industrial production quietly began to decline. This was perhaps the most significant warning sign of all, yet it was almost completely overlooked in the euphoria of the bull market's final manic phase.

The statistics told a clear story for those willing to look. Industrial production peaked in June 1929 and began a slow, steady decline through the summer and early fall. Steel production, often considered a bellwether for overall economic health, fell from 86 percent of capacity in June to 71 percent by September. Automobile production, the crown jewel of 1920s prosperity, declined throughout the summer. Construction, which had been one of the decade's great growth engines, had actually peaked back in 1926 and was in steady decline by 1929.

Yet the stock market, supposedly a forward-looking mechanism that priced in future economic conditions, continued its parabolic rise. Between June and September 1929, as real economic activity contracted, the Dow Jones Industrial Average gained another 20 percent. The disconnect between market valuations and economic reality had become total.

This divergence revealed a fundamental shift in the nature of the market. Stock prices were no longer tied to underlying business conditions or earnings prospects. Instead, the market had become a self-referential bubble, where prices rose because they were rising, and investors bought because others were buying. The market had detached from economic moorings and was floating free in a realm of pure speculation.

Contemporary observers noted the anomaly but explained it away with increasingly tortured logic. Perhaps the stock market was anticipating a recovery that economic statistics had not yet captured. Perhaps new efficiencies would allow companies to maintain profits despite lower production volumes. Perhaps the most dangerous rationalization of all traditional metrics simply didn't apply in the "New Era" of American capitalism.

The inventory data told an even more troubling story. As production declined through the summer, inventories began to accumulate. Warehouses filled with unsold goods, a classic signal that supply was outstripping demand. Any first-year economics student could explain the implication: prices would need to fall, margins would compress, profits would decline, and the economy would contract further. Yet investors, so confident in their financial acumen, missed or ignored this fundamental signal.

Some insiders understood what was happening. Corporate executives, with access to their companies' real-time sales data, began quietly selling shares. But insider selling is a hidden signal, visible only in retrospect when the data is compiled and analyzed. The general public, reading optimistic analyst reports and newspaper editorials celebrating the market's rise, had no idea that those with the best information were heading for the exits.

The phenomenon illustrated a crucial insight about market crashes: the final phase of a bubble is often the most explosive, driven not by improving fundamentals but by pure momentum and the fear of missing out. The greater the disconnect between prices and reality, the more spectacular the eventual correction. Summer 1929 was the perfect storm of deteriorating fundamentals and manic speculation.

Florida's Crystal Ball: The Real Estate Collapse of 1926

Three years before the stock market crash, Florida experienced a spectacular real estate bubble and collapse that served as a perfect miniature preview of what was to come. The Florida land boom of the mid-1920s and its catastrophic bust contained every element of the later disaster: wild speculation, easy credit, greater fool theory, and ultimate collapse. Yet the lesson went unlearned.

The Florida boom began innocently enough, driven by genuine factors: improved transportation making the state more accessible, Americans' growing affluence and leisure time, and Florida's undeniable appeal as a winter destination. But speculation quickly overwhelmed fundamentals. Land prices in Miami and other Florida cities rose at a dizzying pace. Lots purchased for a few thousand dollars sold months later for ten times that amount. Fortunes were made on paper overnight.

The mechanics of the bubble were nearly identical to what would later occur in the stock market. Buyers purchased land with minimal down payments, planning to "flip" the property for a quick profit before the full payment came due. Professional speculators bought and sold the same lots multiple times, each transaction at a higher price, without any actual development occurring. The very act of buying seemed to guarantee profits, as prices only went one direction: up.

Banks, eager to profit from the frenzy, loosened lending standards dramatically. Credit flowed freely to anyone wanting to speculate in Florida real estate. Investment schemes proliferated, allowing small investors to pool money for land purchases. The promise was always the same: easy riches through real estate appreciation that would never end.

Promotional excesses reached absurd heights. Developers advertised underwater lots as "waterfront property." Cities were planned on paper in swampland, complete with elaborate sketches of the grand boulevards and civic buildings that would surely materialize once the development launched. Celebrity endorsements, the influencer marketing of the 1920s hyped various developments. Even William Jennings Bryan, three-time presidential candidate, was hired to promote Miami-area real estate.

The collapse, when it came, was swift and total. By 1926, the boom had exhausted itself. The supply of greater fools willing to pay ever-higher prices simply ran out. Sales slowed, then stopped. Buyers who had purchased on installment plans found themselves unable to flip their properties and defaulted on payments. Banks, holding land as collateral that was now worth a fraction of the loan amount, failed in waves. The mythical cities in the swamps remained nothing but sketches.

A devastating hurricane in September 1926 provided the coup de grâce, destroying thousands of structures and killing hundreds of people. The damage shattered whatever remained of Florida's real estate mystique. Property values collapsed to a fraction of their peak. Fortunes vanished. Many who had become "paper millionaires" during the boom were left bankrupt.

The Florida bust should have served as a national wake-up call. Every element of an unsustainable bubble was present: speculation replacing investment, easy credit, rising prices justifying higher prices, and the conviction that normal rules of valuation didn't apply. The collapse demonstrated that asset bubbles always end badly, regardless of how many people believe "this time is different."

Yet the lesson was not learned. Instead, it was compartmentalized. Florida's problems were dismissed as unique to real estate, to that particular region, to those specific circumstances. Surely the stock market, with its sophisticated investors and professional analysts, operated under different rules. Surely New York was not Florida. This comfortable denial allowed speculation to continue and intensify, setting the stage for a collapse that would make Florida's bust look like a dress rehearsal.

The Prophets Without Honor

Not everyone was blind to the gathering storm. A small group of economists, analysts, and investors warned repeatedly that the market had detached from economic reality and that disaster loomed. Their reward for prescience was mockery, marginalization, and for those who acted on their convictions substantial short-term losses that destroyed their credibility before they were proven right.

Roger Babson, a successful businessman and statistician, was perhaps the most prominent voice of caution. Throughout 1929, Babson warned that the market was overvalued and that a crash was inevitable. On September 5, 1929, at the Annual National Business Conference, Babson delivered his most dire warning yet: "Sooner or later a crash is coming, and it may be terrific." He predicted that stock prices could decline 60 to 80 points.

The market's response was immediate and mocking. Stock prices plummeted that afternoon in what became known as the "Babson Break," but recovered the next day as prominent voices rushed to dismiss his warnings. The Harvard Economic Society, representing the academic establishment, issued a statement declaring that "a severe depression like that of 1920-21 is outside the range of probability." Professor Irving Fisher of Yale, one of the most respected economists of the era, famously declared just weeks before the crash that stocks had reached "what looks like a permanently high plateau."

The financial press treated Babson as a crank. Editorials questioned his motives and his competence. How dare this statistical analyst challenge the collective wisdom of the market and the assurances of distinguished professors? The implicit message was clear: pessimism was not merely wrong but somehow un-American, a betrayal of the nation's manifest destiny for permanent prosperity.

Other voices joined Babson in the wilderness. Paul Warburg, a prominent banker and one of the architects of the Federal Reserve System, warned in early 1929 that the "orgy of speculation" would end in catastrophe. Alexander Noyes, financial editor of the New York Times, consistently cautioned about overvaluation throughout 1928 and 1929. These were not fringe figures but respected establishment voices—yet they were dismissed as dinosaurs who didn't understand the New Era.

The Federal Reserve itself was divided. Some officials within the system recognized the dangers of rampant speculation and advocated for tighter monetary policy to cool the market. But political pressure and the prevailing ideology of limited intervention prevented decisive action. The Fed raised interest rates modestly but proved unwilling to take strong action that might prick the bubble. The institution that had been created to provide financial stability found itself paralyzed by the fear of being blamed for ending the party.

What made the warnings so easy to dismiss was their imprecision. The skeptics could not say exactly when the crash would come or what would trigger it. They could identify the underlying instability but couldn't predict the specific moment of collapse. This imprecision allowed bulls to portray the warnings as perpetual pessimism. After all, if someone predicts a crash every month and is wrong every time, why should anyone listen when they issue the same warning again?

Moreover, the warnings were costly to heed. Investors who sold in 1928 based on valuation concerns watched the market soar another 50 percent in 1929. Those who were cautious missed out on spectacular gains. In a bull market, pessimism doesn't just feel wrong, it is wrong in the sense that it leads to opportunity cost and underperformance. Career risk made it nearly impossible for professional money managers to act on crash warnings even if they believed them.

This created a perverse dynamic: the longer the bubble continued, the more the skeptics were discredited, and the more difficult it became to voice concerns. A self-reinforcing cycle of optimism took hold. Anyone who questioned market valuations was portrayed as bitter about missing the rally, out of touch with modern realities, or motivated by some hidden agenda. The social pressure to conform to bullish sentiment became immense.

The Psychology of Denial

Understanding why warning signs were ignored requires examining the psychological mechanisms that allow intelligent people to disregard obvious risks. The phenomenon is not unique to the 1920s, it recurs in every bubble, including our own era because it emerges from deep patterns in human cognition and group behavior.

Recency bias played a powerful role. The 1920s had been a decade of uninterrupted prosperity and rising stock prices. Young investors and many middle-aged ones had never experienced a bear market, let alone a crash. The recent past became the guide to the future. Every previous dip had been a buying opportunity. Every warning of disaster had proven false. This built confidence that the pattern would continue indefinitely.

The "New Era" narrative provided intellectual cover for ignoring warnings. Proponents argued that fundamental changes in the American economy such as technological innovation, professional management, Federal Reserve stabilization, higher productivity had eliminated the old boom-bust cycle. Past precedents were irrelevant because the economy now operated under different rules. This wasn't speculation; it was rational investment based on transformed fundamentals.

This narrative was emotionally irresistible because it allowed people to feel sophisticated rather than reckless. Investors weren't gambling, they were recognizing a paradigm shift that pessimists were too rigid to see. The New Era theory turned caution into obsolete thinking and speculation into wisdom. It was a flattering self-delusion that justified exactly the behavior people wanted to engage in anyway.

Social proof exerted tremendous influence. When everyone around you is making money in the market, when your neighbors are buying stocks, when dinner party conversation revolves around trading tips, the pressure to participate becomes overwhelming. The fear of missing out (FOMO) is a powerful motivator. Being wrong alongside everyone else is emotionally tolerable; being right alone while watching others prosper is psychologically agonizing.

The media amplified these tendencies. Newspapers filled their pages with success stories of ordinary people who made fortunes in the market. Financial publications provided endless bullish analysis. Radio, the social media of the 1920s, broadcast market updates and investment advice that skewed heavily optimistic. Bearish voices were marginalized or excluded entirely. The information environment created an echo chamber where warnings simply couldn't penetrate.

Confirmation bias led people to interpret every piece of information through a bullish lens. Good economic news confirmed that prosperity would continue. Bad news was dismissed as temporary or irrelevant. Ambiguous data was spun positive. Investors actively sought information that justified their bullish positions while avoiding or discounting anything that challenged their views. The human mind is remarkably skilled at maintaining comfortable beliefs in the face of contradictory evidence.

The sunk cost fallacy also played a role. By 1929, millions of Americans had their savings invested in the market. Acknowledging that prices might be dangerously inflated would require accepting that their wealth was illusory, that their sacrifices to accumulate capital had been squandered on overpriced securities. Psychologically, it was easier to believe the market would continue rising than to face such a painful reality.

Finally, there was the dangerous comfort of unanimous expert opinion. When prestigious economists, successful businessmen, and government officials all proclaimed the market's soundness, who was the ordinary investor to disagree? The illusion of expert consensus silenced individual doubts. Surely all these accomplished people couldn't be wrong. This deference to authority allowed people to abdicate personal responsibility for their financial decisions and silence their own better judgment.

The Ignored Precedents

History offered numerous examples of financial bubbles and their inevitable collapses, yet these precedents were dismissed as irrelevant to the American situation of the 1920s. This historical amnesia is itself a warning sign that appears in every bubble: the conviction that past episodes of excess and collapse bear no relation to the current situation.

The Dutch Tulip Mania of the 1630s was already part of financial lore. The South Sea Bubble of 1720 had been studied by historians. More recently, the Panic of 1907 had demonstrated the financial system's fragility just two decades earlier. Yet these historical episodes were waved away. Tulips were flowers, not industrial securities. The South Sea Company was an 18th-century absurdity, not a modern corporation. The 1907 panic had led to creation of the Federal Reserve, which now provided a stabilizing presence.

Each historical precedent was dismissed through special pleading. The specific circumstances differed, therefore the general pattern of speculation, excessive leverage and inevitable collapse somehow didn't apply. This ability to acknowledge historical facts while denying their implications is a remarkable feat of cognitive gymnastics that appears in every era.

The most relevant precedent was largely forgotten: the Panic of 1837. That crisis followed a period of intense speculation, rapid credit expansion, and transformative new technologies (canals and railroads). The similarities to the 1920s were striking, yet few drew the parallel. The Panic of 1837 led to a depression lasting years, with bank failures, collapsing land values, and widespread unemployment. It demonstrated that American democracy was not immune to financial disaster. But 90 years later, this lesson had faded from collective memory.

This historical amnesia reflects a troubling truth: financial bubbles recur precisely because each generation must learn the same lessons through bitter experience. Knowledge of past crashes is not sufficient to prevent future ones. The psychological and social dynamics that create bubbles are too powerful to be overcome by historical awareness alone. Perhaps this is the ultimate warning sign, not any specific indicator but the very fact that we consistently ignore all warning signs when gripped by speculative mania.

The Final Days: Confidence at the Precipice

By October 1929, the warning signs had multiplied to the point where denying them required willful blindness. Yet confidence remained absolute right up to the moment of collapse. Stock prices continued rising through early September. Professional analysts issued bullish forecasts. Politicians and business leaders proclaimed the economy fundamentally sound. The dissonance between market confidence and underlying reality had never been greater.

This phenomenon, maximum confidence at the point of maximum danger is itself a reliable warning sign. When pessimism has been driven entirely from the market, when bearish voices have been completely silenced or discredited, when unanimous bullishness prevails, the crash is near. The eerie calm of universal confidence typically precedes the storm.

The ignored warnings of the 1920s offer lessons that transcend any particular era. They reveal that crashes are not bolts from the blue but foreseeable results of identifiable excesses. They demonstrate that intelligence and education provide no immunity to bubble psychology. They show that warning signs are most vigorously denied when most urgently relevant.

Most importantly, they teach that it is not the absence of warnings that leads to disaster, but the certainty that this time, whatever the indicators suggest is different. When an entire society convinces itself that old rules no longer apply, that new paradigms justify any price, that warning voices are simply too pessimistic to grasp the transformed reality, that is the moment of maximum peril. The warning signs of 1929 were not obscure. They were ignored by collective choice, rationalized away by narratives that made speculation feel like prudence. This is the pattern that recurs throughout financial history, and it is the pattern we must vigilantly watch for in our own time.

Chapter 4

The Crash and Its Aftermath

The crash did not announce itself with trumpets. There was no singular dramatic event that served as an obvious trigger, no assassination of an archduke, no declaration of war, no natural disaster. Instead, the greatest financial catastrophe in American history began with a subtle shift in psychology, a spreading doubt, a growing unease, a dawning realization that prices had risen too far, too fast, on foundations of sand. What followed was not merely a stock market decline but a cascade of interconnected failures that would reshape American society and haunt the national psyche for generations.

The Cracking Foundation: September's Hidden Tremors

The conventional narrative dates the crash to October, but the market's underlying structure began fracturing in September 1929. On September 3rd, the Dow Jones Industrial Average reached its peak of 381.17, a summit it would not regain for a quarter-century. What appeared to be a healthy correction at the time was actually the beginning of a structural collapse.

The initial decline was modest and orderly, the kind of pullback that had occurred numerous times during the bull market. Experienced traders bought the dip, confident that this was merely another opportunity to profit from temporary weakness. After all, every previous decline had been followed by new highs. The pattern seemed immutable.

But this time was different, the three most dangerous words in finance. The decline continued through September, punctuated by brief rallies that gave false hope. By late September, some of the more speculative stocks had lost 20 percent or more from their peaks. Margin calls began to trickle in. Investors who had borrowed heavily to purchase stocks found themselves facing demands for additional capital to maintain their positions.

The psychology shifted subtly but crucially. The universal confidence that had characterized the summer gave way to nagging doubt. Trading volume remained heavy but changed in character, from eager buying to nervous selling. The market's internal dynamics were deteriorating even as public commentary remained largely optimistic.

On September 20th, the market suffered a sharp one-day decline that rattled nerves. Prominent voices rushed to provide reassurance. Professor Irving Fisher of Yale, perhaps the most respected economist in America, declared that stock prices were not too high and that the economy was on a "permanently high plateau." Charles E. Mitchell, president of National City Bank, proclaimed that "the industrial situation of the United States is absolutely sound." These reassurances worked temporarily, producing a brief rally, but the underlying pressure continued building.

What investors didn't fully grasp was that the market had become extraordinarily fragile. Years of speculation had created a massive pyramid of debt. Investment trusts owned other investment trusts, which owned other investment trusts, creating layers of leverage. Margin debt, money borrowed to purchase stocks had reached unprecedented levels. The entire structure required continuously rising prices to remain stable. Once prices began falling, the pyramid would collapse layer by layer.

Black Thursday: October 24, 1929

Thursday, October 24th, 1929, dawned like any other autumn day in New York, but it would enter history as Black Thursday, the day the bubble finally burst in spectacular fashion. The opening bell at the New York Stock Exchange rang at 10:00 AM, and almost immediately, the deluge began.

Sell orders overwhelmed the market from the opening minutes. There were no buyers at prevailing prices. Stocks gapped down, dropping from one price level to a dramatically lower level with no trades in between. The ticker tape, the technological marvel that allowed investors across the nation to follow market prices in near real-time, began to fall behind almost immediately. By 11:00 AM, it was running an hour late. Investors frantically tried to sell but had no idea what prices their stocks were actually fetching.

The trading floor of the New York Stock Exchange descended into chaos. Traders screamed themselves hoarse trying to execute orders. The noise was described as deafening, like standing inside a waterfall. Paper from order tickets littered the floor ankle-deep. Exhausted messengers ran back and forth until they collapsed. Outside on Wall Street, a crowd gathered, growing larger and more anxious as rumors spread. Police were called to maintain order.

The psychology of panic was setting in. Investors who had held through September's decline now decided to cut their losses. Those who had bought on margin received calls demanding immediate payment of their loans or liquidation of their positions. Many couldn't meet the margin calls, they had no additional capital. Their brokers had no choice but to sell their holdings at whatever price the market would bear, which created more selling, which drove prices lower, which triggered more margin calls, which created more forced selling. The death spiral had begun.

By midday, panic was absolute. Rumors swept through the crowd gathered on Wall Street: the exchange would close, banks were failing, prominent speculators had committed suicide. The ticker was now hours behind, meaning no one knew the current state of their holdings. In the information vacuum, fear filled the void. The unthinkable was happening, the invincible bull market was collapsing.

Then came a moment of high drama that briefly stemmed the tide. At 12:30 PM, a group of the nation's most powerful bankers gathered in the offices of J.P. Morgan & Company, located across the street from the stock exchange. The meeting included Thomas Lamont of Morgan, Albert Wiggin of Chase National Bank, William Potter of Guaranty Trust, Seward Prosser of Bankers Trust, and Charles Mitchell of National City Bank. These men controlled billions in capital and, perhaps more importantly, they controlled market psychology.

The bankers agreed to pool resources and intervene to stabilize the market. Richard Whitney, vice-president of the Exchange and a Morgan man, walked onto the trading floor at 1:30 PM and began placing conspicuously large buy orders for major stocks at prices above the current market. The symbolism was clear: the financial establishment was supporting the market. If the House of Morgan was buying, surely prices had fallen far enough.

The intervention worked, temporarily. Prices stabilized and even recovered somewhat in the afternoon. The market closed down significantly but well off its lows. The bankers were hailed as heroes who had saved the financial system. President Hoover issued a statement that "the fundamental business of the country... is on a sound and prosperous basis." The crisis, many believed, had been contained.

In reality, Thursday had revealed the market's profound weakness. Nearly 13 million shares had traded, a record volume that overwhelmed the exchange's ability to process transactions. Billions in paper wealth had vanished in hours. The psychological damage was severe. Even the dramatic banking intervention could only pause, not reverse, the selling pressure. The facade of invincibility had cracked, and once investors glimpsed the void beneath, no reassurance could restore lost confidence.

The Weekend of Delusion

The weekend following Black Thursday was a study in denial and delusion. Saturday's newspapers carried reassuring headlines. Financial leaders issued bullish statements. The prevailing narrative was that the worst had passed, that Thursday's intervention had marked the bottom, and that those who bought Monday morning would profit handsomely from the recovery.

Behind the scenes, a different reality was unfolding. Brokerage firms worked through the weekend processing the paperwork from Thursday's unprecedented volume. Margin calls went out to thousands of investors. Many of these investors had no additional funds and would be forced to sell on Monday. The pipeline of forced liquidation was full.

Small investors spent the weekend in quiet anguish, contemplating financial ruin. Many had invested their life savings, encouraged by the narrative that everyone was getting rich in the market. Some had borrowed money beyond their margin accounts using second mortgages and personal loans to speculate on stocks. Thursday's collapse had wiped them out, but they didn't yet know it because the ticker had been so far behind that exact losses were still being calculated.

Wealthier investors faced a different calculus. Some recognized that Thursday was just the beginning and resolved to sell Monday morning before prices fell further. Others saw opportunity, believing that stocks were now bargain-priced. Still others were paralyzed by indecision, hoping for guidance that would never come. No one could agree on what had caused Thursday's crash, which made it impossible to predict what would happen next.

What hardly anyone understood was that they were living through a phase transition, a moment when a complex system shifts from one stable state to another. The market had existed in a stable state of rising prices and widespread confidence. That state had been destroyed Thursday. The new stable state would be falling prices and pervasive fear, but the transition between these states would be chaotic and unpredictable. The weekend was merely the eye of the hurricane.

Black Monday: October 28, 1929

The storm returned Monday morning with even greater ferocity. From the opening bell, the market plunged. There was no semblance of order, no pretense of normal trading. Sell orders avalanched into the market. The banking consortium that had intervened Thursday was nowhere to be seen, either they had exhausted their resources or, more likely, they had recognized the futility of fighting the tide.

Monday's decline was relentless and accelerating. Stocks fell not by fractions or single points but by dollars at a time. Companies that had been market darlings, trading at dizzying multiples just weeks before, saw their shares cut in half in a single day. The ticker fell further and further behind, eventually running four hours late. Investors were trading blind, selling at prices they couldn't know into a falling market whose depth they couldn't measure.

The Dow Jones Industrial Average fell 13 percent on Monday, the largest single-day percentage decline to that point in the index's history. But the Dow, composed of thirty large, established companies, actually held up better than the broader market. Speculative stocks, the glamorous names that had led the market higher, were decimated. Shares of investment trusts, those leveraged vehicles that had been the mania's favorite instrument, lost 20, 30, even 40 percent in a single day.

The human element of the disaster became impossible to ignore. Reports spread of investors, their fortunes destroyed, taking their own lives. While these stories were often exaggerated, they reflected a deeper truth: lives were being ruined in real-time. Wealth that had taken years to accumulate vanished in hours. Dreams of retirement, of children's education, of financial security, all gone.

By Monday's close, the illusions of the weekend had been thoroughly shattered. This was not a healthy correction. This was not a buying opportunity. This was a catastrophic collapse of a market that had been built on borrowed money and borrowed time. The only question was how much worse it could get.

Black Tuesday: October 29, 1929

Tuesday answered that question with brutal clarity: much worse. If Monday had been a catastrophe, Tuesday was an apocalypse. October 29, 1929, Black Tuesday would live in infamy as the darkest day in American financial history, the day the bottom fell out completely.

Over 16.4 million shares traded on Black Tuesday, a record that would stand for nearly four decades. The number is almost meaningless without context: the exchange's systems were designed to handle 3-4 million shares per day. The volume was so overwhelming that the ticker ran nearly five hours behind. By the time the closing prices were finally printed, it was after 7:00 PM and the prices were already irrelevant, the damage had been done.

The cascade of selling fed on itself with mechanical inevitability. Margin calls forced selling, which drove prices lower, which triggered more margin calls, which forced more selling. The market had become a machine purpose-built to destroy wealth. No circuit breakers existed to halt trading. No cooling-off periods allowed rationality to reassert itself. The selling continued relentlessly from opening to close.

Entire fortunes vanished on Black Tuesday. John J. Raskob, vice-president of General Motors, lost millions. William Durant, who had founded General Motors and made a fortune in the bull market, was wiped out and would spend years paying off debts. The investment trusts that had allowed ordinary people to leverage themselves into the market collapsed spectacularly. The Goldman Sachs Trading Corporation, which had traded above $326 per share in the summer, fell below $65. It would eventually trade for less than $2.

But Black Tuesday's destruction fell most heavily on those who could least afford it. The small investors who had been encouraged to participate in the market, who had believed the narratives of permanent prosperity and painless wealth, were obliterated. Schoolteachers, shopkeepers, clerks and people who had saved modest sums over years of hard work saw those savings evaporate. Many had not just lost their savings but were deeply in debt, having borrowed on margin or taken personal loans to speculate.

As Tuesday's catastrophic session drew to a close, the scope of destruction was staggering but still not fully comprehended. The market had suffered its worst two-day collapse in history. But the psychological impact exceeded the numerical losses. The belief system that had sustained the bull market of confidence in markets, faith in experts and trust in the future had been shattered. And without that belief system, nothing could prevent the crisis from metastasizing into a broader economic disaster.

The Sickening Spiral: October into November

The immediate aftermath of Black Tuesday brought a strange, stunned calm. The sheer scale of destruction was too vast to process. Many investors were in shock, unable to fully grasp what had happened or what it meant for their futures. The newspapers ran stories of heroism, traders who had worked through the night, bankers who had rushed to support the market. There was talk of recovery, of buying opportunities, of resilience.

But the damage was done and irreversible. The mechanism of destruction, once set in motion, continued grinding forward. Margin calls from

Tuesday's chaos went out over the following days and weeks. Many investors couldn't meet these calls because their collateral was now worthless. Their positions were liquidated, creating new waves of selling that pushed prices even lower.

The immediate week following Black Tuesday saw wild volatility. Wednesday and Thursday brought powerful rallies as bargain hunters stepped in and short-sellers covered positions. These relief rallies created hope that the worst had passed. But then Friday brought renewed selling. The pattern would repeat for weeks: sharp rallies that restored hope, followed by renewed declines that destroyed it.

By mid-November, the Dow had recovered about 20 percent from its October lows. Optimists declared the crash over. President Hoover held meetings with business leaders who pledged to maintain wages and employment. The message from authorities remained consistent: the economy was fundamentally sound, the market decline was a temporary disruption, recovery was inevitable and imminent.

They were catastrophically wrong. What the authorities failed to understand was that the crash had set in motion a chain reaction that would feed on itself for years. The destruction of wealth in the stock market, totaling tens of billions of dollars, had profound real-world consequences. Consumers who had felt wealthy stopped spending. Businesses that had planned expansion based on expected stock market profits cancelled those plans. Banks that had lent against stock collateral faced mounting losses.

The Banking Crisis: When the Foundation Crumbles

The stock market crash transformed into a broader economic depression through the banking system. Banks in the 1920s had been heavily involved in market speculation, both directly through securities holdings and indirectly through loans collateralized by stocks. When stock prices collapsed, the collateral backing these loans became inadequate. Banks faced massive potential losses.

Moreover, many banks had recommended stocks to their customers, had helped them establish margin accounts, had even lent them money beyond margin loans to speculate. These customers were now ruined, unable to repay loans, and often blaming the banks for their losses. Trust in the banking system began eroding.

The first banks to fail were rural banks already weakened by the agricultural depression of the 1920s. These small institutions had been teetering for years; the crash provided the final push. But by early 1930, the banking crisis was spreading to urban areas. Depositors, frightened by news of bank failures and worried about their own savings, began withdrawing funds. These withdrawals forced banks to call in loans and sell assets, often at fire-sale prices, which weakened them further.

Bank runs, the nightmare scenario where depositors rush to withdraw funds simultaneously began occurring with increasing frequency. Once a run started at a bank, it was almost impossible to stop. Even sound banks couldn't survive if all depositors demanded their money at once, because banks operated on fractional reserves, keeping only a portion of deposits as cash while lending out the rest. A bank run became a self-fulfilling prophecy: fear of failure caused withdrawals that caused failure.

The Federal Reserve, created in 1913 specifically to prevent such crises, failed spectacularly in its mission. Rather than providing liquidity freely to stem the banking panic, the Fed worried about inflation and maintaining gold reserves. It kept monetary policy tight even as banks collapsed and credit froze. The Fed's failure to act decisively turned what might have been a severe recession into a depression that would last a decade.

Between 1930 and 1933, over 9,000 banks failed, roughly one-third of all banks in the United States. The consequences were catastrophic. Each bank failure destroyed the savings of depositors, who had no insurance and lost everything. Businesses lost their operating capital when their banks failed. Communities lost their financial infrastructure. The credit system that lubricated the economy seized up completely.

The banking crisis also revealed how interconnected the financial system had become. When banks failed, they defaulted on obligations to other banks. These secondary failures spread like a contagion through correspondent banking networks. A bank failure in Iowa could trigger failures in Chicago, which could trigger failures in New York. The system's complexity, which had seemed like a strength during good times, became a fatal weakness during the crisis.

The Real Economy Collapses

The transition from financial crisis to economic depression occurred through multiple channels, each reinforcing the others in a vicious cycle. The destruction of wealth in the stock market and subsequent banking failures decimated consumer spending. Families that had felt prosperous suddenly felt poor and they were. The psychological impact was as important as the numerical impact. Even those whose wealth wasn't entirely destroyed became cautious, cutting back on spending, increasing savings, delaying major purchases.

This drop in consumer demand hit businesses immediately. Inventories that had been accumulating through summer 1929 now became disasters. Companies couldn't sell their products. They responded by cutting prices, which helped move some inventory but crushed profit margins. More importantly, they cut production. Factories reduced hours, then closed entirely. Workers were laid off by the thousands, then hundreds of thousands.

Unemployment became the Great Depression's defining tragedy. The official unemployment rate, which had been 3.2 percent in 1929, rose to 8.7 percent by 1930, then 15.9 percent in 1931, then peaked at nearly 25 percent in 1933. These numbers don't capture the full horror because they measure only those actively seeking work. Millions more had given up looking. In some cities, unemployment exceeded 50 percent. Men who had supported families comfortably just months before now stood in bread lines.

The multiplier effects magnified the collapse. Unemployed workers couldn't pay rent, so landlords lost income. Landlords then couldn't pay their mortgages, so banks faced more defaults. The unemployed stopped buying anything except bare necessities, which caused more businesses to fail, which caused more unemployment. Each contraction in one sector caused contractions in others, spiraling downward.

Agriculture, already depressed throughout the 1920s, plunged into complete disaster. Farm prices collapsed by an additional 50 percent between 1929 and 1932. Farmers couldn't pay mortgages or taxes. Foreclosures reached epidemic levels. Farmers began destroying crops and livestock rather than selling them at prices below the cost of bringing them to market. In a cruel irony, people were starving in cities while food rotted in the countryside because the price was too low to justify transportation.

International trade collapsed as the depression went global. The Smoot-Hawley Tariff Act of 1930, intended to protect American industry, triggered retaliatory tariffs from other nations. Global trade fell by over 60 percent between 1929 and 1933. This destroyed what remained of the export markets that might have cushioned the depression's impact.

The Social Catastrophe

The Great Depression's economic statistics tell only part of the story. Behind the numbers were human tragedies that scarred a generation. Men who had been productive, proud workers lost not just income but identity. The psychological impact of prolonged unemployment, the shame, the sense of uselessness and the erosion of self-worth devastated millions.

Families disintegrated under the pressure. Marriages collapsed. Birthrates plummeted as couples decided they couldn't afford children. Hundreds of thousands of children were placed in orphanages because their parents couldn't feed them. Young men hopped freight trains, wandering the country looking for work that didn't exist, becoming a generation of homeless transients.

Malnutrition and associated diseases became widespread, particularly among children. Hospitals reported cases of starvation. Public health deteriorated as people couldn't afford medical care and local governments couldn't fund health services. The human cost of the depression would manifest in diminished health and shortened lifespans for those who endured it.

Shanty towns—collections of makeshift shacks built from scrap materials sprang up on the outskirts of cities. These became known bitterly as "Hoovervilles" after President Hoover, who was widely blamed for the depression. The sight of these desperate encampments became symbols of the era's hardship.

Education suffered as local governments, unable to collect property taxes, closed schools. Teachers went unpaid for months. Many children dropped out of school to look for work to help support their families, though work was nearly impossible to find. A generation's education was compromised, with effects that would last decades.

The social fabric frayed in other ways. Crime increased, particularly property crime driven by desperation. Prohibition-era organized crime expanded as legitimate economic opportunities vanished. Political extremism both communist and fascist movements gained adherents among those who had lost faith in democratic capitalism. The system that had promised unlimited prosperity had delivered unlimited misery.

Policy Failures and the Long Road Down

The Great Depression's severity and duration owed much to catastrophic policy failures. President Hoover and his advisors, guided by the conventional economic wisdom of the era, implemented policies that made the situation worse rather than better.

The most fundamental error was adherence to balanced budget orthodoxy. As tax revenues collapsed due to falling economic activity, the government cut spending to avoid deficits. This exactly backwards approach removed government spending from the economy precisely when it was most needed. State and local governments, constitutionally required to balance budgets, cut even more drastically, laying off workers and canceling projects.

Monetary policy remained tight throughout the early depression years. The Federal Reserve, fearing inflation and committed to maintaining the gold standard, refused to expand the money supply even as the economy contracted and prices fell. Deflation, falling prices made debts more burdensome in real terms and incentivized consumers to delay purchases, waiting for even lower prices. The Fed's passivity transformed recession into depression.

Tax policy moved in exactly the wrong direction. The Revenue Act of 1932 raised taxes dramatically to reduce the federal deficit. This removed more purchasing power from an already devastated economy. The timing could not have been worse, raising taxes in the depths of depression was economically suicidal.

International policy failures compounded domestic errors. The Smoot-Hawley tariffs triggered a global trade war that ensured the depression would be worldwide. The international gold standard, which required countries to maintain fixed exchange rates, prevented the currency devaluations that might have stimulated exports. When Britain abandoned gold in 1931, it created pressure on the American system that intensified the crisis.

Perhaps most damaging was the psychological failure of leadership. Hoover's repeated assurances that "prosperity is just around the corner" rang increasingly hollow. His insistence that the depression was a temporary disruption that would correct itself through market mechanisms became cruelly absurd as years passed and conditions worsened. The loss of credibility made it impossible for the government to restore confidence even when it finally attempted stimulus policies.

The Bottom and the Slow Recovery

The depression reached its nadir in early 1933, when Franklin Roosevelt was inaugurated. The banking system was in complete collapse, multiple states had declared bank holidays, closing all banks to prevent runs. The inauguration occurred amid a genuine fear that the economic system itself might not survive.

Roosevelt's first hundred days brought unprecedented government action. The Emergency Banking Act provided a framework for reopening sound banks. The creation of the Federal Deposit Insurance Corporation (FDIC) restored confidence in banks by guaranteeing deposits. The abandonment of the gold standard allowed monetary expansion. Public works programs provided employment. Agricultural programs addressed farm distress.

These interventions stabilized the system and produced a partial recovery. GDP growth returned, unemployment fell from its peak, and confidence gradually rebuilt. But full recovery took far longer than the crash itself. The economy didn't return to 1929 output levels until 1937, and then a secondary recession pushed it back down. Unemployment remained above 10 percent until World War II mobilization finally absorbed the labor surplus.

The stock market's recovery was even slower. The Dow Jones Industrial Average, which had peaked at 381 in September 1929 and bottomed at 41 in July 1932, didn't return to its 1929 peak until November 1954, twenty-five years later. An entire generation of investors never recovered their losses. The psychological scars lasted even longer. Millions of Americans who lived through the Depression remained permanently cautious, never fully trusting markets or financial institutions again.

Lessons Written in Suffering

The crash of 1929 and the Great Depression that followed taught lessons written in human suffering. Financial markets are not naturally self-stabilizing; they require regulation and oversight. Banking systems are inherently fragile and require deposit insurance and lender-of-last-resort facilities. Monetary policy must respond aggressively to economic contractions. Fiscal policy should be countercyclical, expanding deficits during downturns rather than contracting them.

Perhaps the most important lesson was the simplest: asset bubbles end badly. The belief that prices can rise indefinitely, that traditional metrics no longer apply, that new eras have abolished old rules, these beliefs recur with each generation because they are emotionally irresistible. But they are always wrong. The crash of 1929 demonstrated with brutal clarity that gravity always reasserts itself, that what goes up must come down, and that the higher the climb, the more devastating the fall.

The question for our own time is whether we have truly learned these lessons or merely forgotten them during our latest period of prosperity. The warning signs described in the previous chapter were clear in the 1920s but were ignored. Are we ignoring similar warnings today? The mechanisms that created the 1929 crash, excessive leverage, asset price bubbles, regulatory failure and misguided policy remain with us. The names and instruments change, but human nature and the dynamics of speculation remain constant. The crash of 1929 is not merely history; it is a mirror in which we can see our own vulnerabilities if we have the courage to look.

Part II: Today's Financial Landscape

Chapter 5

The Everything Bubble

If the 1929 crash was a devastating storm that destroyed wealth concentrated primarily in stocks, today's financial landscape presents a far more dangerous proposition: a simultaneous inflation of nearly every asset class imaginable. Stocks, bonds, real estate, cryptocurrencies, private equity, venture capital, collectibles and art all have experienced extraordinary price appreciation that has become disconnected from underlying fundamentals. We are living through what historians may someday call "The Everything Bubble," a unique moment when policy decisions designed to prevent another Great Depression may have created the conditions for something potentially worse.

The Genesis: 2008 and the Policy Response

To understand today's Everything Bubble, we must return to its origin: the 2008 financial crisis and the unprecedented policy response it triggered. When Lehman Brothers collapsed in September 2008, the global financial system teetered on the edge of complete meltdown. Banks stopped lending to each other. Credit markets froze. A depression seemed imminent.

The Federal Reserve, led by Chairman Ben Bernanke, a scholar of the Great Depression, was determined not to repeat the policy mistakes of the 1930s. The Fed slashed interest rates to zero and kept them there. But zero wasn't enough. The Fed then embarked on an experimental program called quantitative easing (QE): the central bank would create money electronically and use it to purchase government bonds and mortgage-backed securities.

The logic was straightforward: by purchasing these securities, the Fed would inject liquidity into the financial system, lower long-term interest rates, and encourage investment and consumption. The economic recovery would strengthen, unemployment would fall, and eventually the Fed could unwind these emergency measures and return to normal policy.

The initial rounds of QE were defensible as crisis management. The financial system stabilized. A depression was avoided. But what began as emergency medicine became permanent treatment. QE1 was followed by QE2, then QE3. What was supposed to be temporary became the new normal. The Fed's balance sheet, which stood at about $900 billion before the crisis, swelled to over $4.5 trillion by 2015.

Other central banks followed America's lead. The European Central Bank, the Bank of Japan, the Bank of England all embraced zero interest rates and quantitative easing. The scale was unprecedented in human history: central banks created over $25 trillion in new money in the decade following 2008. This tsunami of liquidity had to go somewhere. Where it went was into assets, all assets.

The Great Distortion: Zero Interest Rates and Asset Inflation

Zero percent interest rates fundamentally distorted the entire pricing mechanism of the financial system. Interest rates are supposed to reflect the time value of money and the risk of lending. They are the most important price in capitalism, affecting every other price in the economy. When central banks artificially suppress interest rates to zero for over a decade, they break the pricing mechanism itself.

Consider the traditional 60/40 portfolio, 60 percent stocks, 40 percent bonds that had served retirees and institutional investors for generations. In a normal interest rate environment, the bonds in this portfolio provided stable income and a cushion against stock market volatility. But with ten-year Treasury bonds yielding less than 2 percent and sometimes under 1 percent, bonds no longer served their traditional function.

Investors faced an impossible choice: accept real returns that were negative after inflation, or take on more risk. Pension funds with fixed obligations had to reach for yield. Insurance companies with guaranteed payouts needed returns. Endowments supporting universities and foundations had to generate income. Savers planning for retirement couldn't live on near-zero interest rates. The entire investor class was forced out on the risk curve.

This migration into riskier assets to achieve acceptable returns became known as the "search for yield." Money poured out of safe government bonds and bank deposits into corporate bonds, high-yield "junk" bonds, dividend-paying stocks, real estate investment trusts, and increasingly exotic securities. Each step up the risk ladder pushed prices higher and yields lower, forcing investors to take on even more risk.

The result was asset price inflation across the board. But unlike the 1920s bubble, which was largely confined to stocks, this bubble inflated everything simultaneously. Stocks reached valuations that made the 1920s look modest by comparison. Bonds traded at prices that guaranteed negative real returns. Real estate in major cities rose to levels that made homeownership impossible for average workers. Even classic cars, fine art, and vintage wine became investment vehicles that soared in price.

The normal relationship between risk and return broke down. Junk bonds, debt issued by companies with questionable credit traded at yields barely above Treasury bonds. Stocks of companies that had never made a profit traded at valuations previously reserved for the most established, profitable corporations. Real estate investors accepted cap rates (the ratio of income to price) that would have been rejected as absurdly low just a decade earlier.

Stock Market Mania: The New Era Redux

The stock market's ascent in the post-2008 era bears uncomfortable similarities to the 1920s. From the March 2009 low to the 2021 peak, the S&P 500 rose over 700 percent, one of the longest and strongest bull markets in history. This extraordinary performance was driven not primarily by earnings growth or economic expansion, but by multiple expansion investors' willingness to pay ever-higher prices for each dollar of earnings.

Valuation metrics reached levels rarely seen outside of extreme bubbles. The Shiller cyclically-adjusted price-to-earnings ratio (CAPE), which smooths earnings over ten years to eliminate short-term distortions, exceeded 38 in late 2021 higher than at any point except the 1999-2000 tech bubble peak. The Buffett Indicator, which compares total stock market capitalization to GDP, exceeded 200 percent, suggesting stocks were trading at twice their historical relationship to the underlying economy.

These valuations were justified through narratives eerily reminiscent of the 1920s "New Era" thinking. Technology was transforming everything, we were told. Software was eating the world. Network effects and winner-take-all dynamics meant dominant companies deserved premium valuations. Zero interest rates meant traditional valuation metrics no longer applied, with discount rates at zero future cash flows were worth infinitely more.

The cult of disruption reached religious fervor. Companies labeled as "disruptors" commanded valuations based not on current profits but on theoretical future dominance. Amazon traded for years with a triple-digit P/E ratio because it was disrupting retail. Netflix commanded premium valuations as it disrupted entertainment. Tesla became worth more than all traditional automakers combined because it was disrupting transportation.

Initially, skeptics questioned these valuations. But as the bull market continued year after year, skepticism itself became discredited. Bears who warned of overvaluation missed out on extraordinary gains. The career risk of pessimism became so severe that institutional investors had little choice but to participate. Being wrong alongside everyone else was acceptable; being right alone was professional suicide.

The stock market became increasingly dominated by passive index investing and a handful of massive stocks. By 2021, the "Magnificent Seven" technology stocks of Apple, Microsoft, Amazon, Alphabet, Meta, Tesla, and Nvidia represented over 25 percent of the S&P 500's market capitalization. This concentration meant the overall market could keep rising even as the majority of stocks declined. Beneath the surface, market breadth was deteriorating, but headline indices kept climbing.

The Bond Market Paradox

Perhaps nothing better illustrates the distortions created by central bank policy than the bond market's behavior. Bonds are supposed to be the safe, boring part of a portfolio, you lend money, you receive interest, you get your principal back at maturity. Risk and return should be positively correlated: riskier borrowers pay higher interest rates.

But in the post-2008 world, sovereign bonds of developed nations traded with negative yields. Investors paid governments for the privilege of lending them money. At the peak in 2020, over $18 trillion in bonds worldwide traded with negative yields. Think about that: you hand someone $100, and at maturity they hand you back $98, and this is considered an investment.

The rationalization was that deflation might make that negative nominal return positive in real terms. Or that even more negative yields were coming, so today's negative yield bond would appreciate in price. Or that regulations required holding government bonds regardless of return. Each explanation had some validity, but collectively they revealed a system that had lost its moorings.

Corporate bonds showed similar distortions. Investment-grade corporate debt traded at spreads over Treasuries that barely compensated for default risk. High-yield junk bonds traded at yields that the term "high-yield" rendered ironic. Companies with weak balance sheets, declining businesses, or speculative prospects could borrow at rates that would have seemed impossible in a functioning market.

The corporate bond bubble enabled the emergence of "zombie companies", firms that earned barely enough to service interest on their debt but not enough to ever pay down the principal or invest in growth. These corporate walking dead survived only because ultra-low interest rates allowed them to continuously refinance. When rates eventually rose, they would face extinction. But in the meantime, they tied up capital, employed workers, and competed with healthier firms, creating a drag on overall economic productivity.

Most perversely, the bond bubble created an inverted relationship between price and risk. As bond prices rose (yields fell), the risk of holding bonds increased because the potential for price appreciation diminished while the risk of reversal grew. Investors holding bonds at near-zero or negative yields faced catastrophic losses if rates rose even modestly. The supposed safe haven had become a powder keg.

Real Estate: From Shelter to Speculation

The real estate market's inflation rivals and in some ways exceeds the stock and bond bubbles. Housing prices in major metropolitan areas rose to levels that severed the traditional relationship between home prices and incomes. In San Francisco, Seattle, New York, Los Angeles, Vancouver, Sydney, London, and dozens of other cities, the median home price reached 10, 15, or even 20 times median household income.

These ratios were unsustainable by any historical standard. Traditional mortgage lending used a rule of thumb that housing should cost no more than three times annual income. The explosion beyond this ratio meant that homeownership was being put out of reach for average workers in the cities where jobs were concentrated. The American Dream of homeownership became accessible only to those who already had wealth or were willing to take on crushing debt burdens.

The drivers of real estate inflation were multiple. Ultra-low mortgage rates made monthly payments affordable even at elevated prices, allowing buyers to rationalize purchases. Foreign capital, seeking safe havens and yield, poured into real estate in global cities. Institutional investors, starved for returns, began buying single-family homes as investment properties. Restrictive zoning and NIMBY (Not In My Back Yard) politics constrained supply in desirable areas.

But underlying all these factors was the monetary policy that made borrowing essentially free. With 30-year mortgages available below 3 percent, the carrying cost of a $1 million home was lower than renting a modest apartment in many cities. The math seemed to make sense until you considered what would happen when interest rates rose.

Commercial real estate told a similar story. Office buildings, retail spaces, industrial properties, and apartment complexes all traded at cap rates (the ratio of net operating income to purchase price) that had compressed to historic lows. A 4 percent cap rate means an investor pays 25 times annual income for a property, a multiple previously reserved for the highest-quality, most irreplaceable real estate. Yet by the 2020s, even mediocre properties traded at cap rates that guaranteed minimal returns and maximum risk.

The real estate bubble created profound social consequences beyond financial risk. Young people couldn't afford to buy homes in the cities where career opportunities existed. Wealth inequality widened as homeowners benefited from appreciation while renters fell further behind. Cities became playgrounds for the wealthy while workers were pushed to distant suburbs or out entirely. The productive economy suffered as workers spent larger portions of income on housing rather than goods and services.

The Cryptocurrency Phenomenon: Digital Tulips or Digital Gold?

No discussion of the Everything Bubble would be complete without addressing cryptocurrencies, perhaps the most spectacular and certainly the most controversial manifestation of speculative excess. Bitcoin, created in 2009 in the wake of the financial crisis as a decentralized alternative to government-issued currency, spawned an entire ecosystem of digital assets that collectively reached a market capitalization of over $3 trillion at its peak in 2021.

The cryptocurrency phenomenon captured all the elements of classic bubble psychology. True believers proclaimed that blockchain technology would revolutionize finance, eliminate middlemen, bank the unbanked, and create a new monetary system free from government manipulation. Skeptics countered that cryptocurrencies had no intrinsic value, consumed enormous energy to secure through mining, facilitated crime, and served primarily as vehicles for speculation.

What was undeniable was the price action. Bitcoin rose from pennies to nearly $69,000. Ethereum grew from an initial coin offering price of $0.31 to over $4,800. Hundreds of alternative coins and tokens emerged, each claiming to solve some problem or improve on predecessors. The total number of cryptocurrencies exceeded 20,000, though the vast majority had negligible trading volume or utility.

The cryptocurrency bubble displayed familiar patterns. Early adopters who understood the technology made fortunes. This success attracted attention from those who understood less but wanted similar gains. Media coverage intensified as prices rose. Celebrities endorsed various coins. Institutional investors, initially dismissive, began adding crypto exposure to portfolios. Retail investors, suffering from FOMO, rushed in during late-stage parabolic moves.

The narrative evolved as needed to justify higher prices. Initially, Bitcoin was promoted as a currency for transactions. When transaction speeds and fees made this impractical, it became "digital gold", a store of value and inflation hedge. When it crashed alongside other risky assets and proved highly volatile, the narrative shifted to "an emerging asset class" that required patience. Each story served the same purpose: rationalizing continued buying regardless of price.

The proliferation of altcoins (alternative cryptocurrencies) mirrored the investment trusts of the 1920s. New coins launched continuously, each promising to improve on Bitcoin's limitations or solve different problems. Initial coin offerings (ICOs) raised billions from investors who received tokens of questionable utility or legality. Many projects were outright scams; others were well-intentioned but technically infeasible. The common thread was that speculators bought tokens not for utility but hoping to sell at higher prices.

The integration of cryptocurrencies into the broader financial system increased systemic risk. Crypto lending platforms offered unsustainably high interest rates by rehypothecating customer deposits using the same collateral for multiple loans. Stablecoins, supposedly pegged to the dollar, grew to hundreds of billions in value with opaque backing. Crypto hedge funds used extreme leverage. When cracks appeared, the dominoes fell quickly. By late 2022, major crypto lenders, hedge funds, and exchanges had collapsed, vaporizing hundreds of billions in value.

Whether cryptocurrencies represented innovation or delusion remained debatable. What was certain was that their extraordinary price appreciation had been fueled by the same forces inflating traditional assets: too much liquidity chasing too few opportunities, desperate search for yield, and faith that central bank money printing would continue indefinitely.

Private Markets: Opacity Breeds Excess

While public market bubbles attracted attention, perhaps the most dangerous inflation occurred in private markets, venture capital, private equity, and private credit where opacity prevented accurate pricing and regulatory oversight remained minimal. Trillions of dollars flowed into these markets, driven by sophisticated investors' conviction that public markets had become too efficient and that alpha (excess returns) could only be found in private deals.

Venture capital funding reached absurd levels. Startups with minimal revenue but attractive narratives raised hundreds of millions at valuations in the billions. The term "unicorn", a private company valued at $1 billion or more, went from rare to commonplace. By 2021, there were over 1,000 unicorns globally, with a collective valuation exceeding $3 trillion. Many of these valuations bore little relationship to financial performance.

The unicorn phenomenon reflected distorted incentives throughout the venture capital ecosystem. VC firms raised enormous funds from institutional investors desperate for returns. These funds needed to deploy capital to justify management fees. The pressure to put money to work led to inflated valuations and funding of marginal companies. Late-stage private rounds occurred at valuations designed to position the company for an IPO, not to reflect actual business value.

Private equity followed a similar trajectory. Firms raised record amounts of capital, "dry powder" waiting to be invested. With public markets expensive, private equity targeted private companies, often using extreme leverage to juice returns. The traditional private equity model of buying undervalued companies, improving operations, and selling at a profit gave way to financial engineering: buying at high prices with borrowed money and hoping to sell to a greater fool at even higher prices.

The proliferation of private credit marked perhaps the most concerning development. As banks retreated from certain lending activities following post-2008 regulations, private credit funds stepped in. These funds, operating with minimal regulatory oversight, made loans to risky borrowers at rates that seemed high until compared to public junk bonds. The problem was opacity: while public bonds traded daily with transparent prices, private credit valuations were marked by the funds themselves with minimal independent verification.

This opacity bred excess. Private equity firms marked up portfolio company valuations based on questionable assumptions. Venture capital funds carried failed investments at initial valuations far longer than appropriate. Private credit funds rarely marked down troubled loans. The fictional valuations fed back into fundraising, strong "performance" on paper attracted more capital, which allowed the game to continue.

The danger was that much of this capital came from pension funds, endowments, and insurance companies, institutions managing money for retirees, students, and policyholders. These institutions had loaded up on illiquid private assets to achieve return targets that public markets could no longer provide. But illiquidity meant they couldn't easily exit if values declined. When the eventual repricing came, these institutions would face devastating losses with no ability to salvage positions.

SPACs and Meme Stocks: The Retail Revolution

The final phase of the Everything Bubble featured two phenomena that perfectly captured the speculative excess: SPACs (Special Purpose Acquisition Companies) and meme stocks. Both represented the democratization of speculation taken to absurd extremes, enabled by technology and fueled by stimulus money looking for a home.

SPACs, blank-check companies that raised money through IPOs with the intention of later acquiring private companies exploded in popularity in 2020-2021. Over 600 SPACs raised more than $160 billion in 2020-2021, more than all previous years combined. The SPAC structure allowed private companies to go public with less scrutiny than traditional IPOs, and it allowed sponsors to make enormous profits regardless of how the acquired companies ultimately performed.

The SPAC boom had all the hallmarks of late-stage bubble behavior. Celebrity sponsors, from athletes to entertainers to politicians launched SPACs despite no investing experience. The deals became increasingly aggressive, with target companies valued at absurd multiples based on distant revenue projections. Many companies taken public via SPACs were early-stage businesses that traditionally would never have qualified for public markets.

As with most bubble excesses, the SPAC boom ended badly. The majority of SPACs traded below their IPO price within a year. Many target companies saw their stock prices collapse by 70, 80, or 90 percent as reality failed to match projections. Lawsuits proliferated. The SEC began investigating misleading projections. But by then, sponsors and early investors had extracted their profits, leaving retail investors holding worthless paper.

Meme stocks represented something unprecedented: social media-driven trading that divorced stock prices entirely from company fundamentals. GameStop, a struggling video game retailer, became a battleground between retail traders coordinating on Reddit's WallStreetBets forum and hedge funds shorting the stock. The retail traders drove GameStop's price from $4 to $483 in weeks, generating billions in losses for short sellers.

The GameStop saga inspired similar moves in AMC Entertainment, Bed Bath & Beyond, and other struggling companies. The common thread was retail traders buying stocks not based on business prospects but to squeeze short sellers or simply for entertainment value. Trading became gamified, with success measured not by investing returns but by social media acclaim.

Commission-free trading apps like Robinhood facilitated this speculation. The platforms, designed to make trading addictive, used psychological techniques borrowed from gaming and social media: confetti animations for trades, push notifications, and leaderboards. Options trading, previously reserved for sophisticated investors, became accessible to anyone with a smartphone. Zero-day expiry (0DTE) options, bets on intraday price movements exploded in volume, turning the stock market into a casino.

Stimulus checks provided fuel for this speculation. When the government distributed trillions in pandemic relief, much of it ended up in trading accounts. Data showed direct correlations between stimulus payment dates and trading volume spikes. People who had lost jobs or businesses gambled stimulus money on meme stocks and cryptocurrencies, chasing the only pathway to quick wealth available to them.

The meme stock phenomenon revealed how technology and monetary policy had combined to create something new and dangerous: a fully democratized speculative mania where millions of amateur traders, armed with free trading apps and stimulus money, could create disconnects between price and value that previously required professional speculators. The wisdom of crowds had given way to the madness of crowds.

The Everything Bubble: A Systemic Risk

What makes today's bubble uniquely dangerous is not the excess in any single asset class but the simultaneous inflation of everything. In 1929, the crash began in stocks but spread to the real economy. Today, interconnections are far more complex and dangerous.

When stock bubbles pop, pension funds and endowments lose value, forcing spending cuts and benefit reductions. When bond bubbles pop, interest rate increases destroy asset values across the board while making debt unserviceable. When real estate bubbles pop, banks face losses on mortgage portfolios while construction employment collapses. When cryptocurrency bubbles pop, contagion spreads to traditional finance through integrated lending and trading platforms. When private market bubbles pop, the opacity means losses remain hidden until they emerge catastrophically.

The Everything Bubble means there's no diversification, no safe haven, nowhere to hide. The traditional portfolio allocation strategies that protected wealth through previous crises such as stocks and bonds, domestic and international, public and private all fail when everything is simultaneously overvalued. The diversification is illusory; everything is simply exposed to the same underlying risk: excessive liquidity that must eventually be withdrawn.

Moreover, the scale of today's bubble dwarfs 1929. Global debt, government, corporate, and household exceeds $300 trillion, over three times global GDP. Global derivatives markets, which barely existed in 1929, total over $600 trillion in notional value. The financial system has become more complex, more leveraged, and more interconnected than at any point in history. The potential for cascading failures is correspondingly higher.

The most troubling aspect is the policy response to the last crisis that created this bubble. When the next crisis comes and history suggests it will, what tools remain? Interest rates are already near zero. Central bank balance sheets are already bloated. Government debt levels are already at peacetime records. The ammunition used to fight the last crisis has been exhausted. The policy options for addressing the next one are dangerously limited.

The Everything Bubble represents not just a financial phenomenon but a societal bet: the wager that central banks can suppress interest rates indefinitely, that debt can grow faster than output forever, that asset prices can rise without limit, and that the traditional rules governing risk and return no longer apply. It is the ultimate "this time is different" narrative, applied not to a single sector or asset class but to the entire financial system.

History suggests this bet will not pay off. The question is not whether the Everything Bubble will end badly, but when, and how severe the consequences will be when a decade of policy distortions unwind. The warning signs are everywhere, for those willing to see them. The question is whether we will heed them this time, or whether, like in 1929, we will dismiss them until disaster strikes.

Chapter 6

Modern Leverage and Financial Engineering

If the 1920s investor who bought stocks on 10 percent margin seemed reckless, they would be astonished by the complexity and scale of leverage embedded in today's financial system. The margin buying that fueled the 1929 crash was straightforward and visible: you borrowed money from your broker to buy stocks. Modern leverage is often hidden, embedded in complex instruments, and amplified through chains of interconnected transactions that even sophisticated investors struggle to understand. The financial engineering that has evolved over the past four decades has created leverage so pervasive and opaque that no one, not regulators, not risk managers, not even the traders themselves fully comprehends the system's total exposure.

The Derivatives Monster: When the Tail Wags the Dog

At the heart of modern financial leverage sits the derivatives market, a $600 trillion colossus that dwarfs the real economy it supposedly serves. To put this in perspective, global GDP is approximately $100 trillion. The notional value of derivatives is six times larger than the entire annual economic output of planet Earth. This is not leverage in the traditional sense; it is leverage on an incomprehensible scale.

Derivatives, financial contracts whose value derives from some underlying asset have legitimate uses. A farmer can hedge crop price risk. An airline can lock in fuel costs. A manufacturer can protect against currency fluctuations. These basic hedging functions have existed for centuries. But the modern derivatives market has evolved far beyond such straightforward risk management into something altogether different: a vast web of interconnected bets that amplifies risk rather than managing it.

The problem begins with notional value versus actual exposure. Defenders of derivatives point out that notional value overstates risk, a $1 million interest rate swap might have only $10,000 of actual risk exposure at any given time. This is true but misleading. The relevant question is not the exposure under normal market conditions but the exposure when markets become disorderly. And history repeatedly demonstrates that derivatives behave very differently when markets are stressed.

Consider credit default swaps (CDS), insurance-like contracts that pay out if a borrower defaults. In theory, CDS's allow risk to be distributed efficiently: those who want to bear credit risk can sell protection, those who want to shed it can buy protection. In practice, CDS created an enormous hidden leverage in the system. By 2007, the CDS market had grown to $60 trillion, with much of it concentrated in mortgage-backed securities.

The leverage came from multiple sources. First, CDS could be purchased without owning the underlying bonds, so-called "naked" CDS that were pure speculation rather than hedging. Second, the same reference entity could have many times more CDS protection written on it than actual bonds outstanding, creating synthetic leverage. Third, CDS were traded over-the-counter with minimal capital requirements, allowing dealers to write enormous amounts of protection without posting adequate collateral.

When the housing market collapsed, this structure revealed its fatal flaw: the losses were concentrated. AIG, which had written hundreds of billions in CDS protection on mortgage securities, faced margin calls it couldn't meet. The company required a $182 billion government bailout to prevent its failure from triggering a cascade of counterparty defaults throughout the financial system. The "insurance" had become a transmission mechanism for contagion rather than a buffer against it.

The lesson should have been that derivatives concentrate rather than disperse risk, and that their complexity makes systemic exposure impossible to measure. Instead, the lesson taken was merely that CDS needed better regulation. The broader derivatives market continued growing, with increasing complexity and opacity.

Interest rate derivatives, currency derivatives, equity derivatives, commodity derivatives each market has grown to enormous size with multiple layers of leverage embedded. An interest rate swap might reference a bond, which is itself leveraged. An option on a futures contract adds leverage on leverage. Structured products bundle derivatives with other derivatives, creating leverage towers where the exposure at the top bears little relationship to the risk at the bottom.

High-Frequency Trading: Speed as Leverage

While traditional leverage multiplies capital through borrowing, high-frequency trading (HFT) achieves leverage through speed and volume. HFT firms use sophisticated algorithms and direct market access to execute thousands of trades per second, profiting from tiny price discrepancies that exist for milliseconds. Individually, these profits are minuscule, fractions of a penny per share. But multiplied across millions of transactions, they generate enormous revenue.

HFT now accounts for roughly 50-70 percent of equity trading volume in U.S. markets, though the percentage fluctuates. The firms engaged in HFT maintain they provide liquidity and tighten spreads, benefiting all market participants. Critics argue they are parasitic, extracting value from other traders while contributing to market instability.

The leverage in HFT is not financial but operational: the same capital is recycled through thousands of trades in a single day. A firm with $100 million in capital might establish and close positions worth billions in a trading session. This creates an illusion of liquidity that disappears precisely when it's most needed. During market stress, HFT firms withdraw, removing the liquidity they supposedly provide and accelerating declines.

The May 6, 2010, "Flash Crash" demonstrated this dynamic perfectly. In roughly 30 minutes, the Dow Jones Industrial Average plunged nearly 1,000 points about 9 percent before recovering most of the loss. The trigger was a large sell order in S&P 500 futures contracts, but the amplification came from HFT algorithms. As prices began falling, HFT programs detected unusual volatility and shut down, removing liquidity exactly when it was needed. Other algorithms, designed to follow momentum, began selling as well. The cascade became self-reinforcing until circuit breakers finally halted trading and allowed human intervention.

Since the Flash Crash, there have been dozens of mini-flash crashes in individual stocks and sectors. Stocks have dropped 90 percent in seconds before recovering. These events, previously impossible in human-mediated markets, are now routine. Each demonstrates that the liquidity provided by HFT is conditional and fragile, present during calm periods but vanishing during stress.

More concerning is the arms race dynamic HFT has created. Firms spend hundreds of millions to shave microseconds off execution times, relocating servers next to exchanges, building microwave towers for faster data transmission, even exploring laser transmission through the atmosphere. This investment in speed provides no social value, markets functioned perfectly well when trades took seconds rather than microseconds. But once some firms achieved speed advantages, others had to follow or be systematically disadvantaged.

The result is that modern markets are dominated by machines executing strategies designed by algorithms based on models that may not account for unusual conditions. When multiple algorithms interact in unexpected ways, unpredictable outcomes emerge. The market has become a complex adaptive system where no individual participant understands the whole, and where emergent behavior can overwhelm any single actor's intentions.

Exchange-Traded Funds: Passive Leverage

Exchange-traded funds (ETFs) are marketed as simple, transparent investment vehicles: baskets of stocks or bonds that trade like individual securities. For basic, broad-market ETFs, this description is accurate. But the ETF market has evolved into something far more complex and potentially dangerous, with over $10 trillion in assets and increasing concentration in passive index strategies.

The concern is not that ETFs themselves are leveraged, but that they create leverage-like effects through concentration and mechanical trading. When investors buy an S&P 500 ETF, they buy all 500 stocks in proportion to their market capitalization. This seems diversified, but it creates passive price-insensitive buying that pushes all stocks higher regardless of fundamentals. More money flowing into passive index funds means more indiscriminate buying of every stock in the index.

This dynamic has grown to dominate markets. Passive investing now comprises over 40 percent of U.S. equity assets, up from less than 10 percent two decades ago. During this period, correlations between stocks have increased dramatically. Individual stock selection matters less because passive flows drive prices more than company-specific factors. The market has become less efficient at price discovery, the core function of capital markets.

The leverage effect emerges during reversals. When markets decline and investors sell ETFs, the ETF must sell all underlying holdings proportionally. This creates indiscriminate selling pressure unrelated to any individual company's prospects. Good companies and bad companies fall together, amplifying volatility. The price-insensitive buying that characterized the upswing becomes price-insensitive selling on the downswing.

Leveraged and inverse ETFs create actual, explicit leverage on top of these dynamics. These products use derivatives to provide 2x or 3x the daily return of an index, or the inverse of that return. They're designed as short-term trading vehicles but have attracted long-term holders who don't understand their mechanics. The mathematical properties of these ETFs guarantee that they decay over time due to volatility, even if the underlying index returns to its starting point. Yet billions flow into them from unsuspecting retail investors.

More exotic ETFs have proliferated: sector-specific, country-specific, strategy-specific, factor-based, actively managed, and on and on. Many of these vehicles are thinly traded with wide bid-ask spreads. Some hold illiquid underlying securities that couldn't be easily sold if redemptions accelerated. The ETF wrapper creates an illusion of liquidity for underlying holdings that may be quite illiquid.

The potential for disruption became apparent in March 2020, when even Treasury bond ETFs, supposedly the safest, most liquid instruments experienced severe dislocations. Premiums and discounts to net asset value widened dramatically. The creation/redemption mechanism that's supposed to keep ETF prices aligned with underlying holdings broke down. Only massive Federal Reserve intervention stabilized the situation.

The systemic risk is that ETFs have created correlation and concentration that amplifies market movements in both directions. Money flows into ETFs drive passive buying that pushes prices higher with no regard to valuation. When flows reverse, passive selling will drive prices lower with no regard to quality. The market has become a momentum machine where ETFs serve as the transmission mechanism, and the leverage comes not from borrowing but from mechanical, price-insensitive flows that overwhelm fundamental analysis.

Corporate Debt: The Zombie Apocalypse

While retail and professional traders employ leverage through margin and derivatives, corporations have gorged themselves on debt to a degree that makes the 1920s look prudent. Total U.S. non-financial corporate debt exceeds $11 trillion, up from roughly $6 trillion in 2008. Relative to GDP, corporate debt has reached 47 percent, near record highs. This debt was accumulated during a decade of near-zero interest rates when borrowing was essentially free.

The concerning question is what corporations did with this borrowed money. In theory, companies borrow to invest in productive assets: new factories, research and development, expansion into new markets. Such investment generates returns that exceed the cost of debt, creating value for shareholders. Reality proved very different.

Corporate America used cheap debt primarily for financial engineering rather than productive investment: share buybacks, dividends, and mergers and acquisitions. Between 2010 and 2020, S&P 500 companies spent over $5 trillion on share buybacks. Many companies borrowed money at low interest rates specifically to repurchase their own stock, shrinking share count to boost earnings per share even as absolute earnings stagnated or declined.

This financial alchemy created an illusion of prosperity. Earnings per share rose not because companies were more profitable but because the denominator (shares outstanding) decreased. Stock prices rose not because business prospects improved but because companies themselves were major buyers. Executive compensation, often tied to stock price or earnings per share, soared even as corporate investment in productive capacity declined.

The consequence is an army of zombie companies, firms that earn barely enough to service interest on their debt but not enough to pay down principal or invest in growth. The Bank for International Settlements estimated that by 2019, roughly 12 percent of publicly traded companies in advanced economies were zombies, up from 2 percent in the 1980s. These companies survive only because interest rates remain low enough to refinance debt as it matures.

Zombie companies are a hidden drag on economic productivity. They tie up capital that could be deployed more productively. They employ workers in declining businesses. They compete with healthier firms, suppressing prices and profits industry-wide. They create the illusion of economic activity while actually representing misallocated resources that should have been liquidated.

The corporate debt bubble also created significant credit market distortion. With companies borrowing not to invest but to engineer financial metrics, credit ratings became less meaningful. A company with an investment-grade rating might have weak cash flow and high leverage, surviving only through continuous refinancing. The migration of firms from investment-grade to junk status, so-called "fallen angels" has created an enormous overhang of questionable credits.

Covenant-lite loans, which provide borrowers with fewer restrictions and protections for lenders, proliferated. By 2020, over 80 percent of leveraged loans were covenant-lite, up from virtually zero in the early 2000s. This means lenders have limited ability to intervene even when borrowers show signs of distress. The shift in bargaining power from lenders to borrowers reflects the desperation for yield that zero interest rates created.

When interest rates finally began rising in 2022-2023, the corporate debt bomb started ticking louder. Companies that had borrowed at 3-4 percent now face refinancing at 8-10 percent or higher. For highly leveraged companies, this difference transforms survivable debt loads into unsustainable burdens. Defaults began rising, and the zombie companies that had survived on life support for a decade faced extinction.

Options Trading: Retail Investors as Leveraged Speculators

The democratization of options trading represents one of the most dangerous developments in modern markets. Options, contracts that give the right but not the obligation to buy or sell securities at specific prices are inherently leveraged instruments. A small move in the underlying stock can generate large percentage gains or losses in options. Historically, options were traded primarily by sophisticated investors and institutions who understood the risks.

The rise of commission-free trading apps and gamification of investing changed this completely. Robinhood and similar platforms made options trading accessible to anyone with a smartphone. Young investors, many with limited financial knowledge and no memory of bear markets, began trading options as their primary investing strategy. The surge was staggering: options trading volume more than doubled between 2019 and 2021, with much of the increase coming from retail traders.

The attraction of options is the leverage: with limited capital, traders can control positions worth far more than their account balance. A trader with $1,000 can control $10,000 or $50,000 worth of stock through call options. When the bet works, returns are spectacular, 10x, 20x, even 100x gains on successful trades. These success stories spread through social media, attracting more participants.

The dark side is that most options expire worthless. The leverage works both ways, spectacular gains are possible but total losses are far more common. Studies show that the vast majority of retail options traders lose money. But the same psychological factors that make gambling addictive make options trading addictive: intermittent reinforcement, near-misses, and the belief that the next trade will be the big winner.

The most dangerous recent development is zero-day expiry (0DTE) options, contracts that expire the same day they're purchased. These ultra-short-term instruments are pure speculation on intraday price movement. There's no investment thesis, no fundamental analysis, no consideration of company prospects, just gambling on whether a stock will rise or fall over the next few hours.

0DTE options volume exploded to over 40 percent of total S&P 500 options volume by 2023. This means that nearly half of options activity involves contracts with hours or minutes remaining until expiration. The leverage is extreme, the risks are total, and the impact on underlying markets is significant. Market makers hedging these options must constantly adjust positions, creating feedback loops that amplify volatility.

The options boom has also affected equity markets in unexpected ways. When retail traders buy call options en masse, market makers who sell those options must hedge by buying the underlying stock. This "gamma squeeze" can drive stock prices higher mechanically, unrelated to fundamentals. The GameStop saga in early 2021 was partially driven by this dynamic, retail call buying forced market makers to buy stock driving prices higher, which attracted more call buying, creating a self-reinforcing loop.

The leverage embedded in options trading means that retail investors, who individually have limited capital, can collectively move markets through leveraged bets. This is unprecedented in financial history. In the 1920s, retail speculation was limited by the capital individuals could borrow. Today, through options, retail traders can achieve leverage ratios of 10:1, 20:1, or higher, multiplying the impact of their collective sentiment.

Structured Products: Complexity as Concealed Leverage

For sophisticated investors and institutions, leverage often comes wrapped in structured products, complex securities engineered to provide specific risk-return profiles. These instruments combine various derivatives, bonds, and equity exposures into packages that most buyers don't fully understand. The complexity itself becomes a source of hidden leverage and concentrated risk.

Collateralized loan obligations (CLOs) are a prime example. These securities bundle hundreds of leveraged loans (debt to already highly-leveraged companies) into tranches with different risk levels. The senior tranches receive investment-grade ratings despite being backed by junk-quality loans, a feat achieved through structural subordination and statistical models.

The models assume that loan defaults will be uncorrelated, that loans to hundreds of different companies in different industries won't all default simultaneously. This assumption works in normal times but fails during systemic crises. When a recession hits and defaults correlate, the structured protections evaporate. The senior tranches that seemed safe are suddenly exposed to massive losses.

The CLO market has grown to over $1 trillion, making it larger than the subprime mortgage market was at its peak in 2007. Many of these securities are held by insurance companies, pension funds, and regional banks, institutions that couldn't directly buy junk-rated loans due to regulatory constraints but can hold "investment-grade" CLO tranches. The structured product allowed them to sidestep restrictions and take on risk they weren't supposed to have.

Other structured products display similar properties: complexity concealing risk, ratings that provide false comfort, and leverage embedded through derivatives. Structured notes sold to retail investors often guarantee principal but cap upside or expose investors to downside through complex formulas. Contingent convertible bonds (CoCos) act like bonds during normal times but convert to equity or write down to zero during stress, creating cliff risks that few holders understand.

The common thread is that structured products take leverage and risk that would be obvious in simple instruments and obscure them through complexity. An investor who buys a junk-rated loan knows they're taking on significant credit risk. An investor who buys an investment-grade CLO tranche thinks they're making a safe investment, but they've actually taken on correlated exposure to hundreds of risky credits, just filtered through a structure that obscures the risk.

The 2008 financial crisis should have ended the structured product boom, it was after all structured mortgage products that nearly destroyed the financial system. Instead, structured products simply migrated to new underlying assets. The techniques that packaged subprime mortgages into AAA-rated securities now package leveraged loans, auto loans, credit card receivables, and esoteric assets into rated securities that investors accept without adequate due diligence.

Algorithmic Risk Management: When Models Meet Reality

Modern financial leverage is managed supposedly through sophisticated risk models and algorithmic systems. These systems monitor positions in real-time, calculate risk exposures using complex mathematics, and execute hedging strategies automatically. The promise is that technology allows greater leverage safely because risks are constantly measured and managed.

The reality is that these systems create new risks even as they manage old ones. Risk models rely on historical data and statistical assumptions that can fail catastrophically during unusual conditions. The famous

Black-Scholes option pricing model assumes markets are continuous and liquid, assumptions that break down precisely when options are most needed as hedges.

Value-at-Risk (VaR) models, used by virtually every major financial institution, calculate the maximum loss expected over a specific time period at a given confidence level. A 99% VaR of $10 million means there's a 99% chance losses won't exceed $10 million in a day. But this also means there's a 1% chance of larger losses and 1% is not rare. In a trading year of 250 days, 1% means two or three days with losses exceeding VaR. And VaR says nothing about how large those exceeding losses might be.

More fundamentally, VaR and similar models assume that extreme events are rare and that markets are efficient. Both assumptions fail during crises. Extreme events cluster, one bad day is often followed by more bad days. And markets become inefficient precisely when risk management is most crucial, with liquidity evaporating and correlations going to one (everything falling together).

Algorithmic risk management also creates feedback loops. When VaR limits are breached, algorithms automatically reduce positions, which means selling during market declines. If many institutions use similar risk models and hit limits simultaneously, they all sell at once, accelerating the decline and triggering more selling. The risk management becomes a source of systemic risk.

Long-Term Capital Management's collapse in 1998 demonstrated these dynamics. LTCM was staffed by Nobel Prize winners using the most sophisticated risk models available. Their models said their positions were safe, with diversified exposures and careful hedging. When the Russian debt crisis created correlations the models hadn't predicted, LTCM's leverage meant that a small move in the wrong direction became catastrophic. Only a Federal Reserve-orchestrated bailout prevented broader systemic collapse.

The lesson, that leverage plus complexity plus model dependence equals systemic risk was temporarily learned and then forgotten. Today's hedge funds, investment banks, and trading desks use even more complex models managing even more leverage. The confidence in these models is likely even greater than it was at LTCM, and the systemic leverage is certainly higher. The next model failure will affect more institutions with larger positions in more interconnected markets.

The Interconnection Web: When Everything Depends on Everything

The final and perhaps most dangerous aspect of modern leverage is how it creates webs of interconnection where every participant depends on every other participant. A hedge fund's leverage depends on prime brokers providing financing, which depends on those brokers managing their own risk, which depends on counterparties meeting margin calls, which depends on markets remaining liquid, which depends on confidence persisting.

This interconnection means that no single institution's leverage can be considered in isolation. A hedge fund might seem modestly leveraged at 3:1, but if its prime broker is leveraged 10:1, and its counterparties are leveraged as well, the effective system-wide leverage is far higher. Moreover, the same collateral often supports multiple transactions through rehypothecation, your collateral becomes someone else's collateral for their transaction, which becomes another party's collateral, creating chains of leverage built on the same underlying assets.

When this web functions smoothly, it's nearly invisible. Everyone meets obligations, liquidity flows freely, and the leverage multiplies productive capacity. But during stress, the web becomes a transmission mechanism for contagion. One party's failure to meet obligations causes problems for their counterparties, which causes problems for those counterparties' counterparties, cascading through the system.

The 2008 crisis demonstrated this clearly: Lehman Brothers' failure immediately created crises for its counterparties, prime brokerage clients, and anyone holding its commercial paper. AIG's troubles threatened every institution that had bought CDS protection from it. Money market funds' exposure to Lehman paper sparked runs that required Treasury intervention. The interconnections meant that a single failure point could threaten the entire system.

Since 2008, regulators have tried to reduce these interconnection risks through higher capital requirements, stress testing, and central clearing of derivatives. These reforms helped on the margins but didn't address the fundamental issue: the financial system has become so complex and interconnected that no one, not regulators, not risk managers, not participants themselves can map all the relationships or predict how a shock will propagate.

This opacity is not accidental. It's a feature of modern financial engineering. Complexity benefits insiders who understand it at the expense of outsiders who don't. Interconnection allows institutions to access leverage they couldn't obtain transparently. The result is a system where true risk is unknowable until crisis reveals it, and by then it's too late to prepare.

The Leverage Ratchet: Easy Up, Impossible Down

Modern financial leverage has a ratchet property: it's easy to increase but nearly impossible to decrease without triggering a crisis. When leverage is building, it's profitable for all participants. Borrowers get capital cheaply, lenders earn fees and interest, intermediaries collect transaction revenues. Everyone benefits from the upward spiral.

But deleveraging, reducing the leverage in the system is painful and dangerous. When entities try to reduce leverage by selling assets, prices fall, which reduces collateral values, which triggers more selling, creating a self-reinforcing downward spiral. The very act of deleveraging accelerates the need for more deleveraging.

This is the trap modern financial engineering has created. The system is viable only with continually increasing leverage. When leverage peaks and reverses, the mechanisms that amplified gains on the way up amplify losses on the way down. The speed and scale of modern leverage means these cycles are more violent and more dangerous than historical precedents.

In the 1920s, deleveraging was brutal but comprehensible: brokers issued margin calls, investors sold stocks, prices fell. The process was transparent and linear. Today's deleveraging is opaque and non-linear: derivatives positions must be unwound, structured products must be priced with no market, algorithmic risk systems trigger cascading sales, interconnected counterparties default simultaneously. The complexity that enabled extreme leverage ensures that unwinding it will be chaotic and unpredictable.

This is the poisoned legacy of modern financial engineering: a system leveraged to such extremes through such complex mechanisms that it cannot safely deleverage. The machine can only run faster and faster until something breaks. When it does, the crash will be amplified by all the leverage that seemed safe during the climb, just as it was in 1929 but with complexity and scale that would have been unimaginable to investors then and remains incompletely understood by investors today.

Chapter 7

The New Investment Trusts

In the 1920s, investment trusts were the financial innovation that democratized speculation and amplified the crash. These vehicles allowed ordinary investors to pool money and leverage it to purchase diversified portfolios of stocks. The trusts proliferated wildly in the late 1920s, with many trusts owning other trusts, creating pyramids of leverage that magnified gains during the boom and catastrophically multiplied losses during the bust. By 1929, there were nearly 750 investment trusts controlling $8 billion in assets, a staggering sum that represented a significant portion of total market capitalization.

Today's financial markets have created structures that serve remarkably similar functions with equally dangerous characteristics. Private credit funds, shadow banking entities, structured investment vehicles, cryptocurrency platforms, and digital asset schemes have become the new investment trusts promising diversification and professional management while actually delivering opacity, excessive leverage, and concentrated risk. The names have changed, but the dynamics remain hauntingly familiar.

Private Credit: Banking Without Banks

The most significant and dangerous parallel to 1920s investment trusts exists in the private credit market, which has exploded to over $1.5 trillion in assets under management. Private credit funds make loans to companies, typically middle-market businesses that are too small or too risky for traditional bank financing but too large for simple bank loans. The pitch to investors is compelling: higher yields than public bonds, diversification across many borrowers, and professional credit analysis that identifies good risks.

The reality is far less reassuring. Private credit operates in the shadows, with minimal regulatory oversight, opaque valuations, and borrowers who couldn't access traditional financing for good reasons. The funds employ significant leverage, often 2:1 or higher multiplying both returns and risks.

They offer quarterly or even less frequent redemption windows, meaning investors cannot easily exit. And most concerningly, they mark their own portfolios' values with little independent verification.

This last feature is particularly troubling. Public bonds trade daily with transparent prices that reflect market participants' collective assessment of value. Private credit funds value their loan portfolios internally, using models and assumptions that almost invariably show steady, positive performance. A loan made at par typically stays marked at par on the books for years, even if the borrower's fortunes deteriorate. Only when a borrower actually defaults does the loan get marked down and often not even then, as restructurings allow the fiction of par value to continue.

The result is return profiles that look magically smooth. While public credit markets fluctuate with volatility that reflects changing risk assessments, private credit funds show steadily accruing returns with minimal volatility. This is pure illusion not evidence of superior risk management but evidence of valuation freedom. The returns are too good to be true because the valuations are too good to be true.

The parallel to 1920s investment trusts is precise. Those trusts reported steady portfolio appreciation even as underlying stocks became overvalued. The trust structure provided a layer of opacity between investors and reality. Investors couldn't easily see what the trusts held or whether valuations made sense. They relied on trust managers' representations and the steady reported returns. When reality eventually intruded, the gap between reported values and actual values was devastating.

Private credit funds have attracted enormous capital from pension funds, endowments, insurance companies, and wealthy individuals all searching desperately for yield in a zero-rate world. These institutions have loaded up on private credit exposure, typically 10-20 percent of portfolios but sometimes much more. They accepted the illiquidity because the reported returns justified it. They accepted the opacity because they needed the yield.

What they've actually purchased is a portfolio of unmarketable loans to leveraged, sub-investment-grade borrowers, valued by the very entities that earn fees on the assets, redeemable only at the fund's discretion, with no independent price discovery mechanism. When the economy turns and defaults rise, the cascade will be brutal. Funds will be forced to mark down loans they've carried at par for years. Investors will seek redemptions. Funds will have to sell assets, except there's no liquid market for these loans. Fire sales will ensue, forcing marks even lower. The "alternative" to public credit markets will reveal itself as simply a way to hide risk until it explodes.

Shadow Banking: The Parallel Financial System

Beyond private credit, a vast shadow banking system has emerged, financial intermediation occurring outside the regulated banking sector. Money market funds, securities lending, repurchase agreements (repos), commercial paper, and structured investment vehicles collectively perform bank-like functions without bank-like regulation, capital requirements, or safety nets.

The shadow banking system is estimated at over $60 trillion globally, nearly as large as the traditional banking system. This parallel financial structure amplifies leverage and systemic risk in ways that are poorly understood and inadequately regulated. The entities look like banks, act like banks, and create bank-like risks, but operate outside the regulatory framework designed to prevent bank runs and systemic crises.

Money market funds exemplify the problem. These funds hold short-term debt securities and aim to maintain a stable $1.00 net asset value, creating the illusion of bank deposits. Investors treat them as cash equivalents, using them for day-to-day liquidity. But unlike bank deposits, money market funds aren't insured. And unlike banks, they don't have access to Federal Reserve emergency lending.

When short-term credit markets seized up in 2008, money market funds faced the equivalent of bank runs. The Reserve Primary Fund "broke the buck", its net asset value fell below $1.00 due to holdings of Lehman Brothers commercial paper. Investors panicked and rushed to redeem, threatening a complete freeze of short-term funding markets. Only emergency Treasury guarantees and Federal Reserve interventions prevented catastrophe.

The lesson should have been that shadow banks create bank-like risks requiring bank-like protections and regulations. Instead, the lesson taken was merely that money market funds needed modest reforms. The shadow banking system continued growing, with risk simply migrating to less-regulated corners.

Securities lending, where investors lend stocks or bonds to short sellers in exchange for collateral and fees has grown into a multi-trillion-dollar business. The practice creates complex webs of dependencies where the same securities serve as collateral for multiple transactions through rehypothecation. When stress hits, these chains can break catastrophically as parties scramble to return securities or recall collateral.

Repurchase agreements (repos) are essentially collateralized overnight loans that grease the wheels of financial markets. Institutions borrow against securities overnight, creating short-term liquidity. The repo market typically functions smoothly but can freeze suddenly if collateral values become uncertain. September 2019 saw repo rates spike from 2 percent to 10 percent intraday when the market temporarily seized up, requiring Federal Reserve intervention. If overnight funding markets can dislocate this severely during a period of economic expansion, what happens during a crisis?

The shadow banking system recreates the fundamental vulnerability of banking, maturity transformation and borrowing short to lend long without the regulatory safeguards. Investment trusts in the 1920s did something similar: they created leverage and liquidity mismatches that looked safe until they weren't. Shadow banks today operate on a far larger scale with vastly more complex interconnections.

Structured Investment Vehicles: Lesson Not Learned

One might assume that after structured investment vehicles (SIVs) and collateralized debt obligations (CDOs) nearly destroyed the financial system in 2008, such structures would have been consigned to history. One would be wrong. While the specific labels have become toxic, the underlying techniques have simply been repackaged with new names and applied to different asset classes.

Collateralized loan obligations (CLOs), which bundle leveraged loans into tranched securities, have grown to over $1 trillion in issuance, larger than the subprime CDO market at its peak. The pitch is that CLOs are safer than mortgage CDOs because corporate loans are less correlated than mortgages, and because post-2008 underwriting is supposedly more rigorous. This is rationalization, not analysis.

CLOs employ the same structural techniques that made CDOs dangerous: tranching (slicing pools into senior and junior pieces), credit enhancement (over-collateralization and subordination), and rating agency alchemy (turning pools of junk into AAA-rated securities). The mathematical models assume diversification benefits that evaporate during stress when defaults correlate. The senior tranches, marketed as safe, are actually exposed to tail risk that the models underestimate.

Who buys CLOs? Insurance companies, banks, pension funds and asset managers, the same institutional investors who bought mortgage CDOs in 2006. They buy the senior AAA-rated tranches, believing the ratings and trusting the models. They rarely perform detailed analysis on the underlying loans because the structure is complex and the loan pools are large. They accept the ratings as sufficient due diligence.

This is the classic mistake: trusting structures over fundamentals, trusting models over judgment, trusting ratings over analysis. The 1920s investment trust investor who bought trusts without examining the underlying holdings is the 2020s institutional investor who buys CLO tranches without analyzing the underlying loans. The complexity provides false comfort, surely something this sophisticated has been carefully designed and validated. But complexity is often a feature, not a bug, designed to obscure risk rather than manage it.

Beyond CLOs, structured finance has spawned endless variations: collateralized bond obligations, bespoke tranche opportunities, synthetic CDOs, and structures so complex they require paragraphs to name. Each claims to provide diversification, yield, and safety through financial engineering. Each is opaque, difficult to value, and vulnerable to correlation risk that models underestimate.

The common thread connecting these structures to 1920s investment trusts is leverage concealed through complexity. An investment trust in 1929 might own other trusts, which owned stocks bought on margin, creating three layers of leverage. A modern CLO investor might own the senior tranche of a CLO, which holds leveraged loans to companies that themselves are highly levered, again creating multiple layers. The labels differ but the economics are identical: leverage on leverage on leverage, with structural complexity obscuring the total exposure.

Cryptocurrency Platforms: Decentralized in Name Only

The cryptocurrency ecosystem has generated its own version of investment trusts through centralized lending platforms, exchanges, and "decentralized finance" (DeFi) protocols. These entities promised to revolutionize finance through blockchain technology, eliminating intermediaries and providing transparency. In reality, they recreated the worst aspects of traditional finance, opacity, leverage, conflicts of interest, and fraud without the regulatory safeguards.

Cryptocurrency lending platforms like Celsius Network, BlockFi, and Voyager Digital offered investors high yields on crypto deposits, often 8-10 percent or more. The pitch was simple: deposit your Bitcoin or Ethereum, earn interest, withdraw anytime. Millions of retail investors, unable to earn meaningful interest from traditional banks, poured billions into these platforms.

Behind the scenes, these platforms were operating as unregulated banks with massive leverage and maturity mismatches. They borrowed short-term from depositors and lent long-term to hedge funds and other borrowers. They accepted crypto as collateral for loans but didn't adequately stress-test what would happen if crypto prices fell sharply. They commingled customer funds with firm capital, creating conflicts of interest. And they provided minimal transparency about their actual operations.

When crypto prices crashed in 2022, the house of cards collapsed. Celsius, which had $12 billion in customer deposits, froze withdrawals and declared bankruptcy. BlockFi and Voyager followed. Customer "deposits" were actually unsecured loans to the platforms, meaning depositors became unsecured creditors in bankruptcy with no insurance and little hope of recovering their funds. Billions in customer money vaporized.

The parallel to 1920s investment trusts is striking. Those trusts promised professional management and diversification while actually delivering opacity and leverage. Crypto lending platforms promised transparency and yield while actually delivering opacity and leverage. Investors in both eras trusted intermediaries without understanding what those intermediaries were actually doing with their money.

Three Arrows Capital, a crypto hedge fund, exemplifies the leverage problem. The fund borrowed billions from lending platforms, using crypto as collateral. It then used that borrowed money to make leveraged bets on various tokens and protocols. When prices fell, the fund faced margin calls it couldn't meet. Its collapse triggered losses at multiple lending platforms, which had lent to 3AC expecting the collateral would protect them. But when everyone tried to sell the same collateral simultaneously, there were no buyers at prices that would make creditors whole.

This is exactly what happened in 1929: margin calls forcing liquidations, collateral proving insufficient, and interconnected failures cascading through the system. The technology differs, blockchain instead of ticker tape but the dynamics are identical.

Decentralized finance (DeFi) protocols claimed to eliminate these centralization risks through smart contracts and automated market makers. In practice, DeFi created new risks while preserving old ones. The protocols used extreme leverage, often 10:1 or higher. They created synthetic assets and derivatives on derivatives. They suffered from smart contract bugs that allowed hacks stealing hundreds of millions. And despite the "decentralized" label, many were effectively controlled by small groups of insiders.

The Terra/Luna collapse in May 2022 demonstrated DeFi's fragility. Terra was an algorithmic stablecoin that maintained its peg to the dollar through a complex mechanism involving Luna tokens. The system was essentially a Ponzi scheme, it worked only as long as new money flowed in. When confidence wavered and redemptions accelerated, the algorithmic mechanism failed catastrophically. Over $40 billion in value evaporated in days.

Investment trusts in the 1920s often employed creative structures that worked beautifully during the boom but failed catastrophically during the bust. DeFi protocols are the modern equivalent: innovative in design, brilliant in execution during good times, catastrophically fragile when tested by stress.

NFTs and Digital Collectibles: Tulips 2.0

Non-fungible tokens (NFTs) and digital collectibles represent perhaps the purest expression of speculative mania in the Everything Bubble. These digital assets, ranging from artwork to trading cards to virtual real estate sold for millions of dollars during the peak, driven entirely by greater fool theory and belief that digital scarcity created value.

The NFT boom reached its zenith in 2021, with $25 billion in trading volume. The most expensive NFT, "The Merge" by digital artist Pak, sold for $91.8 million. Bored Ape Yacht Club, a collection of 10,000 cartoon ape images, saw individual NFTs selling for hundreds of thousands of dollars, with celebrity buyers including Jimmy Fallon, Paris Hilton, and Snoop Dogg.

The investment thesis was that NFTs were the future of digital ownership and that early adopters would profit as the technology gained mainstream acceptance. The reality was pure speculation detached from any economic fundamentals. An NFT provides no cash flow, no productive use, and despite claims of "ownership" often limited actual rights to the underlying asset.

The parallels to historical manias are obvious. Tulip bulbs in 1630s Holland had genuine utility, you could plant them and grow flowers. Yet speculation drove prices to absurd levels before the inevitable collapse. NFTs have even less utility than tulip bulbs, yet reached valuations that made tulip mania look modest. A JPEG file that anyone can right-click and save sold for millions because buyers believed they could sell to someone else for more.

Investment trusts in the 1920s often held stocks that were themselves overvalued. NFT platforms and funds created another layer: structures that held collections of already-speculative digital assets, adding another level of opacity and fees. Fractional ownership platforms allowed investors to buy shares of expensive NFTs, creating investment vehicles that owned digital assets that owned...nothing of fundamental value.

The NFT crash was swift and brutal. By late 2022, trading volumes had fallen over 95 percent from peak. NFTs that sold for hundreds of thousands became unsellable at any price. The celebrity buyers who had promoted NFTs fell silent. Platforms shut down. The billions in "value" that had existed on paper evaporated.

This boom-bust cycle follows the exact pattern of investment trust mania in the 1920s: rapid proliferation of vehicles, celebrity endorsement, prices driven by speculation rather than fundamentals, growing complexity and leverage, and ultimate collapse when greater fools stop appearing. The technology was new but the psychology was ancient.

Private Equity: Fees on Fees on Fees

Private equity firms have become the modern equivalent of investment trust sponsors, collecting multiple layers of fees while promising superior returns. The typical private equity structure charges a 2 percent annual management fee plus 20 percent of profits, the infamous "2 and 20" model. These fees are extracted regardless of whether the investments actually outperform public markets.

The industry has grown to over $5 trillion in assets under management, with capital concentrated in a few dozen major firms. The pitch to institutional investors is that private equity can generate returns exceeding public markets through operational improvements, superior deal selection, and alignment of interests. The reality is more complicated.

Academic research shows that after fees, private equity has historically delivered returns roughly comparable to public equities but with higher risk, less liquidity, and more volatility. The outperformance occurred primarily in earlier decades when the market was less competitive. As capital flooded into private equity, returns compressed while fees remained elevated.

The fee structure creates perverse incentives reminiscent of 1920s investment trust sponsors. Those sponsors earned fees based on assets gathered, not on investor returns, encouraging them to create as many trusts as possible and load them with leverage to boost reported returns. Private equity firms earn management fees on committed capital regardless of returns, encouraging them to raise ever-larger funds whether or not attractive opportunities exist.

Private equity firms have also created secondary layers: funds of funds, which invest in multiple private equity funds, adding another layer of fees. Co-investment vehicles, which allow investors to invest alongside funds in specific deals, with additional fees. Separately managed accounts, customized arrangements with additional layers of fees. The fee extraction has become the business model, with investment returns almost secondary.

The leverage employed by private equity has reached extremes. The typical leveraged buyout now uses 6:1 debt-to-equity ratios or higher, far exceeding historical norms. This leverage amplifies returns during good times but will magnify losses during downturns. Companies acquired at peak valuations with maximum leverage face distress or bankruptcy when the cycle turns.

Moreover, private equity's illiquid nature means that valuation problems can be hidden for years. When a public company's stock price falls, the loss is immediate and transparent. When a private equity portfolio company deteriorates, the fund can maintain its valuation on paper for quarters or years, recognizing losses slowly or not at all until an exit forces honest accounting.

This is precisely what investment trusts did in the 1920s: maintained fictional valuations as underlying holdings deteriorated, allowing sponsors to continue collecting fees while investors remained unaware of true losses. The crash forced honest valuations, revealing the gap between reported and actual values. Private equity faces the same reckoning whenever exit markets close and honest valuation becomes unavoidable.

Venture Capital: Subsidizing Unprofitability

Venture capital has evolved from a small industry funding genuinely innovative startups into a multi-hundred-billion-dollar machine that subsidizes unprofitable business models, creating zombie companies that survive on funding rather than revenues. The transformation mirrors how investment trusts evolved from legitimate investment vehicles into pure speculation vehicles.

The venture capital model traditionally made sense: invest early in genuinely disruptive companies, accept that most will fail, profit enormously from the few winners that achieve liquidity through IPOs or acquisitions. The math worked because entry valuations were low and winners returned 100x or more.

But cheap capital distorted this model. With interest rates at zero and institutional investors desperate for returns, money poured into venture capital at unprecedented rates. Venture firms raised ever-larger funds. Entry valuations for startups rose dramatically. The definition of "early stage" expanded to include companies with hundreds of millions in revenue. And the emphasis shifted from profitability to growth-at-any-cost.

The result was a parade of companies that lost money on every transaction but made it up in volume or tried to. WeWork, valued at $47 billion in private markets, turned out to be a real estate company with a tech company valuation and a business model that didn't work. Uber and Lyft, each valued at tens of billions, have yet to demonstrate they can be consistently profitable. Hundreds of smaller companies raised funding at unicorn valuations despite unprofitable unit economics and questionable paths to sustainability.

Venture capitalists defended these investments by arguing that "blitzscaling", growing as fast as possible regardless of profitability, would allow winners to achieve monopoly positions and eventually dominate their markets. This narrative justified any amount of cash burn as long as growth continued. It didn't matter if the business model was fundamentally flawed; network effects and scale would supposedly solve everything.

This is magical thinking identical to investment trust sponsors in 1929 arguing that traditional valuation metrics didn't matter in the New Era. The names change, network effects instead of permanent prosperity but the logic is the same: this time is different, old rules don't apply, losses don't matter, growth justifies any price.

The venture-funded company ecosystem creates its own version of interconnected leverage. Companies raise Series A funding, which allows them to burn cash growing. They raise Series B at a higher valuation based on that growth, burning more cash. Series C, D, E, and beyond follow, each round at higher valuations. The company "succeeds" by raising money at increasing valuations, not by achieving profitability or proving business model viability.

Eventually the music stops. When IPO markets close or become discriminating, the funding chain breaks. Companies that require continuous capital infusions to survive face down rounds, distressed sales, or bankruptcy. Venture capital funds that marked these investments at the last round valuation must recognize massive losses. The investors who believed they had exposure to innovation discovered they were funding unprofitable business models subsidized by cheap capital.

The Convergence: When All Roads Lead to the Same Cliff

What makes today's investment trust equivalents particularly dangerous is their convergence, they're all betting on the same underlying factors remaining favorable. Private credit needs low default rates and refinancing availability. Shadow banking needs functioning short-term credit markets. Structured products need low correlation and continued liquidity. Crypto platforms need rising token prices and continued speculation. Private equity needs exit markets at high valuations. Venture capital needs funding continuing at any price.

All of these requirements depend on the same foundations: low interest rates, abundant liquidity, functioning credit markets, investor confidence, and continuous flows of new capital. They're all expressions of the Everything Bubble, different structures capturing the same underlying excess.

When the foundations crack, when interest rates rise, liquidity tightens, credit markets seize, confidence wavers, or capital flows reverse all these structures face stress simultaneously. There's no diversification because they all depend on the same conditions. The private credit fund holding leveraged loans, the CLO holding those same loans repackaged, the pension fund owning both the fund and the CLO, the bank providing leverage to the fund, they're all exposed to the same risk through different vehicles.

This is exactly what happened in 1929 with investment trusts. Individual trusts seemed diversified across different stocks and sectors. But all trusts depended on stock prices continuing to rise and credit remaining available. When those conditions reversed, all trusts failed together. The apparent diversification was illusory; they were all expressions of the same underlying speculation.

The new investment trusts have created a financial system where leverage is hidden in complexity, where risks are obscured by opacity, where fees are extracted regardless of performance, and where everything depends on everything continuing to work. Like the investment trusts of the 1920s, they've proliferated wildly during good times, promising sophisticated investors superior returns through professional management and structural innovation.

And like the investment trusts of the 1920s, they will collapse together when conditions change, revealing that the complexity was not sophistication but confusion, that the opacity concealed rather than managed risk, and that the structures were not innovations but simply new ways to package old mistakes. The crash, when it comes, will be amplified through all these interconnected vehicles, just as investment trusts amplified the 1929 crash. The lesson remains unlearned because the profits remain too attractive to resist.

Part III: Striking Parallels

Chapter 8

Psychology and Mania

If financial markets were purely rational mechanisms for allocating capital based on mathematical calculations of risk and return, bubbles and crashes would not exist. Prices would smoothly adjust to new information, always reflecting the aggregate wisdom of millions of informed participants. But markets are not rational mechanisms, they are collective human enterprises, driven by emotions, distorted by cognitive biases, and prone to manias that disconnect prices from fundamentals before violently reconnecting them through crashes.

The psychological dynamics that drove the 1929 bubble and crash are not historical curiosities, they are permanent features of human nature that recur in every speculative episode. Understanding these patterns is crucial not because they allow us to predict the exact timing of the next crash, but because they help us recognize when we are in the grip of the same forces that have destroyed wealth repeatedly throughout history. The names and technologies change, but the psychology remains constant.

"This Time Is Different": The Four Most Dangerous Words

At the heart of every bubble lies a narrative that explains why traditional valuation metrics no longer apply, why historical precedents are irrelevant, and why the current situation represents a paradigm shift that justifies unprecedented prices. This "this time is different" mentality is not merely a symptom of bubbles, it is their essential enabling condition. Without the belief that old rules no longer apply, speculation cannot reach the extremes necessary to produce spectacular crashes.

In the 1920s, the New Era narrative held that technological transformation, professional management of corporations, and Federal Reserve stabilization had fundamentally changed the economic landscape. The business cycle had been conquered. Productivity gains would continue indefinitely. Stock valuations that seemed high by historical standards were actually reasonable given the transformed environment. Anyone who pointed to traditional valuation metrics was dismissed as hopelessly behind the times, unable to grasp the new reality.

The parallels to recent decades are striking. During the late 1990s tech bubble, the narrative was that the internet changed everything, that network effects and winner-take-all dynamics justified extreme valuations for companies with no earnings. Traditional metrics like price-to-earnings ratios were declared obsolete; what mattered was eyeballs, clicks, and market share. When skeptics pointed out that companies needed to eventually make profits, they were dismissed as dinosaurs who didn't understand the New Economy.

The 2020-2021 bubble featured multiple "this time is different" narratives operating simultaneously. For stocks, the story was that zero interest rates meant traditional valuation metrics were irrelevant, with discount rates at zero, future cash flows were worth infinitely more. For real estate, the story was that supply constraints in desirable cities meant prices could only go up. For cryptocurrencies, the story was that blockchain technology represented a monetary revolution that would displace fiat currencies. For meme stocks, the story was that social media coordination had permanently shifted power from institutions to retail traders.

Each narrative contained kernels of truth. Technology did transform business in the 1920s and 1990s. Interest rates did reach unprecedented lows. Blockchain is an interesting technology. But these truths were weaponized to justify extremes that bore no relationship to underlying economic reality. The narrative served to rationalize behavior that participants knew was speculation but wanted to believe was investment.

The psychological function of "this time is different" thinking is to provide intellectual cover for actions driven by greed and fear of missing out. It allows participants to feel sophisticated rather than reckless, informed rather than naive. It transforms gambling into strategy, speculation into vision. The narrative is emotionally irresistible because it flatters those who believe it, they see what others cannot, understand what others miss, grasp opportunities that others overlook.

The danger is that "this time is different" thinking silences doubt and dismisses warning signs. Every cautionary voice, every historical parallel, every traditional metric suggesting overvaluation becomes evidence not of actual risk but of the speaker's failure to understand the new paradigm. Criticism strengthens rather than undermines the narrative because it demonstrates how few people truly "get it." This creates an echo chamber where only confirmatory evidence is acknowledged while contrary evidence is systematically dismissed.

History teaches an unambiguous lesson: it is never different in the ways that matter most. Human nature doesn't change. The mathematics of valuation don't change. The relationship between risk and return doesn't change. The laws of financial gravity don't change. When prices become disconnected from fundamentals, they always reconnect violently. The only question is timing, and the longer the disconnect persists, the more violent the reconnection becomes.

FOMO: Fear as the Dominant Emotion

While "this time is different" provides intellectual justification for speculation, the emotional driver is fear, specifically fear of missing out (FOMO). In a bubble's mature stages, FOMO overwhelms all other considerations. The pain of watching others get rich becomes psychologically unbearable, driving increasingly irrational behavior from people who should know better.

FOMO operates through social comparison. Humans are inherently comparative creatures; we evaluate our status and success relative to peers rather than in absolute terms. When your neighbor, colleague, or brother-in-law is making money in the market, your own prudent savings suddenly feel like failure. When conversation at dinner parties revolves around investment gains, being out of the market becomes socially awkward. The psychological pressure to participate becomes enormous.

In the 1920s, this dynamic drove millions of Americans with no investing experience into the stock market. Stories of secretaries and shoeshine boys making fortunes spread widely, some true, many embellished or fabricated. These stories created the impression that everyone was getting rich except those too timid or too foolish to participate. The fear of being left behind overwhelmed the fear of losing money.

The same pattern repeated in recent bubbles, amplified by social media. During the GameStop mania of early 2021, Reddit's WallStreetBets forum became a showcase for traders posting screenshots of six- and seven-figure gains. These images, some real, some manipulated, all unrepresentative of typical outcomes created intense FOMO among viewers. Thousands of people put life savings into meme stocks at absurd prices, driven entirely by fear of missing out on easy money.

Cryptocurrency forums and social media featured similar dynamics. Images of Lamborghinis and mansions supposedly purchased with crypto gains proliferated. Influencers posed on private jets, attributing their wealth to Bitcoin or altcoin investments. The "when Lambo?" meme captured the expectation that cryptocurrency riches were inevitable for those who held on. Missing out became unthinkable.

The psychological pain of FOMO is often more intense than the pain of actual losses. This counterintuitive reality drives much bubble behavior. Investors who prudently avoided overvalued markets and preserved capital often feel worse than those who participated and lost money, at least the losers tried, at least they took their shot. The regret of inaction exceeds the regret of wrong action.

This creates a perverse incentive structure where rational risk management becomes emotionally intolerable. The professional investor who avoids an overvalued market and preserves capital is punished by career risk and social judgment. Colleagues who participated and lost money are excused, everyone was wrong together. The investor who was right alone by staying out is viewed as having missed the opportunity, their caution reframed as cowardice or incompetence.

FOMO also creates self-fulfilling dynamics. When enough people are driven to participate by fear of missing out, their buying pushes prices higher, which generates more FOMO, which drives more buying. The feedback loop becomes self-reinforcing until it exhausts the supply of new participants. The bubble peaks not when it looks most dangerous but when FOMO has pulled in the last marginal buyer.

The emotional intensity of FOMO explains why bubbles so often end with parabolic blow-off tops, final vertical surges in price that mark the moment of maximum euphoria and maximum risk. These climactic rallies draw in the last holdouts, the skeptics who finally can't stand watching everyone else profit. Their capitulation marks the top because there's no one left to buy. FOMO has consumed all available capital and created the preconditions for crash.

Herd Behavior and Social Proof

Humans are social animals with deep evolutionary programming to follow the herd. This made sense in ancestral environments where the group's collective wisdom about predators, food sources, and dangers exceeded any individual's knowledge. But in financial markets, herd behavior creates and amplifies bubbles because the market is not an external reality to be discovered but a social construction where the herd's beliefs actively shape outcomes until reality imposes itself.

Social proof, the tendency to adopt beliefs and behaviors because others have adopted them is one of the most powerful cognitive biases affecting financial decisions. When we see others buying stocks, we infer that buying stocks is correct. The more people buying, the stronger the inference. This is rational in many contexts but devastating in markets where prices themselves reflect the herd's beliefs.

In the 1920s, social proof manifested through investment clubs where neighbors pooled money to speculate in stocks, through newspaper coverage of market gains, and through visible consumption funded by market profits. Seeing others participate and profit provided validation that overcame individual caution. The collective behavior created its own justification.

Modern technology has amplified social proof to unprecedented degrees. Social media creates constant exposure to others' investment decisions and results. Trading apps show popular stocks and trending investments. Forums like Reddit's WallStreetBets create real-time feedback loops where thousands of people simultaneously see and react to the same information, creating coordinated buying that moves markets.

The GameStop episode perfectly illustrates modern herd behavior. What started as an idiosyncratic trade by a few contrarians became a mass movement as social media spread the story. Hundreds of thousands of retail traders bought GameStop stock simultaneously, not based on fundamental analysis but because others were buying. The collective action pushed the stock from $4 to $483 in weeks, a move that made no economic sense but made perfect sense as an expression of herd behavior.

The cryptocurrency boom similarly reflected herd dynamics. Bitcoin's rise attracted attention, which attracted more buyers, which pushed prices higher, which attracted more attention in a self-reinforcing cycle. Altcoins proliferated because Bitcoin's success proved crypto was legitimate, so any crypto project could attract capital. The herd stampeded from one coin to another, creating and destroying billions in value based purely on collective sentiment shifts.

Professional investors are not immune to herd behavior, in many ways they're more susceptible. Career risk creates powerful incentives to follow the herd. A fund manager who invests like peers and loses money alongside everyone else keeps their job. A manager who invests differently and loses money alone gets fired. This asymmetric risk profile encourages conformity over contrarianism.

Quarterly performance measurement intensifies herd behavior among professionals. When a bubble is inflating, being out of the market means underperforming peers every quarter. The pressure to catch up drives participation even when valuations are obviously extreme. The manager who stayed prudent in 1928 was likely fired in 1929 before vindication came. The manager who participated recklessly and lost everything in the crash at least lost it alongside everyone else.

Herd behavior also explains why bubbles can persist far longer than rational analysis would suggest. As long as the herd keeps buying, prices keep rising, validating the decision to participate. The bubble becomes self-sustaining through collective belief. Only when the herd reverses, when buyers become sellers does the price discovery happen, and it happens violently as the stampede reverses direction.

The shift from buying herd to selling herd is typically sudden and devastating. The same social proof that drove buying drives selling. If others are selling, there must be a reason, better sell too before prices fall further. The information cascade becomes negative rather than positive. The herd that trampled each other rushing in tramples each other rushing out.

Confirmation Bias and Selective Perception

Once investors have committed capital to a bubble, cognitive biases kick in that make rational reassessment nearly impossible. Confirmation bias, the tendency to seek, interpret, and remember information that confirms existing beliefs while ignoring contrary evidence becomes a powerful force maintaining bubble psychology even as warning signs accumulate.

An investor who bought stocks in 1928 or cryptocurrencies in 2021 had powerful psychological incentives to find evidence justifying that decision. Every piece of good news, every bullish analysis, every optimistic forecast received attention and credence. Contradictory evidence was dismissed, reinterpreted, or ignored. The mind is remarkably skilled at maintaining comfortable beliefs despite contrary evidence.

This selective perception creates bubble-specific information diets. Bull market participants read bullish analysts, follow bullish influencers, and congregate in forums with bullish consensus. Bearish voices are dismissed as bitter, jealous, or hopelessly out of touch. The information environment becomes an echo chamber amplifying bullish sentiment while filtering out warnings.

During the 1920s, investors dismissive of warnings from Roger Babson and others weren't being irrational in a vacuum, they were engaging in confirmation bias, giving weight to the many voices saying the market was sound while dismissing the few saying it was doomed. The human mind naturally weighs evidence supporting desired conclusions more heavily than evidence opposing them.

Modern social media has turbocharged confirmation bias. Algorithms show users content similar to what they've previously engaged with, creating filter bubbles. A retail trader who watches one video about meme stocks will be served hundreds more. A crypto enthusiast who follows

Bitcoin promoters will see crypto-bullish content exclusively. The algorithmic curation ensures users see only information confirming their existing beliefs.

Confirmation bias also affects how people interpret ambiguous information. When a company announces mixed earnings, bulls focus on the positive aspects while bears focus on negatives. When economic data is released, each side finds confirmation of their thesis. The same objective information gets filtered through psychological lenses that ensure it confirms rather than challenges existing positions.

The danger is that confirmation bias makes course correction nearly impossible. As a bubble matures and risks mount, participants should ideally become more cautious, reducing positions and raising cash. But confirmation bias ensures they instead double down, finding reasons why warning signs are actually bullish signals. Declining market breadth becomes "healthy rotation." Deteriorating fundamentals become "buying opportunities." Every negative is reframed as a positive.

This creates the paradox where investors become most confident at the point of maximum danger. The late stages of bubbles feature near-universal bullishness precisely because everyone has positions to justify and confirmation bias ensures they find justification. The warnings that should prompt reassessment are instead interpreted as evidence that skeptics don't understand the situation. The bubble peaks with maximum confidence, not maximum doubt.

Recency Bias and Historical Amnesia

Humans are hardwired to weigh recent experience far more heavily than distant history. This recency bias makes intuitive sense, recent conditions are more likely to persist than conditions from decades ago. But in financial markets, recency bias is devastating because it causes participants to extrapolate recent trends indefinitely while dismissing historical patterns that might repeat.

In the 1920s, young investors had no memory of the Panic of 1907 or earlier crashes. Middle-aged investors remembered those crises but found them irrelevant to the transformed New Era economy. The recent experience of steadily rising markets overwhelmed historical knowledge of boom-bust cycles. Each year without a crash increased confidence that crashes were artifacts of the past.

Modern investors display identical recency bias. The generation that came of age after 2008 has known only a world of ultra-low interest rates, endless liquidity, and markets that always recover. "Buy the dip" became an entire investment philosophy based purely on recency, every previous dip had been a buying opportunity, therefore every future dip will be too. The possibility that past patterns might not continue went unconsidered.

The 2010-2021 bull market created extreme recency bias. For over a decade, every correction proved temporary and every bear case proved wrong. This extended period of uninterrupted gains convinced many investors that the Federal Reserve had eliminated serious bear markets, that crashes were preventable through policy intervention, and that long-term holding of risk assets was essentially guaranteed to work.

This recency-driven confidence explains the willingness to buy aggressively during every dip from 2010-2021. Investors weren't being irrational, they were following the pattern that had worked for over a decade. The problem is that recency bias blinds participants to the possibility that the pattern might end. The longer a pattern persists, the more confident participants become, and the more devastating the eventual pattern break.

Recency bias also affects institutional investors and policymakers who should know better. The Federal Reserve, having successfully deployed quantitative easing to fight the 2008 crisis, became overconfident in this tool. Each round of QE "worked" by pushing asset prices higher, reinforcing the belief that monetary policy could solve any problem. The recent success of unconventional policies created confidence that made ever-more-aggressive interventions seem prudent.

Historical amnesia compounds recency bias. Financial crises that occurred decades ago fade from collective memory. The 1929 crash became ancient history by the 1960s. The 1987 crash seemed irrelevant by the 2000s. Even the 2008 crisis, despite being recent, faded from active consideration by 2020. The human mind quickly discounts past disasters, especially when recent experience suggests they won't recur.

This creates the dangerous pattern where each generation must learn the same lessons through painful experience. Knowledge that crashes are possible proves insufficient to prevent them. The psychological impact of recent positive experiences overwhelms intellectual knowledge of historical disasters. Investors know bubbles end badly but convince themselves the current situation is different because their recent experience doesn't match their historical knowledge.

The antidote to recency bias requires conscious effort to study history, to understand that long periods of stability often precede severe instability, and to recognize that patterns that have persisted for years can reverse suddenly. But this intellectual knowledge rarely translates to behavioral change because the emotional pull of recent experience proves stronger than abstract historical knowledge.

The Confidence Cycle: From Fear to Greed and Back

Market psychology follows a predictable cycle from fear to greed and back to fear, with each stage reinforcing itself before transitioning to the next. Understanding this cycle doesn't allow precise prediction of transitions, but it does help identify where we are in the cycle and what behaviors to expect.

The cycle typically begins in the aftermath of a crash, when fear is dominant. Investors who survived the crash are traumatized, having watched wealth evaporate. The pain of losses creates extreme risk aversion. Bargains go unrecognized because buyers remain paralyzed by fear. This represents maximum pessimism and, ironically, maximum opportunity, though few can recognize it.

As the market begins recovering, fear slowly gives way to hope. Those who bought near the bottom see gains and feel validated. Gradually, others gain confidence to participate. The recovery broadens and strengthens. Hope transitions to optimism as gains continue. The psychological memory of the crash fades as positive recent experience accumulates.

Optimism eventually becomes confidence as the bull market matures. Years of gains create conviction that investing in risk assets is safe and profitable. The fear that characterized the bottom seems quaint and excessive. New investors enter the market, having no memory of the crash and seeing only the profitable upward trend. Confidence spreads from early adopters to the mainstream.

In the final stage, confidence becomes greed and ultimately euphoria. Valuation concerns are dismissed. Risk is ignored or rationalized away. Participation shifts from investing to speculating, from earning returns to getting rich quickly. The fear of missing out overwhelms the fear of losing money. This stage features maximum bullishness, maximum leverage, and maximum vulnerability to reversal.

The transition from euphoria to fear happens suddenly, often violently. Something minor that wouldn't matter in calmer times, sparks selling. Leveraged positions face margin calls. Forced liquidations accelerate declines. The psychology reverses: instead of fearing missing out on gains, investors fear losing what they have. The rush for exits overwhelms the market's ability to provide liquidity. Fear cascades through the system.

What makes this cycle dangerous is that each stage feels permanent while you're in it. At the bottom, fear feels like rational risk assessment rather than panic. At the top, euphoria feels like justified confidence rather than mania. Participants can rarely recognize their own position in the cycle because the emotions are so powerful and the social consensus so strong.

The 1920s followed this exact pattern: fear after World War I giving way to hope in the early twenties, optimism as the bull market developed, confidence and greed in the late twenties, euphoria in summer 1929, and sudden terrifying reversal to fear in October. Each stage seemed justified by circumstances until the next stage revealed the previous one as excessive.

Recent decades have shown the same progression. Fear after 2008 gave way to hope as markets recovered, optimism during the mid-2010s, confidence and greed as the bull market aged, euphoria in 2020-2021 with stimulus money flooding into speculation. The cycle repeats because human psychology repeats, responding to circumstances in predictable ways that create self-reinforcing feedback loops until something breaks.

Expert Fallibility and Authority Bias

One of the most dangerous aspects of bubble psychology is the role of experts and authorities in validating speculation. When prestigious voices declare markets fairly valued or reasonably priced, their authority provides cover for continued participation. When those voices later prove catastrophically wrong, the damage spreads far beyond those who blindly followed expert advice, it undermines trust in expertise itself.

Authority bias, the tendency to attribute greater accuracy to the opinions of authority figures is a powerful cognitive bias that serves humans well in many contexts but fails in financial markets where supposed experts often know little more than laypeople. Investors defer to professional analysts, prestigious economists, successful investors, and institutional consensus, assuming these authorities have superior information or analytical capabilities.

In 1929, the most respected economist in America, Irving Fisher of Yale, declared that stocks had reached a "permanently high plateau" just before the crash. His authority gave comfort to investors who wanted to believe valuations were reasonable. When he proved spectacularly wrong, the losses were amplified by the collective belief that if Irving Fisher said stocks were fairly priced, they must be.

The 2008 crisis featured similar expert failures. Ben Bernanke, then Chairman of the Federal Reserve, said in 2007 that subprime mortgage problems were "contained" and would not spread to the broader economy. Rating agencies gave AAA ratings to mortgage securities that proved nearly worthless. Major investment banks declared their portfolios safe until they collapsed. The supposed experts were as blind to the building crisis as ordinary investors, perhaps more blind because their expertise created overconfidence.

Recent decades have seen continued expert fallibility. Economists failed to predict the 2008 crisis. Analysts maintained "buy" ratings on stocks that fell 90 percent. Cryptocurrency proponents predicted Bitcoin would reach $1 million while it crashed from $69,000 to $16,000. Institutional investors loaded up on private credit and structured products without understanding the risks.

The problem is not that experts are malicious but that they operate under constraints that compromise objectivity. Sell-side analysts work for firms that earn fees from the companies they cover, creating incentives to maintain positive ratings. Economists often work for financial institutions with vested interests in bullish outlooks. Fund managers are paid to be invested, not to sit in cash. Their expertise is real, but their incentives compromise its application.

Authority bias causes investors to outsource thinking to experts rather than conducting independent analysis. This might be rational in fields where expertise is clear-cut, you should defer to your doctor on medical issues. But in financial markets, expert consensus is often wrong at important turning points precisely because experts face the same psychological biases as everyone else, amplified by career risk and institutional incentives.

The most dangerous manifestation of authority bias is unanimous expert consensus. When virtually all experts agree on a market direction or valuation assessment, contrarian views get systematically excluded from consideration. The investor who questions the consensus can point to no authoritative voices supporting their position. The psychological pressure to defer to unanimous expertise becomes overwhelming.

Yet history teaches that unanimous expert consensus is often most wrong at critical junctures. In 1929, nearly all respected voices called the market sound. In 2007, few mainstream economists or analysts warned of an impending crisis. The contrarians who were proved right, Roger Babson in 1929 and Michael Burry in 2007 were dismissed precisely because they contradicted expert consensus.

The antidote is humility, recognizing that expertise provides probabilistic advantages, not certainty, and that experts face the same psychological biases as everyone else. Independent thinking requires confidence to question authority, but not arrogance to dismiss all expertise. The balance is difficult to strike, and most investors err toward excessive deference to authority, particularly when that deference validates desired actions.

The Narrative Arc: From Skepticism to Inevitability

Every bubble follows a narrative arc that begins with a small group of true believers, expands through early adopters, reaches the mainstream, and culminates in universal acceptance before collapsing back to skepticism. Understanding this arc helps identify bubble stages, though it doesn't solve the timing problem.

In the earliest stage, a new investment opportunity is viewed with skepticism or ignored entirely. The idea seems implausible, the risks seem large, and the opportunity is dismissed by mainstream investors. Only true believers and contrarians participate. This stage represents actual opportunity, but few recognize it because the narrative hasn't developed to make the opportunity seem obvious.

As early participants profit, the narrative begins developing. What seemed implausible becomes possible. Early adopters, attracted by the pioneers' success, begin participating. The narrative gains sophistication, it's no longer just a hunch but an investment thesis with supporting arguments. Skeptics remain numerous but their voices begin losing authority as results validate the bulls.

The breakthrough moment comes when the narrative reaches mainstream acceptance. What seemed like speculation becomes conventional wisdom. The narrative appears in major media. Institutional investors begin allocating capital. The investment opportunity becomes a frequent topic of conversation. At this stage, the largest gains typically lie in the past, but most participants enter here, driven by the now-compelling narrative and social proof.

The final stage is universal acceptance and assumed inevitability. Skeptics have been silenced or converted. The narrative is treated as obvious truth rather than debatable thesis. "Everyone knows" that this investment will continue appreciating. The phrase "it's a sure thing" enters conversations. This stage represents maximum danger and minimum opportunity, but also maximum participation as even the most cautious investors finally capitulate.

The 1920s stock market followed this exact arc. Early in the decade, stocks were viewed with skepticism after the 1920-21 recession. By mid-decade, the narrative of the New Era economy gained credibility. By 1928-1929, stock ownership had become mainstream and the continued appreciation of stocks seemed inevitable. At the peak, skepticism was virtually non-existent.

Bitcoin's narrative arc illustrates the same pattern. In its early years, Bitcoin was dismissed as a curiosity or scam. By 2013-2014, it had gained early adopter interest and a developing narrative about digital currency disruption. By 2017, mainstream interest had developed. By 2020-2021, institutional investors were participating and the inevitability of cryptocurrency seemed widely accepted. Each stage drew in more participants at progressively worse prices.

The danger of the narrative arc is that it makes psychological sense at every stage. Early skepticism seems prudent when the opportunity is untested. Growing acceptance seems rational as evidence accumulates. Mainstream adoption seems like validation of the thesis. Universal acceptance seems like obvious truth. Each stage transitions naturally to the next, with participants unable to recognize that they're following a pattern that has repeated throughout history.

The crash reverses the narrative arc rapidly and violently. Universal acceptance becomes doubt, then skepticism, then dismissal. The narrative that seemed obviously true becomes obviously false in retrospect. Participants wonder how they could have believed something so clearly speculative was safe. The new conventional wisdom becomes that "everyone knew it was a bubble," though this revisionist history ignores that virtually no one acted on that knowledge.

Understanding the narrative arc doesn't solve the practical problem of when to exit. Being right early feels like being wrong, the skeptic who sold in 1928 missed huge gains in 1929. Being right but early can be financially equivalent to being wrong. But recognizing the narrative's stage at least provides context for decision-making and awareness of psychological forces at work.

The Madness of Crowds: When Rationality Fails

The ultimate lesson from studying bubble psychology is that markets are not rational mechanisms for price discovery but collective human enterprises subject to the madness of crowds. Individually rational people make collectively irrational decisions when caught in manias. Intelligence and education provide no immunity. The psychological forces driving bubbles are powerful enough to overwhelm reason.

This insight is humbling and troubling. It means that knowing about bubble psychology doesn't prevent succumbing to it. Reading about 1929 doesn't protect against repeating 1929's mistakes. Understanding confirmation bias doesn't eliminate its influence on thinking. The psychological forces operate below the level of conscious awareness, shaping perceptions and decisions in ways that feel completely rational at the time.

The madness of crowds explains why bubbles can inflate to extremes that seem obvious in retrospect but were invisible to participants. It wasn't that investors in 1929 were stupider than today's investors, they were experiencing the same psychological forces that affect every bubble. The narratives change, the technologies evolve, but the underlying psychology remains constant because human nature remains constant.

This psychological permanence is why history repeats, why every generation must learn the same lessons, and why warnings are consistently ignored until disaster strikes. The warnings are intellectually understood but psychologically ineffective against the combination of greed, fear of missing out, social proof, confirmation bias, and authority validation. Knowing the danger doesn't prevent walking into it when everyone else is walking in the same direction and being rewarded for it.

The only protection is humility: recognizing that you are not immune to psychological forces, that feeling certain probably means you're wrong, that consensus probably means the opportunity has passed, and that the times when selling seems most difficult are probably the times when selling is most necessary. But even this knowledge provides imperfect protection because the psychological forces are so powerful and the social pressure so intense.

The market will crash again not because we haven't learned the lessons of 1929 or 2008, but because we cannot help but forget them during extended periods of prosperity. The crash will seem obvious in retrospect but will surprise the vast majority who participated in the mania. And the next generation will read about it as history, confident that they would never make such obvious mistakes, unaware that they're already making the same mistakes in different forms. This is not a failure of intelligence but a feature of human psychology that no amount of knowledge seems capable of overcoming.

Chapter 9

Structural Similarities

While psychology explains why bubbles form and how manias spread, structural factors determine how severe crashes become and how deeply they penetrate the real economy. The most disturbing aspect of comparing the 1920s to today is not the psychological parallels, human nature is constant but the structural similarities that create conditions for catastrophic outcomes. When wealth concentration, middle-class speculation, credit expansion, and fundamental disconnects align simultaneously, the result is not a mere correction but a crash that reshapes society for decades.

The structural similarities between the 1920s and today are not superficial resemblances but deep systemic parallels that suggest we have reconstructed the essential conditions that produced the Great Depression. Understanding these structural factors is crucial because they operate independently of psychology or sentiment, they create mathematical inevitabilities that no amount of optimism or policy intervention can overcome indefinitely.

Wealth Concentration: Then and Now

The most striking and troubling structural similarity between the 1920s and today is the extreme concentration of wealth at the top of the income and asset distribution. Wealth inequality reached a peak in 1929 that would not be matched again until the 2010s. This is not coincidence, extreme wealth concentration is both a symptom of speculative excess and a cause of economic instability.

In 1929, the top 0.1 percent of Americans held approximately 25 percent of the nation's wealth. The top 1 percent controlled roughly 45 percent. Meanwhile, the bottom 90 percent of Americans held a shrinking share of national wealth, with many families living paycheck to paycheck despite the decade's overall prosperity. This concentration meant that the benefits of productivity growth and economic expansion flowed predominantly to those at the very top.

The parallels to today are stark. By 2021, the top 0.1 percent of Americans held approximately 20 percent of national wealth, while the top 1 percent controlled roughly 35 percent. These figures are not identical to 1929, but they represent levels of concentration seen only during the late 1920s and today. The decades between roughly 1940 through 1980 featured significantly more equitable wealth distribution.

This wealth concentration creates economic instability through multiple channels. First, it concentrates consumption decisions in a small group whose spending is largely discretionary. When the wealthy feel less wealthy, whether through asset price declines or simply increased caution they cut spending dramatically. This discretionary spending employed significant portions of the labor force in both the 1920s and today: domestic servants then, service workers now.

Second, extreme wealth concentration means that asset price fluctuations have outsized effects on the economy. When 1 percent of the population holds 35 percent of wealth, and much of that wealth exists in the form of securities, a 50 percent market decline doesn't just create paper losses, it destroys real economic demand. The wealthy pull back on spending, investments, and philanthropic activities. The businesses and workers dependent on that spending face immediate distress.

Third, wealth concentration drives asset bubbles by creating enormous pools of capital seeking returns. In the 1920s, the wealthy accumulated capital faster than profitable real investment opportunities could absorb it. The money flowed into financial speculation, bidding up asset prices to unsustainable levels. Today's dynamics are identical: extreme wealth at the top creates capital that cannot be productively deployed in the real economy and instead floods into financial assets, driving valuations to extremes.

The concentration also has political economic implications. In both eras, extreme wealth translated into political influence that shaped policy toward the interests of the wealthy. In the 1920s, this meant limited regulation of financial markets, low top marginal tax rates, and policies that favored capital over labor. Today's dynamics mirror this: financial deregulation, historically low taxes on capital gains, and political gridlock preventing policies that might redistribute wealth or regulate speculation.

The Gini coefficient, a standard measure of inequality where 0 represents perfect equality and 1 represents perfect inequality tells the story numerically. The U.S. Gini coefficient reached approximately 0.45 in 1929, fell to around 0.35-0.36 in the 1960s-1970s, and has climbed back to 0.48 by 2020. This U-shaped pattern captures the extreme inequality of the pre-Depression era, the more equitable postwar period, and the return to Gilded Age levels of concentration.

What makes this structural similarity particularly dangerous is that high inequality creates economic fragility. An economy where the bottom 50 percent has minimal wealth cannot withstand shocks because those households have no cushion. When layoffs come or asset prices fall, they face immediate distress. An economy where the top 1 percent holds enormous wealth tied up in securities cannot withstand asset price crashes because the wealth effect on consumption is massive. The structural similarity suggests today's economy is as fragile as the 1920s economy proved to be.

Middle-Class Speculation: When Everyone's an Investor

A defining feature of the 1920s bubble was the democratization of stock market speculation. For the first time in American history, the middle class participated in securities markets on a mass scale. Secretaries, shop clerks, barbers, and schoolteachers bought stocks, often on margin. This broad participation transformed the stock market from a mechanism for capitalizing productive enterprises into a national casino where ordinary people gambled on securities they barely understood.

The statistics from the 1920s are revealing. The number of Americans owning stocks rose from about 4 million in 1920 to 10 million by 1929, a dramatic increase, though still representing only about 8 percent of the population. More significant was the cultural shift: stock ownership went from being the province of the wealthy elite to being seen as the path to prosperity for ordinary people. Investment clubs proliferated. Newspapers devoted increasing coverage to market movements. Stock tips were exchanged in barbershops and at dinner parties.

This democratization was enabled by margin lending and investment trusts. Margin allowed workers to buy stocks with 10 percent down, borrowing the rest from brokers. Investment trusts allowed pooling small amounts of capital to access diversified portfolios. Together, these innovations made stock ownership accessible to people with limited savings and no investing knowledge. The result was that people who should have been saving in bank deposits were speculating in securities.

Today's parallel is even more extensive. The percentage of Americans owning stocks has increased dramatically, reaching approximately 55-60 percent through direct ownership and retirement accounts. But more significant is the cultural shift toward treating investing as a primary wealth-building strategy for people who lack traditional paths to prosperity.

The democratization of options trading through commission-free apps represents the most direct parallel to 1920s margin buying. Young workers with limited capital use options to gain leveraged exposure to stocks, often without understanding the instruments they're trading. The apps gamify the experience, making speculation feel like a game rather than financial risk. The social media celebration of successful trades creates FOMO that drives more participation.

Cryptocurrency expanded middle-class speculation beyond traditional securities into entirely new assets. People working ordinary jobs invested significant portions of savings into Bitcoin, Ethereum, and obscure altcoins. The participation crossed all demographics: teachers, nurses, construction workers and retail employees all speculating in digital assets they barely understood, often using borrowed money or money they couldn't afford to lose.

The meme stock phenomenon brought the democratization full circle. Retail traders coordinating on social media drove stocks like GameStop and AMC to valuations disconnected from fundamentals. The traders weren't investing based on business prospects; they were speculating on price movements and trying to profit from short squeezes. This is pure speculation, yet it was framed as "democratizing finance" and "taking on Wall Street."

The structural problem with middle-class speculation is identical in both eras: it creates enormous fragility. When wealthy elites speculate and lose, they remain wealthy, they have other assets, income streams, and cushions. When the middle class speculates and loses, they face genuine hardship, lost retirements, wiped-out savings, unpayable debts. The 1929 crash devastated the middle class in ways it merely inconvenienced many of the wealthy.

Moreover, middle-class speculation changes how financial crises affect the real economy. When speculation was confined to the wealthy, a market crash was primarily a redistribution among elites. When the middle class is heavily invested in markets, a crash becomes an economic catastrophe.

Consumer spending collapses because households are poorer. Home equity lines of credit default because the stock portfolios backing them evaporated. Retirement plans are destroyed, forcing people to work longer or depend on social support.

The democratization of speculation also creates political pressures for bailouts and interventions. When only the wealthy are at risk, letting markets clear is politically feasible. When millions of middle-class families face ruin, political pressure for government intervention becomes irresistible. This creates a moral hazard: participants speculate recklessly assuming the government will rescue them. The structural similarity suggests today's crash will force even larger interventions than 2008, with profound implications for fiscal sustainability and moral hazard.

Credit Expansion: The Fuel of Bubbles

Every major financial bubble in history has been fueled by credit expansion, the extension of borrowed money to purchase assets whose values rise partly because of the borrowed money being extended. This self-reinforcing dynamic is the engine of bubbles, and both the 1920s and today feature credit expansion on extraordinary scales.

In the 1920s, margin lending exploded. By 1929, margin debt reached $8.5 billion, a figure equal to roughly 10 percent of the U.S. GDP at the time. This borrowed money flowed into stocks, pushing prices higher, which made margin lenders more comfortable extending additional loans since the collateral (stocks) kept appreciating. The feedback loop was powerful and ultimately destructive.

Beyond margin loans, consumer credit proliferated during the 1920s. Installment buying allowed Americans to purchase automobiles, appliances, and furniture on credit. By 1929, approximately 60 percent of cars and 80 percent of radios were purchased on installment plans. This debt-fueled consumption created an illusion of prosperity while actually making households more fragile. When income disruptions came, indebted households couldn't service their loans, leading to defaults and repossessions.

Today's credit expansion dwarfs the 1920s in both absolute and relative terms. Total U.S. debt, government, corporate, and household exceeds $90 trillion, or roughly 350 percent of GDP. This compares to total debt of approximately 150-180 percent of GDP in 1929. The scale is unprecedented, and the debt has been accumulated across all sectors simultaneously.

Household debt, while lower than its 2008 peak relative to income, remains elevated by historical standards. More concerning is the composition: student loan debt exceeds $1.7 trillion, auto loan debt exceeds $1.5 trillion, and credit card debt exceeds $1 trillion. These debts burden middle-class households with payments that constrain consumption and eliminate financial cushions. The parallel to 1920s installment debt is precise, consumption funded by borrowing rather than income growth.

Corporate debt has exploded to over $11 trillion for non-financial corporations, reaching nearly 50 percent of GDP. This debt was accumulated not primarily to invest in productive capacity but to fund financial engineering: share buybacks, dividends, and M&A. The interest payments on this debt consume earnings that might otherwise support employment or investment. When refinancing comes at higher rates, many companies will face distress.

Government debt has also ballooned. Federal debt held by the public exceeds $25 trillion, roughly 100 percent of GDP. State and local government debt adds another $3 trillion. The debt accumulated during the pandemic was necessary to prevent immediate collapse, but it leaves governments with limited fiscal space to address the next crisis. The structural similarity to the 1920s is not debt levels, government debt was actually lower then but the exhaustion of policy options.

The most concerning parallel is margin debt for securities purchases. By 2021, margin debt exceeded $900 billion, representing approximately 4 percent of GDP, lower than the 1929 ratio but significant in absolute terms. This understates leverage because it ignores options trading, which provides equivalent leverage, and synthetic leverage through derivatives. The total effective leverage in the financial system likely exceeds 1929 levels significantly.

Credit expansion creates bubble dynamics through straightforward mathematics. When borrowed money flows into assets, it pushes prices higher. Higher prices make lenders comfortable extending more credit because collateral values have risen. More credit flows in, pushing prices higher still. The cycle continues until the supply of new credit is exhausted, at which point prices can no longer rise. Once prices stop rising, the entire structure reverses: collateral values fall, lenders demand repayment, forced selling pushes prices lower, which triggers more deleveraging in a death spiral.

The structural similarity is that both the 1920s and today feature credit expansion across multiple sectors simultaneously. It's not just stock market leverage or just household debt or just corporate debt, it's all of them together. This synchronized leverage means that when deleveraging begins, it cascades across the entire economy. The margin calls affect not just speculators but also households, corporations, and even governments that have borrowed excessively.

Disconnect Between Asset Prices and Economic Fundamentals

Perhaps the most fundamental structural similarity between the 1920s and today is the enormous disconnect between asset prices and the underlying economic fundamentals those assets supposedly represent. In both eras, securities markets climbed to valuations that bore little relationship to earnings, cash flows, or economic output, justified through narratives that assumed future growth would catch up to present valuations.

In the late 1920s, the price-to-earnings ratio of the overall market reached levels that were unprecedented at the time, approaching 30 or higher for many leading stocks. These valuations assumed that the high earnings growth of the mid-1920s would continue indefinitely. In reality, corporate earnings peaked in 1929 and would not reach those levels again for over a decade. Investors paid 1940s prices for 1929 earnings.

The dividend yield on stocks fell below the yield on safe bonds by 1929, a warning sign that was dismissed at the time. Historically, stocks yielded more than bonds because stocks were riskier. The reversal suggested either that stocks had become overvalued or that investors had become irrationally confident in continued appreciation. The latter proved true, with devastating consequences.

Today's disconnect is even more extreme. The Shiller CAPE ratio exceeded 38 in 2021, a level reached only briefly at the peak of the 1999-2000 tech bubble. This meant investors were paying 38 times the average earnings of the past decade for stocks, assuming extraordinary growth would justify such valuations. The historical average CAPE is approximately 17, meaning recent valuations were more than double the long-term norm.

Market capitalization to GDP, the Buffett Indicator exceeded 200 percent in 2021, meaning the total value of stocks was twice the annual economic output of the nation. Warren Buffett has called this measure "probably the best single measure of where valuations stand at any given moment." The historical average is approximately 80-90 percent. A reading of 200 percent suggests either that stocks are wildly overvalued or that a new paradigm has permanently altered the relationship between market values and economic output.

The disconnect extends beyond stocks. Real estate prices in major cities reached 10-20 times median household income, far above historical ratios of 3-4 times income. This meant that workers in those cities could not afford housing without taking on crushing debt burdens or leaving the cities where jobs were located. The disconnect between housing prices and incomes was mathematically unsustainable.

Corporate debt trading at extremely low yields despite high leverage represented another disconnect. Companies with weak balance sheets could borrow at rates barely above Treasury yields, suggesting either that default risk had disappeared or that investors were mispricing risk dramatically. The rating agencies that blessed these low yields were the same agencies that gave AAA ratings to subprime mortgage securities in 2006.

The cryptocurrency boom featured perhaps the most extreme disconnect of all: digital tokens with no earnings, no cash flow, and no productive use trading at market capitalizations in the hundreds of billions. The valuations were justified through narratives about future adoption and use cases that remained perpetually just beyond the horizon. When Bitcoin reached $69,000, its total market cap exceeded $1.3 trillion larger than most companies in the S&P 500, despite generating no earnings.

These disconnects create structural instability because they cannot persist indefinitely. Asset prices are ultimately constrained by the cash flows those assets generate. A stock worth 40 times earnings needs earnings to grow dramatically to justify that price. A house worth 15 times income needs incomes to rise dramatically or prices to fall. A bond yielding 4 percent on a company with 8:1 leverage needs that company to never face economic stress.

The 1929 crash demonstrated what happens when disconnects resolve. Stock prices didn't just decline, they collapsed to levels that reflected depression-era earnings and economic output. The Dow fell 89 percent from peak to trough. Companies that seemed like blue-chip investments went bankrupt. The resolution was so violent because the disconnect had grown so large and because the debt financing the inflated prices had to be unwound.

Today's disconnects are larger and more pervasive than 1929's. Stocks, bonds, real estate, private assets, and cryptocurrencies are all simultaneously disconnected from fundamentals. The resolution of these disconnects will not be orderly. Prices will fall until they reach levels justified by underlying fundamentals, and those fundamentals will themselves deteriorate during the adjustment, driving prices even lower. The structural similarity suggests a resolution of comparable or greater magnitude to 1929.

Blind Faith in New Technologies

Both the 1920s and today feature widespread belief that technological innovations have fundamentally altered economic laws and justify unprecedented asset valuations. This technological optimism is not wrong, the innovations are real but it becomes dangerous when used to rationalize speculative excess and dismiss traditional valuation metrics.

The 1920s witnessed genuine technological revolution. Electrification transformed manufacturing and home life. The automobile revolutionized transportation and spurred massive infrastructure investment. Radio created instant mass communication. These innovations were real, transformative, and economically significant. The error was assuming that their transformative nature justified any stock price.

Radio Corporation of America (RCA) exemplified the era's technological optimism. The company represented cutting-edge technology and dominated the radio industry. Investors bid RCA stock from $85 in early 1928 to $549 by September 1929, a six-fold increase in less than two years. This appreciation reflected not business performance but pure speculation on radio's future. When reality intruded, RCA ultimately fell to $2.50 in 1932. The technology was real; the valuation was insane.

Automobile stocks displayed similar dynamics. General Motors and other auto manufacturers were building genuinely transformative businesses that would dominate the 20th-century economy. But investors in 1929 paid prices that assumed growth and profitability that would not materialize for decades. The technology was revolutionary; the timing was wrong; the valuations were catastrophic.

Today's technological optimism centers on artificial intelligence, blockchain, biotechnology, and clean energy, all genuinely transformative technologies with real economic significance. The parallel to the 1920s is using these technologies to justify valuations disconnected from current or foreseeable earnings.

Tesla exemplifies modern technological optimism. The company makes electric vehicles and has genuine technology advantages. Investors valued Tesla at over $1 trillion at its peak, more than all traditional automakers combined despite selling a fraction of their volume. The valuation assumed Tesla would not just dominate the auto industry but would expand into robotics, artificial intelligence, and energy storage, achieving profit margins no automaker has ever sustained. The technology is real; the valuation assumes perfect execution of optimistic scenarios.

Numerous software companies trade at extreme valuations justified by "software eating the world" narratives. Cloud computing, SaaS business models, and network effects are real advantages. But companies with minimal revenue and no profits trade at multi-billion dollar valuations because "growth at all costs" and "land grab dynamics" supposedly justify negative cash flows. This is 1920s radio stocks rebranded for the 21st century.

The cryptocurrency boom represented faith in blockchain technology justifying trillion-dollar valuations for tokens with no underlying business. The technology has potential applications, but the valuations assumed it would displace entire sectors of the financial system, assumptions with little evidence to support them. Many blockchain projects promised to revolutionize industries but delivered little beyond white papers and speculation.

The structural problem with technological optimism is that it makes speculation feel like investing. Buying RCA in 1929 or Tesla in 2021 doesn't feel like reckless gambling it feels like participating in the future, supporting innovation, and positioning for transformation. The narrative transforms speculation into vision, gambling into foresight. This makes the speculation more widespread and more persistent than it would be with transparently speculative assets.

Moreover, technological optimism makes traditional valuation metrics seem obsolete. Why does price-to-earnings matter when the company is disrupting entire industries? Why worry about current profitability when network effects will lead to dominance? Why focus on today's fundamentals when the future will be radically different? These questions sound sophisticated but function psychologically to dismiss caution and justify speculation.

The 1929 lesson is that technological transformation and stock valuation are separate questions. Electrification and automobiles did transform the economy, but that didn't make 1929 stock prices reasonable. Today's technologies will likely transform the economy, but that doesn't make recent valuations reasonable. The structural similarity is dangerous because it suggests that genuine technological progress is being used to rationalize speculative excess that will end as badly as previous episodes.

Policy Dependence and Central Bank Put

A final crucial structural similarity, though one that distinguishes recent decades more than paralleling the 1920s directly, is the market's dependence on central bank support and the widespread belief that policymakers will not allow serious market declines. This "Fed put" has become a structural feature of modern markets that paradoxically increases systemic risk while seeming to reduce it.

The 1920s featured some degree of policy accommodation. The Federal Reserve, still learning its role, kept interest rates relatively low through much of the decade. This easy money contributed to speculation, though the Fed was not yet engaging in active market support. When the crash came, the Fed failed to provide adequate liquidity, deepening the depression. The policy error was passivity, not excessive intervention.

Today's markets have evolved in the opposite direction. Since at least 1987, when the Fed cut rates following the October crash, and especially since 2008, the Fed has consistently intervened to support asset prices during declines. Quantitative easing, zero interest rates, direct asset purchases, and explicit forward guidance have created the expectation that the Fed will not allow serious bear markets.

This creates a structural dependency where market functioning requires continuous policy support. Investors make decisions based not on fundamentals but on expectations of Fed actions. "Don't fight the Fed" has evolved from a trading maxim into an investment philosophy. Markets rise when policy is accommodative and fall when policy tightens, with fundamentals playing a secondary role.

The structural problem is that this dependency makes markets increasingly fragile. Each intervention must be larger than the last to have equivalent impact. The Fed's balance sheet has grown from $800 billion pre-crisis to over $8 trillion at the peak, a ten-fold increase in a decade and a half. Interest rates have been at or near zero for most of the past 15 years. These extraordinary measures have become normal, and markets cannot function without them.

More concerning is that the Fed's credibility itself has become an asset price support mechanism. Investors believe the Fed will intervene, so they buy dips aggressively, which prevents serious declines, which reinforces belief in the Fed put. This creates a self-fulfilling prophecy during good times but a self-fulfilling catastrophe when belief eventually cracks.

The structural parallel to the 1920s is that policy has enabled speculation beyond what market forces alone would support. In the 1920s, easy money contributed to the bubble. Today, explicit central bank support for asset prices is a primary driver. Both create structural dependencies that make the system fragile. The difference is that today's dependence is far more extreme and explicit, suggesting that when the support fails or is withdrawn, the consequences will be correspondingly more severe.

The Convergence of Structural Risks

What makes the structural similarities between the 1920s and today particularly dangerous is their convergence. Wealth concentration alone creates problems but might be manageable. Middle-class speculation alone is concerning but potentially containable. Credit expansion alone is dangerous but theoretically controllable. Fundamental disconnects alone eventually resolve but need not cause catastrophe.

But when these factors converge, extreme wealth inequality, mass middle-class speculation, extraordinary credit expansion, massive fundamental disconnects, technological optimism dismissing valuation concerns, and central bank dependency all occurring simultaneously the result is a system primed for catastrophic failure. The structural conditions are not merely similar to 1929; they are similar in ways that compound and reinforce each other.

The 1929 crash became the Great Depression because the structural factors created systemic fragility. The concentration of wealth meant that asset price declines had outsized effects on demand. The middle-class speculation meant that losses spread throughout society rather than being confined to elites. The credit expansion meant that deleveraging became a death spiral. The fundamental disconnects meant that prices had to fall dramatically to reach equilibrium. The policy errors meant that the system received no support during the crisis.

Today's structural similarities suggest similar fragility with potentially larger magnitude. The wealth concentration is comparable. The middle-class speculation is more extensive. The credit expansion is far larger. The fundamental disconnects are more extreme. The technological optimism is equally powerful. And the policy dependency adds a new dimension of fragility, faith in central bank omnipotence that will eventually prove misplaced.

These structural factors operate independently of sentiment or policy. They are mathematical realities that create inevitable consequences. Debt must be serviced or defaulted on. Asset prices disconnected from fundamentals must eventually reconnect. Credit-fueled speculation must eventually unwind. Concentrated wealth means concentrated risk. These are not matters of opinion but matters of arithmetic.

The structural similarities to 1929 suggest we are not merely facing another correction or even another 2008-style crisis. We are facing a potential structural unwinding of financial excess that has accumulated over decades, enabled by policies that seemed prudent in the moment but have created systemic fragility. The question is not whether these structures will fail, mathematics suggests they must but when the failure will occur and how severe it will be. The structural parallels to 1929 suggest the answer to the second question is: very severe indeed.

Chapter 10

Key Differences

After examining the disturbing parallels between the 1920s and today, it's essential to acknowledge the significant differences that might prevent or at least mitigate a 1929-style catastrophe. These differences are real and substantial. Modern financial markets, regulatory frameworks, and policy tools have evolved considerably over the past century. The question is not whether differences exist, they clearly do but whether they are sufficient to prevent or meaningfully reduce the severity of the inevitable crash that structural excesses make probable.

Some differences represent genuine improvements that should reduce crash severity. Others are double-edged swords that prevent small crises but may amplify large ones. Still others are differences in form rather than substance, new names for old problems. Understanding which differences matter, how they matter, and what they cannot prevent is crucial for preparing for what comes next.

Circuit Breakers and Trading Halts: Preventing Panic or Postponing It?

Perhaps the most visible difference between 1929 and today is the existence of circuit breakers, automatic trading halts triggered when markets decline by specified amounts. These mechanisms, implemented after the 1987 crash, are designed to prevent the kind of cascading panic selling that characterized Black Tuesday, when there were no pauses and no cooling-off periods during the entire catastrophic trading session.

The current circuit breaker system operates at three levels. A 7 percent decline in the S&P 500 from the previous day's close triggers a 15-minute trading halt. A 13 percent decline triggers another 15-minute halt. A 20 percent decline halts trading for the remainder of the day. Additional protections exist for individual stocks, with "limit up-limit down" rules preventing trades beyond certain price bands.

These mechanisms successfully prevented panic during several near-crises. In March 2020, when pandemic fears gripped markets, circuit breakers triggered multiple times, pausing trading and theoretically allowing rational reassessment. Defenders argue that without these pauses, panic selling would have been far worse. The mechanisms force a timeout during which cooler heads can prevail.

However, circuit breakers are not panaceas; they may simply postpone rather than prevent panic. Trading halts cannot change underlying fundamentals; they only delay price discovery. If a market is genuinely overvalued and needs to fall 50 percent to reach equilibrium, circuit breakers might transform one terrible day into ten bad days, but the destination remains the same. They affect the path but not the outcome.

Moreover, circuit breakers can create perverse effects. Knowing that trading will halt at 7 percent down creates incentives to sell aggressively before the halt triggers. The pause may increase rather than reduce selling pressure as investors rush to exit before they're locked in. When trading resumes, the backlog of sell orders may cause immediate gaps down to the next circuit breaker level.

The 1929 crash unfolded over several days, Black Thursday, Black Monday, and Black Tuesday with wild intraday swings. Circuit breakers would have halted trading multiple times but wouldn't have changed the fundamental problem: prices were too high, leverage was excessive, and forced liquidation was inevitable. The mechanism might have spread the pain over more days, but it's unclear whether that would have been better or worse for participants and the economy.

Perhaps most concerning is that circuit breakers may create false confidence, encouraging risk-taking under the assumption that crashes are preventable. If investors believe circuit breakers will prevent 1929-style catastrophes, they may take on more risk than they would in a truly unprotected market. This moral hazard means circuit breakers might reduce small crashes while enabling larger bubbles that eventually produce crashes of equal or greater magnitude.

The March 2020 experience is instructive. Circuit breakers triggered four times in ten days, a record. Despite these pauses, the S&P 500 still fell 34 percent from peak to trough in just 33 days, one of the fastest bear markets in history. Only unprecedented Federal Reserve intervention far beyond circuit breakers prevented further decline. Circuit breakers bought time for policy intervention but didn't prevent the crisis or ensure recovery.

Deposit Insurance: Protection or Subsidy for Risk?

The Federal Deposit Insurance Corporation (FDIC), created in 1933, represents perhaps the most important financial innovation distinguishing today from 1929. Deposit insurance guarantees bank deposits up to $250,000, preventing the bank runs that devastated the financial system during the Great Depression. Over 9,000 banks failed between 1930 and 1933, wiping out depositors' savings. Since FDIC's creation, such catastrophic bank runs have become rare.

The psychological effect of deposit insurance cannot be overstated. In 1929, depositors had rational reasons to panic when rumors of bank troubles spread, the first to withdraw got their money while those who waited might lose everything. This created self-fulfilling bank runs where even sound banks could fail if depositors panicked. Deposit insurance eliminated this dynamic by removing the incentive to panic-withdraw. Knowing deposits are guaranteed, depositors remain calm even during banking stress.

The FDIC has been extraordinarily successful by this measure. Few Americans worry about their bank deposits disappearing overnight. The confidence deposit insurance provides has enabled financial stability impossible in the pre-FDIC era. The 2008 financial crisis demonstrated this: despite massive banking sector distress, retail depositors largely remained calm, preventing the cascade of bank failures that amplified the 1930s depression.

However, deposit insurance is not without costs and risks. By removing depositor discipline, it creates a moral hazard. If depositors know their money is guaranteed regardless of their bank's soundness, they have no incentive to monitor their bank's risk-taking. This allows banks to take excessive risks without losing deposits. Depositors become complacent, and banks become reckless, each enabled by the government guarantee.

The insurance also creates hidden taxpayer liabilities. The FDIC insurance fund holds only about $120 billion to cover approximately $10 trillion in insured deposits, a ratio of roughly 1.2 percent. This is sufficient for normal bank failures but could be overwhelmed by systemic crises. During such a crisis, the federal government would need to inject capital into the FDIC, effectively transferring bank losses to taxpayers. Deposit insurance is not free, it shifts risk from depositors to taxpayers.

Recent banking stress has revealed another issue: the insurance limit of $250,000 is inadequate for businesses and wealthy individuals who maintain larger balances. When Silicon Valley Bank failed in March 2023, many startup companies had uninsured deposits far exceeding the limit. The government ultimately guaranteed all deposits, not just insured amounts, setting a precedent that all deposits are effectively insured regardless of the legal limit. This ad-hoc expansion of guarantees creates uncertainty and moral hazard.

Moreover, deposit insurance doesn't protect against all forms of bank vulnerability. It prevents traditional bank runs but doesn't prevent wholesale funding runs when institutions lending to banks in short-term markets refuse to roll over loans. In 2008, many banks failed not because depositors withdrew money but because wholesale funding markets froze. Deposit insurance protected retail depositors but didn't prevent the broader banking crisis.

The more fundamental question is whether deposit insurance prevents crashes or simply shifts where they occur. Banks are less vulnerable, but other financial institutions such as shadow banks, investment funds and pension funds remain vulnerable and have grown to rival banks in systemic importance. The protection is real but incomplete. A 1929-style collapse emanating from the banking system is less likely, but collapses originating elsewhere remain entirely possible.

The Federal Reserve as Lender of Last Resort

Perhaps the most significant difference between 1929 and today is the Federal Reserve's evolved role as lender of last resort. In 1929, the Fed was young, its mandate was unclear, and it failed catastrophically to provide liquidity during the banking panic. Today's Fed has internalized the lessons of that failure and stands ready to inject unlimited liquidity to prevent financial collapse. This is an enormous difference but whether it's enough remains uncertain.

The Fed's modern playbook, developed after 2008, is comprehensive. Quantitative easing allows the Fed to purchase virtually any asset, government bonds, mortgage-backed securities, even corporate bonds and ETFs. Swap lines with foreign central banks provide dollar liquidity globally. Emergency lending facilities can provide capital directly to banks, corporations, and municipalities. The Fed has demonstrated willingness to expand its balance sheet without limit when crisis threatens.

This unlimited liquidity provision prevented the 2008 financial crisis from becoming another Great Depression. When Lehman Brothers failed and credit markets froze, the Fed's aggressive intervention provided the liquidity that allowed the system to continue functioning. Without Fed action, the crisis would have been catastrophically worse. The intervention was imperfect and created its own problems, but it prevented depression-scale unemployment and economic collapse.

The March 2020 crisis further demonstrated the Fed's power and willingness to intervene. When pandemic fears triggered market crashes and credit market freezes, the Fed moved with unprecedented speed and scale. Within weeks, the Fed had slashed interest rates to zero, announced unlimited quantitative easing, and created numerous emergency lending facilities. Markets stabilized almost immediately. The Fed had effectively demonstrated it would not allow a 1929-style cascade.

However, the Fed's power has limits that may become apparent in the next crisis. First, the Fed can provide liquidity but not solvency. It can lend to illiquid but solvent institutions, but it cannot (legally) rescue insolvent ones. If a crisis features widespread insolvency rather than mere illiquidity, the Fed's tools are limited. The distinction between illiquidity and insolvency becomes blurred during crises, but it matters enormously for the Fed's legal authority and practical ability to help.

Second, the Fed's interventions have created enormous moral hazard and dependency. Financial institutions take excessive risks assuming the Fed will rescue them. Asset prices are propped up by expectations of Fed support rather than fundamentals. Each crisis requires larger interventions to have an equivalent effect. The Fed has become trapped in a cycle where it must continually escalate interventions to maintain the system it has created.

Third, the Fed's balance sheet and credibility are not infinite. At some point, the scale of necessary interventions may overwhelm even the Fed's capacity. Or confidence in the Fed itself may crack, particularly if interventions consistently favor wealthy asset holders over ordinary citizens. Central bank independence and credibility are fragile; once lost, they're difficult to restore. A Fed that has deployed all its ammunition and failed would face a crisis far worse than one where tools remained available.

Fourth, the Fed cannot control fiscal policy, and financial crises increasingly require fiscal rather than just monetary responses. The Fed can provide liquidity and lower rates, but it cannot directly put money in households' pockets or fund government programs. The COVID response required massive fiscal stimulus alongside Fed actions. If political gridlock prevents adequate fiscal response during the next crisis, Fed actions alone may prove insufficient.

The most concerning possibility is that the Fed's very power and willingness to intervene has enabled the everything bubble. By consistently preventing small crises, the Fed may have created conditions for a mega-crisis beyond its capacity to manage. The institution designed to prevent 1929 may have instead created conditions for something potentially worse.

Global Interconnection: Diversification or Contagion?

One of the most profound differences between 1929 and today is the degree of global financial interconnection. In 1929, financial markets were largely national, with limited cross-border capital flows. The crash originated in the United States and spread internationally, but the transmission mechanisms were relatively slow and indirect. Today's markets are globally interconnected in real-time, with capital flowing instantly across borders and financial institutions operating as truly global entities.

This interconnection offers both benefits and risks. On the positive side, global diversification means that problems in one country or region might be offset by strength elsewhere. An American investor can hold European or Asian equities, spreading risk geographically. Companies can access capital from global sources rather than depending solely on domestic funding. The global capital pool is vastly larger than any national pool, theoretically providing more cushion against shocks.

During several recent crises, global interconnection provided stability. When Japan's economy stagnated in the 1990s, global investors could avoid Japanese assets while maintaining portfolio returns. When European sovereign debt created stress in the 2010s, capital flowed to U.S. assets. The ability to shift capital globally reduced the impact of regional problems, at least for mobile capital.

However, global interconnection also creates contagion channels unknown in 1929. The 2008 crisis demonstrated how problems originating in U.S. subprime mortgages could rapidly metastasize globally. European banks held U.S. mortgage securities. Asian institutions had purchased structured products. When these assets collapsed, the crisis spread instantaneously worldwide. What began as a domestic housing bubble became a global financial crisis within months.

The mechanisms of global contagion are multiple and powerful. Financial institutions operate globally, meaning problems at one institution affect their operations worldwide. Derivatives create direct linkages between markets, with correlations approaching one during stress. Currency markets can amplify rather than buffer shocks. Capital flight from emerging markets during crises can create secondary crises. The interconnection means that diversification offers less protection than it appears to provide.

High-frequency trading and algorithmic systems amplify global contagion. When algorithms detect unusual volatility in one market, they often reduce risk across all markets simultaneously. This creates synchronized selling that can cascade globally within minutes. The 2010 flash crash began in U.S. equity futures but almost instantly affected currencies, commodities, and international equities. Global interconnection meant that panic could spread at the speed of light.

Perhaps most concerning is that global interconnection has occurred alongside a concentration of systemically important institutions. A handful of global banks, JP Morgan, Goldman Sachs, HSBC, Deutsche Bank and BNP Paribas have operations across dozens of countries and exposure to virtually every market. The failure of any one could trigger cascading failures globally. These institutions are "too big to fail" not just nationally but globally, creating unprecedented moral hazard.

The European sovereign debt crisis of 2010-2012 illustrated these dynamics. Problems in Greece, a small economy representing less than 2 percent of European GDP, nearly destroyed the euro and triggered a global financial crisis. The interconnection through banking exposures, sovereign debt holdings, and currency mechanisms meant that a problem in one small country threatened the entire global system. Only coordinated intervention by the ECB, IMF, and national governments prevented catastrophe.

Whether global interconnection is a net positive or negative during crashes remains uncertain. It may provide diversification during small shocks but amplify contagion during large ones. The 1929 crash was devastating but remained primarily an Anglo-American phenomenon for several years. Today's crash would likely be globally simultaneous, affecting all markets and all regions at once. Whether this makes the system more or less stable is an open question, but it certainly makes the system more complex and unpredictable.

Speed of Information Flow: Enlightenment or Panic Acceleration?

The speed of information flow represents perhaps the most obvious difference between 1929 and today. In 1929, information traveled via telegraph, newspaper, and radio, fast by historical standards but glacially slow compared to today. Stock prices were disseminated by ticker tape that could lag reality by hours during heavy trading. Investment decisions were made with incomplete, delayed information.

Today's information environment is radically different. Stock prices, news, and analysis flow instantaneously via the internet, smartphones, and financial terminals. Social media provides real-time sentiment and crowdsourced analysis. High-frequency trading firms make thousands of decisions per second based on data feeds measured in microseconds. The information gap between professionals and retail investors has narrowed dramatically.

This information democratization offers clear benefits. Retail investors can access research, data, and tools that would have been impossible in 1929. Price manipulation is harder when information spreads instantly to millions. Corporate fraud is more difficult when scrutiny is immediate and widespread. The transparency should theoretically make markets more efficient and fair.

However, information speed can also accelerate rather than prevent panics. In 1929, the crash unfolded over several days, with information spreading gradually and unevenly. Today's crash would likely be far more compressed. Social media can spread panic instantly to millions. Algorithmic trading can execute massive sell programs in milliseconds. The lag that might have dampened 1929's panic has been eliminated, potentially making modern panics more sudden and severe.

The March 2020 crash illustrated this dynamic. The pandemic threat went from concerning to crisis in less than two weeks. Markets that had been at all-time highs fell 34 percent in 33 days, one of the fastest bear markets ever. The speed of information about the pandemic translated directly into speed of market reaction. There was no gradual adjustment, no time for measured response, just immediate violent repricing.

Social media adds new dynamics unknown in 1929. Rumors, fears, and panics can spread virally before facts are established. During bank runs on Silicon Valley Bank and other regional banks in March 2023, social media accelerated the panic. Depositors saw tweets about problems and immediately moved to withdraw funds electronically. What might have taken days in 1929 took hours in 2023. The electronic bank run was faster and more devastating than any physical line outside a bank.

Moreover, information speed doesn't necessarily mean information quality. The flood of real-time data, analysis, and commentary can overwhelm rather than inform. Distinguishing signal from noise becomes harder when noise is overwhelming. Retail investors have more information than ever but not necessarily more understanding or better outcomes. The democratization of information hasn't prevented bubbles; if anything, it may have facilitated them by spreading speculative narratives faster.

The speed advantage of high-frequency traders creates new inequalities. Retail investors may have better information than in 1929, but they're still disadvantaged compared to firms with microsecond-faster data feeds and algorithmic execution. The playing field isn't level; it's just tilted differently than it was in 1929. Speed benefits those with the fastest technology, potentially at the expense of others.

The fundamental question is whether information speed stabilizes or destabilizes markets. Theory suggests that faster information flow should improve efficiency and reduce volatility. But empirical evidence suggests the opposite: modern markets feature frequent flash crashes, sudden gaps, and volatility spikes that were impossible in the slower 1929 era. Speed may have reduced some forms of inefficiency while creating new forms of instability.

Government Intervention Willingness and Capacity

Perhaps the most important difference between 1929 and today is the government's demonstrated willingness to intervene aggressively during financial crises. The 1930s featured policy paralysis and adherence to balanced-budget orthodoxy even as the economy collapsed. Modern governments, having learned from that catastrophic error, now intervene quickly and massively when a crisis threatens.

The 2008 response demonstrated this changed approach. The government rescued major banks, guaranteed money market funds, bailed out AIG and the auto industry, and passed the $700 billion TARP program. The Federal Reserve slashed rates and launched quantitative easing. The response was imperfect and favored wealthy asset holders, but it prevented depression-scale economic collapse.

The COVID-19 response was even more aggressive. Within weeks, the government passed over $5 trillion in fiscal stimulus, roughly 25 percent of GDP. Enhanced unemployment benefits, direct checks to households, business loans and grants, and countless other programs flooded money into the economy. Combined with the Fed's unlimited QE and emergency lending facilities, the intervention was unprecedented in speed and scale.

This willingness to intervene is a genuine difference from 1929, when governments adhered to laissez-faire principles even as the economy imploded. Modern governments will not allow 25 percent unemployment or a decade-long depression if policy tools can prevent it. This commitment is real and provides meaningful protection against worst-case scenarios.

However, intervention capacity has limits that may become apparent in the next crisis. First, debt levels constrain fiscal capacity. Federal debt now exceeds 100 percent of GDP, up from roughly 40 percent before 2008. Each crisis requires additional borrowing. At some point, debt levels may constrain governments' ability or willingness to borrow trillions more. Bond markets may demand higher interest rates or simply refuse to lend at acceptable terms.

Second, political polarization may prevent timely intervention. The 2008 and 2020 responses, while imperfect, featured bipartisan support for emergency measures. Future crises may occur in more divided political environments where agreement proves impossible. Gridlock during a crisis could prevent adequate response, transforming a manageable problem into catastrophe.

Third, intervention fatigue may limit public support. The 2008 bailouts were deeply unpopular, seen as rescuing wealthy bankers while ordinary people suffered. Future interventions may face intense political opposition, particularly if they again favor asset holders over workers. Governments may have the theoretical capacity to intervene but lack the political capital to do so.

Fourth, moral hazard from repeated interventions may create larger eventual crises. Each rescue teaches market participants that risk-taking will be rewarded and losses will be socialized. This encourages ever-greater speculation until an eventual crisis overwhelms intervention capacity. The government's willingness to intervene may have planted seeds for a mega-crisis beyond its ability to manage.

Most concerning is the combination of exhausted monetary policy and constrained fiscal capacity. Interest rates are already near zero, the Fed has little room to cut. The balance sheet is already massive, QE has diminishing effectiveness. Debt levels are already high, fiscal space is limited. The next crisis may occur with policy tools already largely depleted, making intervention far more difficult than in 2008 or 2020.

A Double-Edged Reality

The differences between 1929 and today are real and substantial. Circuit breakers, deposit insurance, the Fed's lender-of-last-resort function, global interconnection, information speed, and government willingness to intervene all distinguish today's financial system from the fragile, unprotected system of 1929. These differences matter and should prevent exact repetition of the Great Depression.

However, these differences are double-edged. Circuit breakers may postpone rather than prevent crashes. Deposit insurance creates moral hazard while shifting risk to taxpayers. The Fed's power has enabled bubbles while creating dependency. Global interconnection provides diversification but enables contagion. Information speed can accelerate rather than prevent panics. Government intervention capacity may be exhausted or politically unavailable when most needed.

Most importantly, these differences may have prevented small crises while enabling a larger one. By consistently intervening to prevent corrections, policymakers may have created conditions for a crash of unprecedented scale. The protections are real, but they may simply have changed the crash's character rather than preventing it. Instead of a 1929-style cascade, we may face something different but equally devastating: a crisis of confidence in the institutions and policies that were supposed to prevent crashes.

The question is not whether differences exist, they clearly do but whether they're sufficient to overcome the structural similarities discussed in previous chapters. Extreme wealth concentration, middle-class speculation, massive credit expansion, fundamental disconnects, and policy exhaustion are powerful forces. The protective mechanisms are real but may prove inadequate against the scale of imbalances that have accumulated. The next chapter will examine how crashes typically unfold and what warning signs might indicate that protective mechanisms are about to be overwhelmed.

Part IV: Warning Signs and Predictive Indicators

Chapter 11

Market-Based Indicators

While understanding structural vulnerabilities and psychological dynamics is essential for recognizing bubble conditions, investors need concrete metrics to monitor, quantifiable indicators that signal when markets transition from expensive to dangerous. Market-based indicators are the vital signs of the financial system, and learning to read them can mean the difference between preserving wealth and watching it evaporate.

The challenge is that no single indicator provides perfect warning. Markets can remain expensive longer than seems rational. Valuations can stay elevated for years. Warning signs can flash for months or quarters before the crash arrives. The indicators are probabilistic rather than deterministic, they increase the odds of identifying danger but cannot predict exact timing. Nevertheless, certain market-based signals have proven remarkably consistent across historical crashes, and monitoring them provides crucial intelligence about systemic health.

Valuation Metrics: When Price and Value Diverge

Valuation metrics are the foundation of market analysis, measuring whether current prices are justified by underlying fundamentals or have detached into speculative excess. While dozens of valuation measures exist, several have proven particularly reliable across multiple market cycles and should be monitored continuously.

The Shiller Cyclically Adjusted Price-to-Earnings Ratio (CAPE)

Perhaps the most comprehensive valuation metric is the Shiller CAPE ratio, developed by Nobel laureate Robert Shiller. Unlike simple P/E ratios that can be distorted by single years of unusually high or low earnings, CAPE divides current price by the average inflation-adjusted earnings of the previous ten years. This smoothing eliminates short-term earnings volatility and provides a more stable measure of fundamental valuation.

Historical data shows that CAPE has remarkable predictive power for long-term returns. When CAPE has been above 25, subsequent ten-year returns have averaged approximately 3 percent annually. When CAPE exceeded 30, as it did in 1929, 2000, and 2021 subsequent returns were often negative. At the 1929 peak, CAPE reached approximately 33. At the 2000 tech bubble peak, it reached 44. In late 2021, it exceeded 38.

The CAPE ratio's warning is clear: when stocks trade at extreme multiples of long-term average earnings, subsequent returns are likely to be poor and the risk of crashes is elevated. The metric doesn't predict exact timing, CAPE was elevated for years during the 1990s before the 2000 crash but it identifies periods of elevated risk with impressive consistency.

Critics argue that CAPE may be less relevant in a low-interest-rate environment where higher multiples are justified. This rationalization should be familiar from previous chapters, it's the "this time is different" narrative applied to valuation. While interest rates do affect appropriate valuation levels, the relationship is not linear or unlimited. Even at zero rates, there are limits to reasonable valuation, and CAPE levels above 30 have historically led to poor outcomes regardless of interest rate environment.

The Buffett Indicator: Market Cap to GDP

Warren Buffett has called the ratio of total stock market capitalization to GDP "probably the best single measure of where valuations stand at any given moment." The logic is straightforward: stock market value should bear some reasonable relationship to the size of the economy producing the earnings that justify stock values. When the market cap exceeds GDP by large margins, stocks are likely overvalued relative to economic reality.

Historical norms place the Buffett Indicator at approximately 80-90 percent market cap roughly equal to or slightly below GDP. At the 2000 peak, the ratio reached approximately 140 percent. At the 2021 peak, it exceeded 200 percent. Only twice in history has the indicator breached 200 percent: briefly in 2000 and more substantially in 2021-2022.

The Buffett Indicator faced the same "low interest rates justify higher valuations" critique as CAPE. And as with CAPE, while some adjustment for interest rates may be warranted, a doubling of the historical ratio requires explanation beyond merely lower rates. The indicator suggests that in recent years, the stock market was valued at twice the level historically justified by economic output.

Price-to-Sales and Other Secondary Metrics

Price-to-sales ratios provide another valuation perspective less susceptible to earnings manipulation. Unlike earnings, which can be adjusted through accounting choices, revenue is more difficult to distort. High price-to-sales ratios suggest investors are paying premium prices even for modest revenue streams, often justified by assumptions of future margin expansion that may not materialize.

The median price-to-sales ratio for the S&P 500 has historically ranged between 1.0 and 1.5. By 2021, it had reached approximately 3.0, double the historical norm. This meant investors were paying twice as much for each dollar of sales as historical precedent suggested was reasonable. The metric provides confirmation of the overvaluation signaled by CAPE and the Buffett Indicator.

Dividend yields offer another perspective. Historically, stocks have yielded more than bonds because stocks are riskier. When this relationship inverts and bond yields exceed stock yields it suggests stocks have become expensive relative to their safer alternatives. By 2021, the S&P 500 dividend yield had fallen below 1.5 percent, far below historical norms of

3-4 percent and well below even low Treasury yields, suggesting overvaluation.

The consistent message across multiple valuation metrics is that markets reached extreme overvaluation by 2021, comparable to or exceeding the 1929 and 2000 peaks. No single metric is perfect, but when CAPE, the Buffett Indicator, price-to-sales, and dividend yields all signal extreme overvaluation simultaneously, the probability of poor future returns and elevated crash risk increases dramatically.

Credit Spreads: The Canary's Song

Credit spreads, the difference in yield between risky bonds and safe Treasury bonds provide crucial intelligence about market participants' perception of risk. When spreads are wide, investors demand substantial compensation for bearing credit risk, suggesting caution and concern. When spreads are narrow, investors accept minimal additional yield for taking substantial credit risk, suggesting complacency and reaching for yield.

High-yield bonds, formerly known as junk bonds, typically yield 3-5 percentage points more than Treasuries during normal times. This spread compensates investors for the meaningful risk that these companies might default. During periods of stress or caution, spreads widen to 7-10 percent or more as investors demand greater compensation for risk. During periods of euphoria and complacency, spreads compress to 2-3 percent as investors desperate for yield accept inadequate compensation.

The pattern across market cycles is consistent: spreads compress to dangerous levels during bubble peaks, signaling that investors have stopped pricing risk appropriately. In 2007, high-yield spreads compressed below 3 percent just before the financial crisis. In early 2022, spreads were similarly compressed, suggesting complacency despite obvious risks.

Investment-grade corporate bond spreads provide a similar signal. These companies have better credit ratings and lower default risk, so spreads are typically narrower, perhaps 1-2 percentage points above Treasuries normally. When spreads fall below 1 percent, as they did in 2021, it suggests investors are accepting minimal compensation for lending to companies that, while investment-grade, still carry meaningful credit risk.

The compression of credit spreads reflects the search for yield that near-zero interest rates created. With Treasuries yielding almost nothing, investors accepted progressively riskier credits for minimal additional yield. This dynamic is profoundly dangerous because it means that when defaults rise as they inevitably do during economic downturns investors will be inadequately compensated for losses they suffer.

Moreover, compressed spreads create feedback loops. Companies can borrow cheaply, which allows them to service debt, which keeps defaults low, which keeps spreads compressed, which allows more cheap borrowing. The system appears stable until some shock triggers the first wave of defaults. Then spreads widen, refinancing becomes difficult, more companies default, spreads widen further, and the feedback loop reverses into a death spiral.

Credit spreads also signal changes in risk appetite. When spreads begin widening from compressed levels, it indicates that investors are starting to demand appropriate compensation for risk, a major shift in psychology. The transition from compressed spreads to widening spreads often precedes broader market problems by weeks or months. Monitoring this transition provides early warning of changing risk perceptions.

The challenge is distinguishing between normal spread fluctuation and the beginning of a dangerous widening trend. Spreads widen and narrow constantly in response to economic data and events. The key is observing persistent widening that continues across multiple weeks or months, suggesting a fundamental shift in risk appetite rather than temporary volatility.

Yield Curve Inversions: The Most Reliable Predictor

Few indicators have proven as reliably predictive as yield curve inversions. The yield curve plots interest rates across different maturities, from overnight to 30 years. Normally, longer maturities yield more than shorter ones, reflecting both time value and risk. When this relationship inverts and short-term rates exceed long-term rates it signals that something is wrong with market expectations.

The most-watched inversion is the spread between 10-year Treasury yields and 2-year Treasury yields. When 2-year yields exceed 10-year yields, the curve has inverted. This inversion has preceded every recession since 1970 without a single false positive. The lead time varies, sometimes the recession follows within months, other times more than a year passes but the signal has been remarkably consistent.

Inversions occur when the Federal Reserve raises short-term rates to combat inflation or cool an overheating economy. If the Fed tightens too aggressively or the economy is more fragile than apparent, short-term rates rise above long-term rates as the market prices in eventual rate cuts in response to the recession the tightening will cause. The inversion reflects the market's expectation that today's higher rates are temporary because recession and Fed easing are coming.

The 2022-2023 period featured one of the deepest and most prolonged yield curve inversions in modern history, with the 2-10 spread inverted for over a year. This followed the Fed's aggressive rate-hiking campaign to combat inflation. The depth and duration of the inversion suggested significant recession risk, though as of this writing, the recession many expected has not yet materialized, though the lag between inversion and recession can extend 12-18 months.

Some analysts distinguish between inversions caused by Fed tightening and those caused by economic weakness. The former, policy-induced inversions are considered more benign than inversions occurring despite Fed accommodation, which suggest organic economic weakness. However, this distinction provides limited comfort; both types have preceded recessions with similar reliability.

Critics argue that quantitative easing distorted the yield curve, making inversions less meaningful. Central bank purchases of long-term bonds artificially depressed long-term yields, potentially creating inversions that don't carry the historical signal. This critique has validity, QE did distort yield curves but it doesn't eliminate the inversion signal entirely. Even with QE effects, inversions still reflect something wrong with either policy or economic fundamentals.

The yield curve also provides information beyond simple inversion. The slope of the curve, how steeply it rises from short to long maturities indicates expectations for growth and inflation. A steep curve suggests expectations of strong growth and rising inflation. A flat curve suggests uncertainty or expectations of weak growth. A deeply inverted curve suggests expectations of imminent recession.

For crash prediction, yield curve inversions are most useful in combination with other indicators. An inverted curve alone signals recession risk but doesn't necessarily predict market crashes. However, an inverted curve combined with extreme valuations, compressed credit spreads, and elevated leverage suggests that recession will trigger financial crisis rather than mere economic slowdown.

Volatility Compression: The VIX and Complacency

The VIX, the Chicago Board Options Exchange Volatility Index measures expected volatility in the S&P 500 based on options prices. Often called the "fear gauge," the VIX rises during market stress and falls during calm periods. Counterintuitively, extremely low VIX readings often precede crashes rather than signaling safety. Complacency, not fear, is the most dangerous market condition.

Historical analysis shows that VIX levels below 12 indicate extreme complacency. At such levels, options are cheap because investors see little risk of market volatility. This complacency often marks late-stage bubbles when everyone assumes stability will persist indefinitely. The VIX fell below 10 in 2017 and early 2018, levels rarely seen outside of extreme complacency. The 2018 "Volmageddon" event demonstrated what happens when volatility suddenly spikes from compressed levels.

The VIX's behavior during crashes is predictable: it spikes dramatically as fear replaces complacency. During the 2008 financial crisis, the VIX exceeded 80. During the March 2020 pandemic crash, it exceeded 85. These spikes reflect the panic that emerges when markets that seemed stable suddenly aren't. The magnitude of VIX spikes often correlates with the degree of prior complacency, the lower the VIX during calm periods, the higher it spikes during crisis.

Monitoring the VIX's level relative to historical norms provides useful information about market psychology. Extended periods of VIX below 15 suggest markets are complacent, potentially underpricing risk. When the VIX begins rising from compressed levels, it may signal changing psychology even before market prices reflect it. A rising VIX combined with declining prices suggests fear is entering the market, a dangerous combination.

However, the VIX has limitations as a predictive tool. Low VIX can persist for years without crashes occurring. High VIX can persist during corrections that don't become crashes. The VIX is better at measuring current sentiment than predicting future events. Its primary utility is identifying complacency that makes markets vulnerable rather than predicting when that vulnerability will be exploited.

The term structure of volatility, comparing near-term to longer-term expected volatility provides additional information. When short-term implied volatility exceeds long-term, it suggests immediate stress that markets expect will pass. When the relationship is normal and short-term volatility is below long-term it suggests calm conditions. Persistent inversion of the volatility term structure indicates sustained stress.

Realized volatility, actual price movements rather than expected movements provides another perspective. When realized volatility is low for extended periods, it suggests markets are stable but potentially building complacency. When realized volatility suddenly spikes after extended calm, it often marks the beginning of serious market disruption.

Margin Debt: Leverage Reaching Extremes

Margin debt, money borrowed to purchase securities provides direct measurement of leverage in the system. When margin debt rises relative to market capitalization, it signals that investors are borrowing more to speculate, increasing systemic fragility. Major market peaks have consistently coincided with margin debt reaching extremes relative to market size.

NYSE margin debt is reported monthly with a lag, providing concrete data on borrowing for stock purchases. The absolute level matters less than the ratio to market capitalization as markets grow, some increase in margin debt is natural. But when margin debt exceeds 2.5-3.0 percent of market cap, historical experience suggests danger. At the 2000 peak, margin debt reached approximately 2.8 percent of market cap. At the 2007 peak, approximately 2.5 percent. In 2021, it exceeded 3.0 percent, a record level.

These extremes create mechanical vulnerability. When prices fall, margin calls force selling, which pushes prices lower, triggering more margin calls in a self-reinforcing cascade. The 1929 crash followed this pattern, as did the initial panic in 2008 and March 2020. High margin debt doesn't cause crashes, but it amplifies them when they begin.

The psychology of margin debt is equally important. High margin debt indicates confidence, investors are comfortable borrowing to buy stocks, assuming prices will continue rising. This confidence often peaks near market tops. When confidence cracks and margin investors begin reducing leverage, the forced selling creates selling pressure unrelated to fundamental business conditions.

Margin debt also has asymmetric effects on market dynamics. Rising margin debt supports prices during bull markets, the borrowed money flows into stocks, creating buying pressure. But falling margin debt creates disproportionate selling pressure because it's forced rather than discretionary. The natural selling from declining margin debt overwhelms any discretionary buying, creating conditions where markets can fall much faster than they rose.

The challenge with margin debt as an indicator is the lag in reporting and the exclusion of leverage through derivatives. Reported margin debt understates total leverage because it excludes options, futures, and other leveraged products. Nevertheless, the reported figures provide a minimum bound on leverage and have proven reliable indicators of excessive speculation.

Monitoring the rate of change in margin debt provides early warning. When margin debt growth accelerates relative to market gains, it signals increasing leverage and speculation. When margin debt begins declining while markets are still elevated, it suggests that either confidence is wavering or forced deleveraging has begun, both concerning signals.

Market Breadth: When the Few Carry the Many

Market breadth measures how many stocks participate in market moves. Healthy bull markets feature broad participation, most stocks rising together. Unhealthy late-stage bubbles feature narrow participation, a small number of stocks driving index gains while most stocks lag or decline. Deteriorating breadth is one of the most reliable signs that market leadership is exhausted and crashes are approaching.

The advance-decline line tracks the cumulative difference between advancing and declining stocks. When this line rises steadily alongside market indices, breadth is healthy. When indices reach new highs while the advance-decline line fails to confirm, a bearish divergence signals that fewer stocks are participating in gains. This deterioration often precedes broader market declines by weeks or months.

New highs versus new lows provide similar information. In healthy markets, the number of stocks reaching new 52-week highs expands as indices rise. In deteriorating markets, fewer stocks reach new highs even as indices climb, driven by a handful of large-cap stocks. When new lows begin outnumbering new highs while indices remain elevated, it signals serious internal weakness.

Sector performance offers another breadth perspective. Late-stage bull markets often feature leadership rotating to defensive sectors such as utilities, consumer staples and healthcare as investors unconsciously seek safety. When high-beta, economically-sensitive sectors lag while defensive sectors lead, it suggests deteriorating confidence beneath the surface even if headline indices don't yet reflect it.

The concentration of market gains in a small number of stocks creates both statistical and mechanical problems. Statistically, when a handful of stocks drive index gains, the median stock may be declining even as the index rises. Investors who don't own the leaders underperform dramatically, creating performance pressure to chase the leaders regardless of valuation. This concentration in already-expensive stocks amplifies overvaluation.

Mechanically, concentrated leadership creates fragility. When leadership is broad and the market eventually declines, buyers may support various stocks at various levels, creating natural resistance to further declines. When leadership is narrow, there are few supporters at lower levels for most stocks, and the handful of leaders that have carried the market become too expensive for value buyers. The market becomes an all-or-nothing proposition.

The 2021-2022 period featured extreme concentration, with the "Magnificent Seven" technology stocks representing over 25 percent of S&P 500 market capitalization and contributing disproportionately to index gains. Beneath the surface, many stocks peaked in 2021 and declined substantially through 2022 even as the indices initially held up. This deteriorating breadth signaled internal weakness long before the broader market acknowledged it.

Monitoring breadth indicators requires patience. Breadth can deteriorate for months before affecting major indices. But the signal is valuable precisely because it provides warning before the obvious signs appear. When multiple breadth indicators flash warnings simultaneously, advance-decline line diverging, new highs collapsing, sector rotation defensive and leadership narrowing the probability of significant market decline rises substantially.

Putting It Together: The Dashboard Approach

No single market-based indicator provides perfect warning. Valuation metrics can stay elevated for years. Credit spreads can remain compressed through multiple Fed meetings. Yield curve inversions can lag recessions by over a year. The VIX can stay low during extended bubble periods. Margin debt can reach records and climb higher. Breadth can deteriorate without immediate consequence.

The power comes from monitoring multiple indicators simultaneously and recognizing when they align. When valuation metrics show extreme overvaluation AND credit spreads are compressed AND the yield curve inverts AND volatility is compressed AND margin debt is elevated AND breadth is deteriorating, the probability of severe market decline approaches certainty. The question becomes not if but when.

This dashboard approach requires discipline. Individual indicators will flash warnings at different times. Valuation might signal danger for years before other indicators join. The yield curve might invert months before credit spreads widen. Maintaining conviction in the face of rising markets while indicators flash warnings requires psychological strength that few investors possess.

The historical record provides guidance. Major market peaks in 1929, 1987, 2000 and 2007 featured multiple indicators flashing warnings simultaneously. In each case, investors who heeded the warnings avoided catastrophic losses, though they likely underperformed during the final manic phase. Those who dismissed the warnings as perpetual pessimism suffered devastating losses.

The key insight is that market-based indicators measure systemic fragility rather than predicting timing. They identify conditions where crashes become probable rather than specifying when crashes will occur. This is not a weakness but a fundamental limitation, timing is inherently unpredictable because crashes require catalysts whose timing is unknowable. But recognizing fragility allows appropriate positioning: reducing leverage, increasing cash, avoiding the most speculative investments, and preparing psychologically for volatility.

In the end, market-based indicators serve as the financial system's vital signs. Doctors don't need to know exactly when a patient with terrible vital signs will suffer organ failure to recognize the patient is critically ill. Similarly, investors don't need to know exactly when crashes will occur to recognize when markets are critically overvalued, overleveraged, and fragile. The indicators provide the intelligence needed to act prudently even when precise timing remains elusive. The next chapter will examine economic indicators that complement these market-based signals, providing a fuller picture of systemic health and vulnerability.

Chapter 12

Economic Red Flags

While market-based indicators flash their warnings in the language of prices and volatility, economic red flags speak in the dialect of the real world such as production, employment, consumption, and credit. These indicators are often less dramatic than a sudden market correction, but they're frequently more reliable. They tell us not what investors *think* about the economy, but what the economy is actually *doing*. And history shows that when these fundamental measures begin deteriorating while asset prices continue climbing, the gap between perception and reality eventually closes with brutal efficiency.

The challenge with economic indicators is their complexity and their tendency to provide false signals. The economy is not a simple machine with straightforward cause and effect. It's a vast, interconnected organism where millions of actors make billions of decisions daily. But certain patterns emerge repeatedly before major crashes, and learning to recognize them can provide crucial months of warning or at minimum, heighten your awareness that risk is elevated.

Leading Economic Indicators Rolling Over

The Conference Board's Leading Economic Index (LEI) is perhaps the most watched composite indicator, designed specifically to predict economic turning points. It combines ten different metrics from building permits to consumer expectations to manufacturing orders into a single number that historically turns down before recessions begin.

Before the 2008 crisis, the LEI peaked in July 2007, sixteen months before the recession officially started and fifteen months before Lehman Brothers collapsed. Before the 2001 recession, it peaked in January 2000, just as the dot-com bubble reached its zenith. The pattern repeats with remarkable consistency: the LEI rolls over while the stock market is still celebrating, sometimes for many months.

But here's the crucial subtlety: not every LEI decline signals an imminent crash. The index declined in 2011 without triggering a recession. It wobbled in 2015-2016 during the oil price collapse and industrial recession, yet the broader economy avoided contraction. The key is not a single month's decline but a sustained trend; three to six consecutive months of negative readings create a pattern that demands attention.

Within the LEI, pay particular attention to the manufacturing components. New orders for capital goods (excluding aircraft and defense) tell you whether businesses are investing in future production capacity. When these orders decline, companies are signaling their pessimism about demand six to twelve months out. They're not buying new equipment because they don't expect to need it. The manufacturing workweek, the average hours worked by production employees provides similar forward-looking insight. When manufacturers cut hours before laying off workers, they're testing whether a slowdown is temporary or structural.

The ISM Manufacturing Index, released monthly, provides granular detail about industrial activity. Readings above 50 indicate expansion; below 50 signals contraction. But the devil lives in the components. New orders falling below 50 while inventories remain elevated creates a particularly dangerous combination, companies have built up stock they can't sell, production cuts will follow, and layoffs won't be far behind. This exact sequence played out in 2000-2001 and 2007-2008.

In 2023 and 2024, the ISM Manufacturing Index spent most months below 50, yet the stock market powered to new highs. This disconnect, service sector strength masking manufacturing weakness created fierce debate among economists. Is manufacturing too small a share of the modern economy to matter? Or is it a leading indicator for broader weakness ahead? History suggests the latter. Manufacturing employs a relatively small portion of workers but drives demand throughout the supply chain. When it weakens persistently, the contagion spreads.

The yield curve inversion, discussed in the previous chapter as a market indicator, also functions as an economic red flag. But the economic story it tells is about credit transmission. When short-term rates exceed long-term rates, banks face a profitability squeeze, they borrow short and lend long, and an inverted curve compresses their net interest margin. This makes them less willing to lend, which restricts credit flow to businesses and consumers, which slows economic activity, which justifies the bond market's pessimism. It's a self-fulfilling prophecy, but that doesn't make it less real.

Corporate Earnings Quality Deterioration

Reported earnings can be a mirage. Companies have tremendous latitude in how they present their financial results, and during boom times, aggressive accounting becomes endemic. Revenue recognition gets stretched, expenses get reclassified as "one-time" or "non-recurring," and adjusted earnings bear increasingly little resemblance to actual cash flow. When earnings quality deteriorates broadly across the market, it signals that companies are struggling to meet expectations through operational performance and have resorted to financial engineering instead.

One of the clearest quality indicators is the gap between GAAP earnings (Generally Accepted Accounting Principles) and non-GAAP adjusted earnings. Companies argue that adjustments provide a clearer picture of "ongoing operations" by excluding unusual items. Fair enough in theory. But when the gap widens dramatically, when every quarter brings new "one-time" charges that somehow recur every period, credibility evaporates.

In the years leading to the 2008 crisis, financial companies made extensive use of adjusted earnings to hide mounting losses in their mortgage portfolios. They'd exclude writedowns as non-recurring, even as those writedowns happened quarter after quarter. By late 2007, the gap between reported and adjusted earnings in the financial sector had become a chasm, yet most analysts continued using the adjusted figures. Those who focused on GAAP earnings and actual cash flow saw the disaster coming.

Accrual accounting provides another window into earnings quality. Companies record revenue when earned, not necessarily when cash is collected. This creates opportunities for manipulation, aggressive revenue recognition, lenient credit terms to boost sales, reserves that can be released to manufacture earnings. The ratio of cash flow to net income should hover around 1.0 over time. When it drops significantly below 1.0, when companies report strong earnings but weak cash flow skepticism is warranted. They're reporting profits they haven't actually collected.

Watch particularly for deterioration in accounts receivable. The "days sales outstanding" (DSO) metric tells you how long it takes to collect payment from customers. Rising DSO suggests companies are offering easier credit terms to maintain sales volume, a classic late-cycle behavior. If revenues are growing 10% but receivables are growing 20%, that's not growth it's desperation.

Share buybacks present a related red flag. Buybacks per se aren't problematic; returning capital to shareholders is a legitimate use of cash. The warning sign is when companies borrow money to fund buybacks while operating cash flow stagnates or declines. They're using cheap debt to artificially boost earnings per share by reducing the share count, creating the illusion of per-share earnings growth without actual profit growth. This corporate financial engineering reached spectacular levels in the 2015-2019 period, as companies took advantage of ultra-low interest rates to issue bonds and buy back stock, often at elevated valuations.

The ultimate earnings quality test is simple: compare net income to free cash flow over a multi-year period. Free cash flow, operating cash flow minus capital expenditures represents the actual cash a company generates that's available for shareholders. If a company consistently reports rising earnings while free cash flow stagnates or declines, something's wrong. Either their accounting is aggressive, their business model is deteriorating, or they're overinvesting in projects with poor returns. None of these scenarios is bullish.

Consumer Confidence vs. Consumer Behavior Divergence

The consumer drives roughly 70% of the U.S. economy, so understanding consumer health is critical. But consumers are complicated, they don't always do what they say, and they don't always say what they do. The divergence between what consumers report (confidence surveys) and how they actually behave (spending patterns) often signals underlying stress that hasn't yet surfaced in the data.

The Conference Board Consumer Confidence Index and the University of Michigan Consumer Sentiment Index measure how consumers feel about current conditions and future prospects. These surveys have reasonable predictive power, when confidence plunges, spending typically follows. But the relationship isn't perfect, and the most interesting signals come from divergences.

In late 2007, consumer confidence remained relatively elevated even as spending on big-ticket items had begun declining. People told surveys they felt fine, but they'd stopped buying cars and appliances. This behavioral caution while maintaining verbal optimism suggests consumers were already responding to stress, perhaps rising debt burdens or stagnant wage growth even if they weren't consciously acknowledging it.

The opposite pattern can be equally revealing. In the late 1990s, consumer confidence soared to record levels, but much of the spending increase was debt-fueled. The personal savings rate dropped to historical lows below 2% as households spent stock market gains (the wealth effect) and ran up credit cards. Consumers felt confident, they were spending freely, but the foundation was unsustainable. When the market corrected, the wealth effect reversed, and heavily indebted consumers had to retrench sharply.

Dig deeper into spending patterns for additional insight. The ratio of discretionary to non-discretionary spending shifts predictably with economic cycles. When consumers start cutting back on restaurants, entertainment, and travel while maintaining spending on groceries and utilities, they're entering defensive mode. Credit card data, available with only a few weeks' lag, provides real-time insight into these shifts.

The personal savings rate itself is a crucial metric. When it declines toward zero, consumers have no buffer. They're spending every dollar earned, leaving no room for error. Any shock such as a job loss, unexpected expense or market decline forces immediate spending cuts. This creates economic fragility. Conversely, a rising savings rate might seem like weakness (less spending) but actually builds resilience.

Student loan, auto loan, and credit card delinquency rates tell you how stressed consumers are beneath the surface. These metrics lag, people fall behind on payments after stress has built for months but they're reliable. In 2006-2007, subprime mortgage delinquencies began rising well before the crisis went mainstream. Auto loan delinquencies started ticking up in 2015-2016 as subprime auto lending boomed, though broader economic strength masked the problem. By 2023-2024, credit card delinquency rates were rising, particularly among younger borrowers, even as unemployment remained low. This suggested wage growth wasn't keeping pace with inflation and debt burdens.

Look for divergence between headline unemployment (seemingly strong) and measures of consumer financial stress (rising). This combination is particularly dangerous because it creates complacency, policymakers and investors believe the economy is healthy while stress builds underground.

Commercial Real Estate Stress

Commercial real estate deserves its own section because it's both an economic indicator and a potential crisis catalyst. CRE connects the real economy (businesses needing space) to the financial system (banks holding CRE loans) to the market (REITs and commercial mortgage-backed securities). Weakness in CRE can trigger a cascade that spreads far beyond the property sector.

Office real estate post-pandemic illustrates the dynamic perfectly. Vacancy rates in major cities climbed above 20% as remote work became permanent for many companies. Property values declined 30-40% or more from pandemic-era peaks. But the real danger lies in the debt. Many office properties were purchased or refinanced in 2020-2022 when valuations were high and interest rates were near zero. Now those properties generate insufficient cash flow to service debt taken out at higher values, and refinancing means much higher interest rates.

The "extend and pretend" phase, where banks and borrowers agree to extend loan terms rather than recognize losses can last years. But eventually, reality intrudes. When properties sell for 50 cents on the dollar in distressed transactions, it establishes new comparable values that force mark-to-market losses throughout the sector. Banks holding significant CRE exposure face capital problems. Small and regional banks are particularly vulnerable, CRE loans represent over 25% of assets for many institutions, well above the regulatory comfort zone.

The office sector is obvious, but watch retail and industrial properties too. Retail has been challenged for years by e-commerce, with struggling malls and shopping centers. The pandemic accelerated trends that were already underway. Industrial and warehouse space boomed during the pandemic as e-commerce exploded, but much of that demand proved transitory.

Overbuilding in some markets created excess capacity just as e-commerce growth normalized.

The key indicator is the gap between property-level income and debt service requirements, the debt service coverage ratio (DSCR). When DSCRs drop below 1.0, properties don't generate enough income to cover their loans. This forces either capital injections from owners (unlikely in falling markets), refinancing (difficult with higher rates), or default. Track DSCR trends across property types and geographies for early warning.

Commercial mortgage-backed securities (CMBS) spreads provide market-based insight. When spreads widen, when investors demand higher yields to hold CRE debt it signals rising concern about credit quality. The CMBS market seized up in 2008-2009 as mortgage stress spread from residential to commercial. If spreads widen sharply again while other credit markets remain calm, CRE stress could be the canary in the coal mine.

Pay attention to REIT behavior and pricing. Real estate investment trusts provide liquid access to commercial real estate. When REIT prices diverge significantly from their net asset values (NAV), trading at steep discounts it suggests the market anticipates future NAV write-downs. REITs also provide monthly and quarterly operating data with relatively short lags, offering current insight into occupancy, rent trends, and property performance.

Bank Lending Standards and Credit Availability

Banks sit at the heart of credit creation, and their willingness to lend or reluctance to lend largely determines credit availability. The Federal Reserve's Senior Loan Officer Opinion Survey (SLOOS) asks banks quarterly about their lending standards and demand for loans. This survey is remarkably predictive: when large percentages of banks report tightening standards, recession typically follows within 12-18 months.

The mechanism is straightforward. Banks tighten standards when they perceive rising credit risk, deteriorating borrower financial conditions, falling collateral values, or economic uncertainty. This makes credit less available, which slows business investment and consumer spending, which weakens the economy, which validates banks' initial caution. The feedback loop accelerates.

In 2007, banks began tightening standards for mortgages and commercial real estate loans as delinquencies rose. By late 2007, standards were tightening across categories. By 2008, credit was essentially unavailable except to the strongest borrowers. This credit freeze turned a housing recession into a systemic crisis. In 2023-2024, banks tightened lending standards significantly following the regional bank failures in March 2023, creating what some economists called a "credit crunch" even though the Fed hadn't raised rates further.

The SLOOS also tracks loan demand. When banks report both tightening standards AND weakening demand, the economy is entering dangerous territory. Businesses aren't seeking credit because they don't see profitable investment opportunities. Consumers aren't borrowing because they're uncertain about their financial futures. The combination of restricted supply and falling demand creates a credit contraction that's difficult to reverse.

Watch commercial and industrial (C&I) loan growth at banks. When year-over-year growth turns negative, businesses are paying down debt faster than they're taking on new borrowing. This typically happens only during recessions or immediately before them. Companies deleverage when they're pessimistic about growth prospects and want to preserve financial flexibility for uncertain times ahead.

Consumer credit growth tells a similar story from the household side. When credit card balances, auto loans, and other consumer lending contracts, consumers are either unable to access credit (lenders won't approve) or unwilling to take it on (borrowers are cautious). Either way, consumption growth will slow.

The shadow banking system adds complexity. When traditional bank lending tightens, borrowers often turn to non-bank lenders such as private credit funds, business development companies, and specialty finance companies. This can mask underlying credit stress temporarily. But shadow bank lending comes with higher costs and less favorable terms. When even shadow banks pull back, options have truly disappeared.

Covenant-lite loan issuance provides insight into credit quality. "Cov-lite" loans have fewer protective provisions for lenders, making them riskier. When cov-lite loans represent 80-90% of the leveraged loan market, as they have in recent years, lenders are desperate for yield and unconcerned about risk. This suggests late-cycle exuberance. When cov-lite issuance drops sharply, lenders have remembered that risk exists, often because losses have already started materializing.

The Zombie Company Problem

Perhaps no economic red flag is more indicative of structural fragility than the proliferation of zombie companies, firms that earn less than their debt service obligations and survive only through continuously refinancing or taking on additional debt. These corporate walking dead aren't growing or innovating; they're limping along, consuming resources that could be deployed more productively elsewhere.

The Bank for International Settlements defines zombies as companies ten years or older with interest coverage ratios (earnings before interest and taxes divided by interest expense) below 1.0 for three consecutive years. By this definition, the percentage of zombie companies among listed firms in developed economies rose from about 2% in the 1980s to roughly 12-15% by 2020.

Ultra-low interest rates enabled this zombie proliferation. When borrowing costs are near zero, even barely profitable companies can service their debts. But this represents a hidden tax on the economy. Zombies constrain healthy competitors by keeping prices low and capacity high. They tie up labor and capital in unproductive uses. They prevent the creative destruction that drives economic dynamism.

The danger becomes acute when interest rates rise or credit conditions tighten. Suddenly, zombies can't refinance on favorable terms. Their business models, barely viable at 2% interest rates, become impossible at 6%. A wave of defaults begins, spreading through credit markets and potentially triggering a broader crisis as lenders scramble to manage losses.

During the 2022-2023 rate hiking cycle, many analysts predicted a zombie apocalypse that didn't immediately materialize. Many companies had refinanced during the ultra-low rate period, locking in cheap financing for years. The reckoning was delayed, not canceled. As those bonds and loans mature in 2024-2026, the refinancing wall approaches. Companies that issued 10-year bonds at 3% in 2014 must now refinance at 7-8% or higher. The math doesn't work for marginal businesses.

Track high-yield bond default rates for insight into zombie stress. Historically, default rates below 2% indicate benign credit conditions. Rates of 4-5% signal rising stress. Above 10%, you're in crisis territory. Default rates remained remarkably low through 2023 despite rising rates, but forecasts consistently predicted increases in 2024-2025 as refinancing pressures mounted.

The composition of defaults matters too. When defaults concentrate in obviously struggling sectors, retail bankruptcies during the e-commerce transition, for example its sector-specific evolution. When defaults spread across multiple unrelated sectors, systemic stress is building. When previously investment-grade companies get downgraded to junk and then default, the credit quality deterioration has spread to supposedly safe borrowers.

Putting It All Together

Economic red flags work best not in isolation but in combination. A single indicator can mislead; multiple indicators confirming the same story create conviction. When you see leading indicators rolling over, earnings quality deteriorating, consumer behavior diverging from confidence, commercial real estate stress, tightening lending standards, and zombie companies struggling all at once, the probability of serious economic contraction rises dramatically.

The sequence matters too. Economic weakness typically precedes market crashes by months, sometimes more than a year. The economy begins slowing, credit begins tightening, earnings begin disappointing all while the market remains in denial, trading at or near all-time highs. Investors focus on backward-looking data (last quarter's strong earnings) while economic indicators are forward-looking (next quarter's anticipated weakness).

This lag creates opportunity for those watching the economic indicators. You won't time the market perfectly, no one does. But you can recognize that risk has shifted from theoretical to probable to imminent. You can begin reducing leverage, raising cash, and positioning more defensively while your peers are still enjoying the party.

The hardest part is maintaining conviction when the market continues rising despite red flags. In 2007, economic indicators began deteriorating in the spring and summer. The market peaked in October, then rallied back to near those highs in early 2008 before collapsing. Many who reduced risk in mid-2007 felt foolish by year-end as the S&P 500 finished roughly flat. They felt vindicated in 2008, but enduring those months of looking wrong required conviction.

This is why developing your own systematic approach to monitoring economic red flags is crucial. Don't rely on financial media or Wall Street strategists, who have institutional biases toward bullishness and face career risk from bearish calls. Build a dashboard of indicators you trust. Update it regularly. Decide in advance what combination of signals will trigger defensive action. Then follow your plan, even when it's uncomfortable.

The economy is not the market, and the market is not the economy. But over time, prices must reconnect with underlying economic reality. When economic red flags are waving, that reconnection will be painful. Your goal isn't to predict the exact timing, it's to ensure you're not fully exposed when it happens.

Chapter 13

Behavioral Signals

Markets are not rational computing machines that efficiently process information and arrive at correct prices. They are collections of human beings, emotional, social, prone to manias and panics, subject to cognitive biases that have been hardwired into our brains over millennia of evolution. These psychological patterns repeat with remarkable consistency across centuries and cultures. Understanding behavioral signals, the collective psychology of market participants can provide some of the most reliable warnings that a market has detached from reality and a crash is approaching.

The beauty of behavioral indicators is their visibility. Unlike economic data that arrives with lags or corporate financials that can be manipulated, behavioral signals happen in real-time and in public view. The challenge is separating normal market enthusiasm from dangerous euphoria, and recognizing when optimism has crossed into delusion. This chapter explores the behavioral patterns that emerge repeatedly before major crashes, from the South Sea Bubble to the Roaring Twenties to the dot-com boom to today.

Retail Investor Sentiment Extremes

Professional investors, fund managers, institutional traders and strategists are often wrong, but they're usually wrong within a reasonable range. Retail investors, by contrast, display far greater sentiment volatility. They become extremely bullish at tops and extremely bearish at bottoms, making them reliable contrarian indicators. When retail sentiment reaches euphoric extremes, danger is near.

The American Association of Individual Investors (AAII) conducts a weekly sentiment survey asking members whether they're bullish, bearish, or neutral on the stock market for the next six months. The historical average is roughly 38% bullish, 30% bearish, and 32% neutral. When bullish sentiment exceeds 55-60%, especially for multiple consecutive weeks, the market is often near a local or major top. When bearish sentiment exceeds 50-55%, capitulation has typically occurred and a bottom is forming.

The pattern is striking. In October 2007, just before the financial crisis began in earnest, AAII bullish sentiment was above 50%. By March 2009, at the absolute market bottom, bullish sentiment had collapsed to the teens while bearish sentiment exceeded 70%. Those who bought when everyone was terrified and sold when everyone was euphoric captured the entire subsequent bull market.

The mechanics are straightforward: retail investors have limited capital and tend to be fully invested during euphoric periods. They've already bought, so incremental buying power is exhausted. Meanwhile, professional investors and smart money have been distributing shares to eager retail buyers at elevated prices. When sentiment is extreme, there's no one left to buy, and any negative catalyst triggers selling into a vacuum.

But raw sentiment numbers can be misleading without context. Bullish sentiment of 50% during a healthy bull market is different from 50% after a decade-long rally with valuations at extremes. Look for sentiment extremes that coincide with other warning signals, expensive valuations, deteriorating breadth, economic weakness. The confluence matters more than any single indicator.

Brokerage account activity provides additional insight into retail behavior. When discount brokers report record account openings, massive increases in trading volume, or surges in options trading by retail clients, speculative fever is running hot. During the 2020-2021 meme stock phenomenon, major brokers reported millions of new accounts opened by young, first-time investors. Many had never experienced a bear market. Many believed stock prices only went up. This flood of inexperienced capital, armed with zero-commission trading and fractional shares, created exactly the conditions that precede painful corrections.

The retail options boom deserves particular attention. Options are leveraged instruments that can generate outsized gains or total losses. Historically, options were the domain of sophisticated traders hedging positions or implementing complex strategies. But in 2020-2021, retail options trading exploded. Zero-days-to-expiration (0DTE) options, contracts that expire the same day, became wildly popular allowing traders to make huge bets on tiny market moves. When retail investors are actively trading the most complex, most leveraged, shortest-dated instruments, prudent investors should be moving toward the exits.

The "Dumb Money" Confidence Indicators

The financial industry has developed various composite measures that attempt to quantify "dumb money" behavior, the collective actions of typically unsophisticated market participants who historically buy tops and sell bottoms. While the terminology is harsh, the concept is useful: certain market participants have reliably wrong timing, and their extreme actions provide contrarian signals.

The Investors Intelligence survey tracks the predictions of newsletter writers, individuals who publish investment advice for retail subscribers. The survey categorizes newsletters as bullish, bearish, or expecting a correction. Historically, when bulls exceed 55-60% of advisors and bears drop below 20%, major tops are near. When bears exceed 50-55%, bottoms are forming. In January 2000, at the dot-com peak, bulls exceeded 60%. In March 2009, bears exceeded 50%.

The National Association of Active Investment Managers (NAAIM) surveys active money managers about their equity exposure. When average exposure exceeds 100% (meaning managers are using leverage), aggressive positioning suggests euphoria. When exposure drops below 20%, defensive positioning suggests fear or capitulation. This indicator is less contrarian than retail sentiment, professional managers aren't purely "dumb money" but extreme readings still provide useful signals.

The put-call ratio measures the volume of put options (bets on decline) versus call options (bets on rises). A low ratio indicates far more calls than puts, suggesting bullish positioning and complacency. An extremely high ratio indicates hedging or bearish positioning. The equity put-call ratio typically hovers around 0.6-0.7. When it drops below 0.5 for extended periods, complacency is extreme. When it spikes above 1.0-1.2, panic has set in.

But perhaps the most telling "dumb money" indicator is retail money market fund flows. When retail investors are flooding into money market funds, the safest and lowest-return investment, they're terrified. This typically happens near bottoms. When they're pulling money out of safe investments to chase returns in risk assets, greed has overtaken caution. This happens near tops.

In 2007-2008, retail investors consistently bought equity funds even as the market deteriorated, while institutional investors were selling. Retail buying accelerated into early 2008, even after Bear Stearns collapsed. Only after Lehman failed and the market was already down 40% did retail capitulation occur. The smart money had exited a year earlier, selling to retail investors who were confident "it was just a correction."

The danger of dumb money indicators is their potential for self-righteousness. Everyone thinks they're the smart money. The retail investor buying a hot tech stock believes professional fund managers are dinosaurs who don't understand innovation. The professional fund manager believes retail investors are foolish gamblers. Both can be wrong simultaneously. Use these indicators with humility, as data points about collective positioning and sentiment, not as moral judgments about intelligence.

IPO and SPAC Quality Degradation

Initial public offerings represent the interface between private markets and public markets, and their quality varies dramatically with market cycles. During healthy markets, strong companies go public at reasonable valuations. During manias, anything goes public at any price, and investors suspend disbelief.

The late 1990s saw a parade of unprofitable internet companies going public at multi-billion dollar valuations despite having minimal revenue and no path to profitability. Companies with ".com" in their names saw shares triple on the first day of trading. Pets.com, Webvan and eToys, these companies became symbols of the excess. They had flashy websites and Super Bowl ads but unsustainable business models. When the music stopped, they vanished.

The quality degradation follows a pattern. Early in a bull market, IPOs are legitimate companies with real revenues and profits. As the bull market matures, increasingly speculative companies go public, perhaps profitable but at expensive valuations, or in trendy sectors with uncertain futures. Near the peak, outright frauds and complete fantasy businesses go public and are enthusiastically received.

WeWork provides a perfect case study. The company attempted to IPO in 2019 at a $47 billion valuation despite massive losses, corporate governance issues, and a business model (leasing office space long-term and subleasing short-term) that was obviously vulnerable to economic downturns. When the prospectus was released and analysts actually read it, the valuation collapsed. The IPO was pulled. Yet even after this disaster, investors had funded WeWork to that insane valuation in private markets. The willingness of supposedly sophisticated venture capitalists and institutional investors to suspend disbelief was the signal, not whether the IPO ultimately succeeded.

SPACs, Special Purpose Acquisition Companies represent an even more extreme version of quality degradation. SPACs are blank-check companies that raise money in IPOs with no business, then seek to merge with a private company to bring it public. They became wildly popular in 2020-2021, with over 600 SPAC IPOs raising more than $160 billion in 2021 alone. Celebrities and athletes launched SPACs. The average SPAC investor had no idea what company they were ultimately investing in, trusting the sponsors to find something good.

The quality of companies brought public via SPACs was atrocious. Many had no revenue. Many made absurdly optimistic projections that they missed by 70-80%. Some were outright frauds. Electric vehicle SPACs were particularly popular and particularly disastrous, Nikola, Lordstown Motors, and Faraday Future all came public via SPACs with grand promises and delivered failure. By 2022-2023, the average SPAC that completed a merger had lost 70-80% from its initial price.

When the IPO and SPAC markets are wide open and accepting anything, it signals that capital is abundant, investors are indiscriminate, and quality discipline has disappeared. These conditions don't persist. Eventually, reality intrudes. Some high-profile failures occur. The IPO window slams shut. Companies that delay going public miss their chance. Private valuations collapse. Venture capital funding dries up. The transition from "everything gets funded" to "nothing gets funded" happens with remarkable speed.

Watch for the point when IPOs start breaking, when newly public companies trade below their IPO price shortly after listing. In healthy markets, most IPOs trade up. Near market peaks, an increasing percentage trade down, often dramatically. When the majority of IPOs are underwater within months, the primary issuance market has broken, and the secondary market often follows.

Celebrity and Influencer Market Participation

When celebrities with no investing expertise become vocal market bulls and pitch specific investments, the end is near. When social media influencers with no qualifications are giving stock tips to millions of followers, prudent investors should be reducing risk. Celebrity involvement in financial markets is a near-perfect indicator of excess.

The 1920s featured celebrities endorsing stocks and investment trusts. Showmen like Groucho Marx and Eddie Cantor were publicly talking about their market gains and encouraging others to invest. Cantor famously lost his fortune in the 1929 crash. In the late 1990s, day trading became so mainstream that people quit their jobs to trade full-time, and CNBC became essential viewing. Books about day trading topped bestseller lists.

The 2020-2021 period saw unprecedented celebrity market participation. Rappers promoted cryptocurrencies. Athletes launched NFT collections. Reality TV stars shilled meme stocks on social media. Elon Musk's tweets moved markets dramatically, Bitcoin surged or plunged based on his pronouncements, Dogecoin became a multi-billion dollar asset because he joked about it, and meme stocks rallied when he tweeted vaguely supportive messages.

The influencer phenomenon added a new dimension. Financial influencers on YouTube, TikTok, and Instagram attracted millions of followers by sharing trading tips, investment strategies, and market analysis. Many had minimal qualifications, perhaps a few years of experience, sometimes less.

But they were engaging, charismatic, and posting content during a period when everything was going up, making everyone look like a genius.

The problem isn't that celebrities or influencers are necessarily giving bad advice (though many are). The problem is that their mass participation indicates that investing has become entertainment, that speculation has gone mainstream, and that people who have no business risking capital in complex markets are doing so because it's become culturally popular. When your rideshare driver or hairdresser is giving you stock tips, a famous warning sign that dates back to the 1920s you're in a bubble.

The crypto market illustrated this perfectly. In 2020-2021, crypto influencers emerged as quasi-celebrities, hosting podcasts and conferences, launching tokens, and promising followers that they'd get rich by following their advice. Many of these influencers were promoting projects they were secretly paid to promote or had early positions in. When Bitcoin reached $69,000 in November 2021, celebrities from Paris Hilton to Tom Brady were promoting crypto platforms and NFTs. By 2022, Bitcoin had fallen to $16,000, multiple crypto platforms had collapsed, and several celebrity promoters faced lawsuits.

The celebrity indicator works because celebrities optimize for attention, not returns. They get involved when markets are already the topic of conversation, when everyone is already participating, when the gains have already been made. Their involvement marks the exhaustion point, not the beginning of opportunity, but the end.

Google Search Trends and Social Media Sentiment

The internet age provides unprecedented access to collective consciousness through search behavior and social media activity. Google Trends data shows what millions of people are searching for in real-time. Social media sentiment analysis reveals what they're talking about and how they're feeling. Both provide behavioral signals about market psychology.

Google search volume for terms like "buy stocks," "how to invest," and "stock market crash" varies dramatically with market conditions. Searches for "how to invest" and "buy stocks" surge near market tops as new participants seek to join the party. Searches for "stock market crash" spike during crashes but also sometimes increase before crashes as anxiety builds.

Academic research has found that increased Google search volume for stock tickers correlates with higher subsequent trading volume and often precedes short-term price increases, evidence of retail attention driving demand. But when search volume for speculative assets reaches extreme levels, it often marks a local peak. In late 2017, Google searches for "Bitcoin" reached all-time highs as Bitcoin approached $20,000. It then crashed 80% over the following year. In early 2021, searches for "Dogecoin" and "GameStop" spiked as those assets went parabolic. Both subsequently crashed.

The pattern suggests retail attention is finite and follows performance. Something starts going up, people notice, they search for information, they buy, which pushes prices higher, which attracts more attention and more buyers. This feedback loop continues until everyone who is going to buy has bought. Then momentum stalls, early buyers take profits, late buyers panic, and the crash unfolds.

Social media sentiment provides similar signals. The field of "social sentiment analysis" uses natural language processing to gauge whether discussion of stocks, sectors, or markets is positive or negative. When sentiment becomes extremely positive across broad portions of social media, when bulls dominate conversation and bears are mocked or ignored contrarian signals are flashing.

Reddit's WallStreetBets provides a case study. The forum became famous during the January 2021 GameStop short squeeze, where coordinated buying by retail traders drove the stock from $20 to $480 in a matter of weeks. The sentiment on WallStreetBets during the peak was euphoric, members believed they were changing the financial system, punishing Wall Street, and getting rich simultaneously. Positions were referred to as "diamond hands" (holding no matter what) versus "paper hands" (selling too soon). The memes were elaborate and funny. The sentiment was pure, unfiltered bullishness.

When GameStop crashed from $480 to $40, sentiment became defensive and angry. Many members had bought near the peak and lost substantial money. The tone shifted from triumphant to bitter. This transition from euphoria to despair happened in weeks, but it follows the same emotional arc that plays out over months or years in broader markets.

Twitter (now X) sentiment about markets overall provides similar signals. When finance Twitter, "FinTwit" is uniformly bullish, when prominent accounts are posting rocket ship emojis and "up only" memes, when bearish accounts are quiet or ridiculed, sentiment extremes are in place. Conversely, when FinTwit is pessimistic, when doom scenarios dominate discussion, when bullish posts are attacked, contrarian buying opportunities may be emerging.

The challenge with social media sentiment is signal versus noise. Markets generate endless chatter, most of it meaningless. The key is identifying sustained shifts in sentiment that represent genuine changes in collective psychology, not day-to-day volatility in discussion. Multi-week or multi-month trends in sentiment are meaningful; daily fluctuations are not.

The "This Time Is Different" Syndrome

Perhaps the most dangerous behavioral signal is the widespread belief that historical patterns don't apply because something fundamental has changed. "This time is different" are the four most expensive words in investing. Every bubble convinces itself it's not a bubble because the circumstances are unique.

In the 1920s, the "New Era" thinking held that electricity, automobiles, and radio had fundamentally transformed the economy, justifying permanently higher valuations. Herbert Hoover declared that poverty was near elimination. Irving Fisher, one of the most respected economists of the era, stated in October 1929 that stocks had reached "a permanently high plateau." The crash began days later.

In the late 1990s, the internet was going to change everything. Old metrics like earnings and cash flow were obsolete. Revenue growth was all that mattered. Companies were valued on "eyeballs" and "clicks." Anyone who questioned absurd valuations was dismissed as a dinosaur who didn't understand the new economy. Until the new economy collapsed and the old rules reasserted themselves.

In the mid-2000s, sophisticated financial engineering and risk models had supposedly eliminated risk from mortgage lending. "Housing prices never go down nationally," experts assured us. Securitization had dispersed risk so widely that no single institution was vulnerable. Credit default swaps provided insurance. The models said everything was safe. The models were catastrophically wrong.

In 2020-2021, multiple "this time is different" narratives emerged simultaneously. The Federal Reserve had learned from previous crises and would never again allow a major market decline, the "Fed put" was ironclad. Passive investing had changed market dynamics fundamentally. Inflation was obsolete due to technology and globalization. Cryptocurrencies represented a new asset class uncorrelated to traditional markets. Each narrative had superficial plausibility, and each proved wrong when tested.

The psychological mechanism behind "this time is different" is powerful. Humans are pattern-recognition machines, but we're also motivated reasoners. When we have money invested and are making gains, we desperately want to believe the gains will continue. When everyone around us is making money and insisting the boom is justified, disagreeing requires intellectual courage and social willingness to be excluded. It's easier to agree, to rationalize, to convince ourselves that we're smarter than those who lost money in previous bubbles because we understand what makes this time different.

Listen for specific linguistic markers that indicate "this time is different" thinking. Phrases like "the old rules don't apply," "this is a paradigm shift," "we're in a new era," or "fundamentals don't matter anymore" should trigger alarm bells. When experts start citing reasons why valuation metrics are obsolete or why certain risks aren't actually risky, skepticism is warranted.

The contrarian position is not that nothing ever changes. Innovation happens, economies evolve, and markets adapt. But human psychology doesn't change. Fear and greed remain constant. The tendency toward excess remains constant. The pattern of euphoria followed by panic remains constant. In this sense, it's never different, the manifestations vary but the underlying dynamics repeat with remarkable consistency.

Putting Behavioral Signals to Work

Behavioral signals are most useful when they reach extremes and confirm other indicators. Moderate retail optimism during a healthy bull market isn't concerning. Extreme retail optimism coinciding with expensive valuations, deteriorating breadth, and weakening economic data is concerning. One behavioral indicator at an extreme might be a false signal. Multiple behavioral indicators at extremes simultaneously creates a compelling case for caution.

The practical challenge is maintaining objectivity about your own psychology while observing others. You are not immune to the behavioral biases you're trying to identify in market participants generally. When you feel the urge to mock bears, when you're certain the market will keep rising, when you're checking your portfolio every hour and feeling like a genius, you've become part of the mania. The behavioral signals are flashing red, but you can't see them because you're inside the bubble looking out rather than outside looking in.

Building a systematic approach helps. Define in advance what behavioral extremes look like using specific metrics, AAII sentiment above X%, put-call ratio below Y, IPO break rate above Z%, etc. Check these metrics regularly. When multiple indicators flash warning signals, take them seriously regardless of how the market is performing. Your future self, observing in hindsight after the inevitable crash, will appreciate your present discipline.

Remember that behavioral signals can remain extreme for extended periods. Manias last longer than rational observers expect. The late 1990s bubble continued for years after skeptics declared it unsustainable. The 2020-2021 excess persisted through multiple waves of stimulus and Fed intervention. Being behaviorally early looks like being wrong and costs opportunity. But being late costs capital. The goal isn't perfect timing, it's ensuring you've reduced risk before the behavioral extremes resolve in the only way they ever do: with a painful reversion to sanity.

Chapter 14

The Canaries in the Coal Mine

In the literal coal mines of centuries past, miners carried canaries into the depths. The small birds, more sensitive to toxic gases than humans, would show distress or die before miners were affected, providing crucial early warning to evacuate. Financial markets have their own canaries, obscure corners where stress appears first, small failures that signal systemic problems, technical breakdowns that precede broader chaos. These early warning signs often go unnoticed by mainstream investors focused on major stock indices and headline news. But for those paying attention, they offer precious time to prepare.

The challenge with financial canaries is interpretation. Markets experience countless small disruptions that lead nowhere. A minor liquidity event here, a small hedge fund failure there, most are isolated incidents that get contained and forgotten. The art is distinguishing between routine turbulence and true warning signals. This chapter explores the specific types of breakdowns that have historically preceded major crises, and why they deserve your urgent attention when they occur.

Liquidity Crises in Obscure Markets

Liquidity, the ability to buy or sell an asset quickly without dramatically affecting its price is the lifeblood of financial markets. When liquidity evaporates in small, specialized markets before spreading to mainstream markets, it's the canary gasping for air.

The commercial paper market provides a perfect example. Commercial paper consists of short-term unsecured debt issued by corporations to fund daily operations such as paying suppliers, making payroll and managing cash flow. It's boring, technical, and invisible to most investors. It's also essential to the functioning of corporate America. When the commercial paper market seizes up, companies suddenly can't fund basic operations, regardless of their long-term financial health.

In August 2007, a full year before Lehman Brothers collapsed, the commercial paper market experienced severe stress. Asset-backed commercial paper notes backed by various debt securities including mortgages began to freeze. Investors who had routinely rolled over this paper suddenly refused. The total outstanding fell by over $200 billion in a matter of weeks, a staggering contraction. This happened while the stock market was still near all-time highs and most investors were oblivious.

The commercial paper crisis signaled that sophisticated investors had lost confidence in the safety of debt backed by mortgages and other assets. They didn't trust the ratings agencies. They didn't trust the banks that structured the products. They didn't trust the underlying collateral. This was the canary dying, over a year before the general public understood that a crisis was underway.

The repo market, where financial institutions borrow short-term using securities as collateral offers similar early warnings. Repo is the plumbing of the financial system, a market measured in trillions of dollars that turns over daily. When repo rates spike suddenly, when lenders demand higher quality collateral or larger haircuts (lending less against the same collateral), when certain securities become difficult to finance, stress is building in the system.

September 2019 saw a mysterious repo market seizure. Overnight rates that typically traded around 2% suddenly spiked to 10%. The Federal Reserve had to intervene with emergency liquidity. The exact causes were debated, corporate tax payments draining reserves, Treasury issuance, technical factors. But the spike revealed fragility in market plumbing. While markets continued rising through 2019 and into early 2020, the repo warning suggested the system was more vulnerable than it appeared. When COVID-19 hit in March 2020, markets experienced one of the fastest crashes in history, and the Fed ultimately intervened on an unprecedented scale.

Watch for liquidity stress in municipal bonds, corporate bonds, emerging market debt, and other fixed income markets. Equity markets often ignore these signals because stock investors don't follow bond markets closely. But bonds are the adult in the room, more sensitive to credit risk, more attuned to economic reality and less prone to irrational exuberance. When bond markets signal stress through widening spreads or liquidity problems, equity investors should pay attention even if stock prices aren't reflecting concern yet.

Failed Auctions in Bond Markets

Governments and municipalities regularly issue bonds through auctions, where investors submit bids and the issuer accepts offers at the lowest yield (highest price) necessary to sell all the bonds. These auctions almost always succeed, investors show up, bonds get sold, and the process is unremarkable. When auctions fail or nearly fail, when bids don't materialize or yields spike to unexpectedly high levels to attract buyers, it signals a fundamental breakdown in market confidence.

In February 2008, several auctions of auction-rate securities (ARSs), long-term bonds with interest rates reset through periodic auctions, failed spectacularly. These securities were marketed to investors as cash equivalents, highly liquid instruments that could be easily sold. Suddenly, nobody bid in the auctions. Investors who thought they owned liquid assets discovered they were frozen, unable to sell. The ARS market, which exceeded $300 billion, collapsed virtually overnight.

The ARS failures occurred months before the general financial crisis but signaled that liquidity was disappearing in structured products. Sophisticated investors were backing away from anything complex or hard to value. This "flight to quality" would intensify throughout 2008, ultimately freezing credit markets entirely.

Government bond auctions rarely fail outright, but weak auctions provide clear warnings. When the bid-to-cover ratio (total bids divided by bonds offered) drops significantly, when indirect bidders (foreign central banks and other large institutions) reduce their participation, when dealers have to take down larger portions of auctions because end-investor demand is weak, confidence is eroding.

The British gilt market experienced severe stress in September-October 2022 following the UK government's proposed budget. Gilt yields spiked violently, and pension funds faced margin calls on liability-driven investment strategies. The Bank of England had to intervene as an emergency buyer to prevent a broader collapse. While this was UK-specific, it demonstrated how quickly bond markets can destabilize when investor confidence breaks, and how contagion can spread through interconnected financial systems.

Pay attention to Treasury auctions in the United States. When demand weakens for the world's supposedly safest asset, when foreign buyers reduce participation, when yields have to spike to attract sufficient bids, it suggests deep concerns about U.S. fiscal sustainability, inflation, or broader market conditions. Given that Treasury bonds serve as collateral throughout the global financial system, any significant stress in Treasury markets has systemic implications.

Flash Crashes Increasing in Frequency

A flash crash is a sudden, severe price decline that occurs in minutes or even seconds, typically followed by a rapid recovery. They're caused by algorithmic trading systems responding to each other, creating feedback loops that overwhelm normal market functioning. The first major flash crash occurred on May 6, 2010, when the Dow Jones Industrial Average dropped nearly 1,000 points in minutes before recovering most of the loss by the end of the day.

While flash crashes can be triggered by specific events, a fat-finger error, a large sell order, a glitch, their increasing frequency signals underlying market fragility. Markets with healthy liquidity and diverse participants absorb shocks smoothly. Markets dominated by algorithmic systems following similar strategies, with reduced human oversight and limited liquidity, are vulnerable to cascading breakdowns.

The 2010 flash crash was initially mysterious, later attributed to a large sell order in S&P 500 futures that triggered algorithmic selling. But the deeper problem was market structure. High-frequency trading firms, which provide much of the market's liquidity, are programmed to withdraw during extreme volatility to limit risk. When they all withdraw simultaneously, liquidity vanishes, and prices gap wildly.

Since 2010, flash crashes have occurred with increasing regularity in various markets. Individual stocks have crashed from $50 to $0.01 and back in seconds. Exchange-traded funds have traded at massive discounts to their net asset values. Currency markets have experienced sudden 10% moves that reverse within minutes. Each incident gets investigated, attributed to specific technical factors, and supposedly addressed with new circuit breakers or trading rules. Yet the incidents continue.

The proliferation of flash crashes suggests markets are increasingly fragile and prone to non-linear behavior. Small disturbances trigger disproportionate responses. Safety mechanisms designed to prevent cascades sometimes trigger them instead. The very technologies designed to increase efficiency and liquidity have created tightly coupled systems where failures propagate instantly.

When flash crashes begin occurring across multiple markets, not just equities but also bonds, currencies, and commodities it signals that the infrastructure underlying all markets is stressed. The crashes may be quickly reversed, but each one exposes the fragility. Eventually, a flash crash occurs during an already stressed period, when buyers don't return, when the recovery doesn't happen, when the crash becomes real and permanent.

Prime Broker Failures or Stress

Prime brokers provide essential services to hedge funds and institutional investors in executing trades, financing positions, clearing transactions, and providing custody. They're the interface between investors and markets, and their health is crucial to market functioning. When prime brokers fail or show signs of severe stress, the canary isn't just sick, it's dying.

Bear Stearns' collapse in March 2008 was fundamentally a prime brokerage failure. Hedge funds and other clients lost confidence in Bear's ability to safeguard their assets and began withdrawing. This run on the prime broker drained liquidity, forcing Bear into a weekend rescue acquisition by JPMorgan Chase, facilitated by the Federal Reserve. The precedent was ominous: if a major investment bank could collapse in days, no institution was truly safe.

The mechanics of prime broker stress are important to understand. Prime brokers use client assets as collateral to finance their own operations, a process called rehypothecation. When confidence erodes, clients demand their assets back. But those assets are tied up in the broker's operations, creating a liquidity crisis. The broker must rapidly unwind positions to meet redemptions, often at terrible prices, which creates losses that further erode confidence. The spiral accelerates.

Lehman Brothers' failure six months after Bear Stearns followed a similar pattern. Prime brokerage clients withdrew, confidence collapsed, and the firm couldn't meet its obligations. But Lehman wasn't rescued, and its bankruptcy filing triggered the acute phase of the financial crisis. Money market funds, which held Lehman commercial paper, "broke the buck" (traded below $1 per share). Credit markets froze globally. The prime broker failure metastasized into a systemic crisis.

Watch for signs of prime broker stress well before outright failure. Widening credit default swap spreads on major banks signal that sophisticated investors are hedging against default risk. Stock prices of financial institutions declining while broader markets remain stable suggest sector-specific concerns. News reports of hedge funds moving assets from one prime broker to another, even if presented as routine, may indicate underlying confidence problems.

The interconnectedness of prime brokers means stress spreads quickly. If one major broker fails, clients at other brokers often panic and withdraw preemptively, creating liquidity problems at healthy institutions. This happened repeatedly in 2008. The system has become more regulated since then, with higher capital requirements and stress testing. But the fundamental fragility that prime brokers operate with leverage and depend on client confidence remains.

Hedge Fund Blowups

Hedge funds are supposed to be sophisticated, professionally managed pools of capital with strict risk controls. When major hedge funds blow up spectacularly, losing massive sums or collapsing entirely, it reveals that risk was far greater than acknowledged, that models were flawed, that leverage was excessive, or that fraud was occurring. These failures often precede broader market disruptions.

Long-Term Capital Management's 1998 collapse became a case study in systemic risk. LTCM was run by Nobel Prize-winning economists and legendary traders. They employed complex mathematical models to identify arbitrage opportunities in bond markets. They used enormous leverage of 30:1 or more to magnify returns from small price discrepancies.

For years, it worked brilliantly. Then Russia defaulted on its debt in August 1998, creating market dislocations that LTCM's models said were statistically impossible.

LTCM's positions were so large and so leveraged that its failure threatened to create a cascade through the entire financial system. The Federal Reserve orchestrated a private sector bailout, with major banks and securities firms contributing billions to stabilize LTCM and unwind its positions orderly. The incident revealed how a single hedge fund could become systemically important through leverage and interconnectedness.

Amaranth Advisors' 2006 collapse, losing $6 billion on natural gas futures trades, demonstrated that massive losses were still possible despite supposed risk controls. The fund had concentrated positions and used leverage to amplify bets on gas price movements. When prices moved against them, margin calls forced liquidations at terrible prices, accelerating losses. Amaranth wasn't systemically important enough to threaten the financial system, but its failure signaled that risk management remained inadequate even at supposedly sophisticated institutions.

Archegos Capital Management's March 2021 implosion created over $10 billion in losses, most of which fell on prime brokers like Credit Suisse and Nomura. Archegos used total return swaps, derivatives that provided synthetic exposure to stocks without actually owning them, to build highly concentrated, highly leveraged positions in a handful of stocks. When those stocks declined, margin calls triggered forced liquidations, and the positions were so large that selling crashed the stocks further, creating a death spiral.

The Archegos failure revealed multiple system weaknesses. Prime brokers failed to understand their aggregate exposure because Archegos used multiple brokers, each unaware of positions at other firms. Leverage was excessive. Concentration was extreme. Risk controls failed at both the fund and prime broker levels. And this happened during a bull market, when risk was supposedly well-contained.

When hedge fund blowups occur, analyze the causes carefully. Is it a single idiosyncratic failure of one manager's fraud or incompetence? Or does it reveal broader problems of excessive leverage across the industry, crowded trades where many funds hold similar positions, faulty risk models, inadequate prime broker oversight? The failures that matter are those that expose systemic vulnerabilities, not isolated instances of poor judgment.

Money Market Fund Stress

Money market funds are supposed to be the safest investment vehicles, maintaining a stable $1.00 net asset value while providing slightly better returns than bank deposits. They invest in ultra-safe, short-term instruments such as Treasury bills, high-grade commercial paper and certificates of deposit. When money market funds experience stress, redemptions surge and NAVs decline below $1.00, or funds require support it signals that investors are panicking and that supposedly safe assets aren't actually safe.

The Reserve Primary Fund "broke the buck" on September 16, 2008, the day after Lehman Brothers filed for bankruptcy. The fund had held $785 million in Lehman commercial paper, which became worthless. This created losses that reduced the NAV to $0.97. Investors rushed to redeem, and the fund couldn't meet withdrawals. The Treasury Department had to create an emergency guarantee program for money market funds to stop the run.

The significance of a money market fund breaking the buck cannot be overstated. These funds are where corporations park cash between payrolls, where individuals keep emergency savings, where the financial system stores short-term liquidity. When even money market funds aren't safe, there's nowhere to hide. The only truly safe asset becomes cash itself, physical currency or deposits at the most creditworthy banks. This creates a catastrophic contraction in credit availability.

March 2020 saw renewed money market stress during the COVID-19 market crash. Prime money market funds, those that invest in corporate debt rather than just Treasuries experienced massive outflows as investors fled to safety. Funds had to sell assets to meet redemptions, but buyers had disappeared. The Fed intervened with emergency facilities to support commercial paper and corporate debt markets, stabilizing the funds.

Watch for early signs of money market stress even before funds break the buck. Rising yields on money market funds relative to Treasury bills suggest funds are taking more risk to generate returns. Declining assets under management indicate investors are withdrawing. Funds holding increasing percentages of weekly liquid assets (securities that mature within seven days) signal they're preparing for redemptions. SEC filings sometimes reveal that funds received support from their sponsors to avoid NAV declines, socializing losses before they become visible.

The psychological impact of money market stress is profound. When the safest vehicles outside of government-guaranteed deposits become unsafe, panic accelerates. Investors abandon risk assets entirely, credit markets freeze, and the financial system seizes up. This is why central banks respond so aggressively to money market stress, they understand it's the early stage of a liquidity crisis that can spiral out of control within days.

The Pattern Recognition Challenge

Identifying canaries in the coal mine requires constant vigilance and broad market awareness. Most investors focus narrowly, stock pickers analyze companies, macro investors watch GDP and inflation and technical traders study charts. Few maintain the peripheral vision necessary to notice stress in obscure corners of the market.

Building a monitoring system helps. Financial media reports some of these warning signs, though often buried in niche publications or specialized market reports. The Federal Reserve's financial stability report, published semiannually, discusses many of these vulnerabilities. Market commentators who focus on market structure and plumbing, rather than just price movements often catch these signals early.

But raw information isn't enough. The critical skill is pattern recognition, understanding which disruptions are routine and which signal deeper problems. A single repo rate spike might be technical. Repeated spikes over weeks signal fragility. One hedge fund failure might be idiosyncratic. Multiple failures using similar strategies suggest crowded trades and systemic leverage. A flash crash in a small-cap stock might be a glitch. Flash crashes across multiple markets suggest infrastructure problems.

Context matters enormously. A liquidity event during an otherwise healthy market environment might be contained. The same event during a period when valuations are extreme, sentiment is euphoric, economic indicators are deteriorating, and other warning signs are flashing demands immediate attention. The canaries die when the mine is already full of gas, not when the air is clear.

The behavioral challenge is acting on these signals. By definition, canaries die before the obvious danger arrives. Acting on early warning signs means reducing risk while markets are still rising, while peers are still making money, while your caution looks foolish. The pressure to ignore the canaries and stay fully invested is intense. Career risk for professional investors is substantial, being early looks identical to being wrong, and clients don't reward caution during bull markets.

Yet history is unambiguous: the canaries reliably die before the miners. Commercial paper stress preceded the financial crisis by over a year. Prime broker concerns about Bear Stearns circulated for months before the collapse. LTCM's failure preceded broader market stress in 1998. The pattern repeats across decades and across markets. The investors who survive major crashes are those who took the canaries seriously, even when doing so was uncomfortable and costly in the short term.

Developing Your Early Warning System

You don't need to monitor every obscure market corner personally. But you should develop a systematic approach to staying informed about the types of stress that historically matter. Subscribe to financial news sources that cover market structure and plumbing, not just stock prices. Follow commentators who focus on risk and liquidity, not just investment opportunities. Read the financial stability reports from the Fed, the Bank for International Settlements, and other regulatory bodies.

Create a mental checklist of canary indicators and review them periodically. Are there reports of liquidity stress in any credit markets? Have any significant auctions failed or struggled? Are flash crashes becoming more frequent? Is there unusual stress at any major financial institutions? Have there been any significant hedge fund failures or reports of funds limiting redemptions? Are money market funds experiencing outflows or requiring sponsor support?

When you identify a potential canary, investigate further. What caused the stress? Is it isolated or part of a broader pattern? Are other warning signs from previous chapters, valuation metrics, economic indicators, behavioral signals also flashing red? The most dangerous scenarios are when multiple types of warning signs align, when the canaries are dying while valuations are extreme and sentiment is euphoric and economic data is deteriorating.

Most importantly, decide in advance how you'll respond when canaries start dying. Will you reduce equity exposure by 20%? 50%? Will you raise cash, buy protection, or shift to defensive sectors? Making these decisions in advance, based on clear criteria, prevents paralysis and rationalization when signals arrive. The stress of watching markets continue rising while you're defensive is real, but it's manageable if you've committed to a plan based on sound reasoning.

The canaries have saved countless miners over the centuries by providing early warning of invisible danger. In financial markets, they can save your capital by providing early warning of crashes. But only if you're watching, only if you take them seriously, and only if you act on their warnings before the obvious danger arrives.

Part V: What to Watch For

Chapter 15

The Critical Sequence

Market crashes don't happen in a vacuum, nor do they strike like lightning from a clear sky. They follow patterns, not identical patterns but rhyming sequences that have repeated throughout financial history. Understanding this critical sequence is perhaps the most valuable knowledge an investor can possess, even though it comes with a frustrating caveat: recognizing the pattern doesn't mean you can time it perfectly.

The anatomy of a market crash unfolds in distinct phases, each with its own characteristics, psychology, and market behavior. These phases don't have clean boundaries, and they vary in duration from one crash to another, but the sequence itself is remarkably consistent across centuries of financial markets.

Phase One: The Warning Phase

The warning phase is characterized by a curious paradox: warning signs accumulate while the market continues to rise, often accelerating to new heights. This is the phase that torments thoughtful investors and rewards the reckless. It's the period when value investors like Jeremy Grantham or John Hussman begin issuing warnings, only to watch the market climb another twenty, thirty, or even fifty percent higher.

During this phase, certain cracks begin to appear in the facade of perpetual prosperity. Credit spreads start to widen, even if only slightly. High-yield bonds begin to underperform. The advance-decline line which measures how many stocks are participating in the rally starts to deteriorate, meaning fewer and fewer stocks are responsible for pushing the major indices higher. Market leadership rotates toward increasingly speculative names. The safest, highest-quality companies with strong balance sheets and steady earnings begin to lag, while the riskiest companies with no earnings, questionable business models, or extreme valuations lead the charge.

Corporate insiders, the CEOs, CFOs, and board members who know their companies best begin selling their shares in earnest. The ratio of insider selling to buying reaches extremes. Smart money, or at least cautious money, starts positioning more defensively. Hedge funds reduce gross exposure. Legendary investors raise cash levels. Warren Buffett's Berkshire Hathaway sees its cash pile grow to record levels because he can't find attractively priced opportunities.

Meanwhile, retail investors and institutional momentum funds pile in with increasing enthusiasm. Options activity explodes, particularly in call options that bet on continued gains. Margin debt, money borrowed to buy stocks climbs to new records relative to GDP or market capitalization. The financial media celebrates new paradigms. Conference panels discuss why old valuation metrics no longer apply. This time really is different, they insist, because of technology, or globalization, or monetary policy, or some other factor that supposedly changes the fundamental nature of investing.

The warning phase can last months or even years. In the late 1920s, serious economists and investors began warning about speculation as early as 1927 and 1928, yet the market continued its manic climb into September 1929. Before the 2000 dot-com crash, warnings about extreme valuations began in earnest in 1998, but the NASDAQ would nearly double again before its March 2000 peak. Prior to the 2008 crisis, concerns about subprime mortgages and excessive lending surfaced in 2006, well before the market peak in October 2007.

This extended warning phase creates a dangerous psychological dynamic. The longer the market continues to rise after warnings are issued, the more those warnings appear foolish. Those who heed them and position defensively suffer the pain of opportunity cost, watching others get rich while their own conservative portfolios lag badly. The siren song grows louder: maybe the worriers really are wrong this time. Maybe things have changed. Maybe you should stop overthinking and just join the party.

The warning phase ends not with a clear signal, but with a transition so subtle that it's only recognizable in hindsight. Some seemingly minor event occurs, a single hedge fund failure, a spike in defaults, a disappointing economic report, a geopolitical flare-up and the market's reaction seems disproportionate. Instead of shrugging off bad news as it has for months or years, the market stumbles. The dip might be bought quickly, but something has shifted. The armor of invincibility has been scratched.

Phase Two: The Denial Phase

After the first real crack appears, markets enter a phase of collective denial that can be even more treacherous than the warning phase. This is when volatility increases, but the prevailing narrative remains bullish. Corrections are dismissed as "healthy" or "overdue profit-taking." Each decline is met with eager buyers convinced they're getting a bargain. The phrase "buy the dip" becomes a mantra, a strategy that has worked flawlessly for so long that it seems foolish to question it.

During the denial phase, market behavior becomes choppier and more unpredictable. The smooth, steady grind higher gives way to sharp moves in both directions. Intraday reversals become common, the market might drop two percent in the morning only to close up one percent, or vice versa. These violent swings are often interpreted as evidence of a "healthy" market working off excess, but they actually reflect something more ominous: a fundamental disagreement about value that's beginning to surface.

The financial media during this phase oscillates between reassurance and alarm, often within the same broadcast. One segment features a permabull explaining why concerns are overblown and this is a buying opportunity. The next segment interviews a strategist who outlines worrying developments. Viewers are left confused, which is precisely the problem.

The clarity of the uptrend has been replaced by genuine uncertainty, even if most participants aren't ready to admit it.

Key technical support levels begin to break. A market that once bounced reliably off its 50-day moving average suddenly cuts through it like it isn't there. Breadth deteriorates further, not only are fewer stocks participating in rallies, but more stocks are making new lows. Sector rotation accelerates as money flows erratically, seeking safety in one moment and reaching for yield or growth in the next.

Corporate earnings reports during this phase often deliver the first real disappointments. Revenue misses, margin compression, guidance cuts the fundamental justification for high valuations begins to crack. But markets are remarkably resilient in this phase, finding reasons to dismiss bad news as company-specific or temporary. The overall narrative of economic strength remains intact, even as more and more data points contradict it.

Central banks often provide crucial support during the denial phase, either through actual policy changes or simply through reassuring rhetoric. A Federal Reserve chairman might emphasize patience, flexibility, and a willingness to support the economy. These verbal interventions can spark powerful rallies that temporarily silence the skeptics. The "Fed put", the belief that central banks will always step in to prevent serious market declines provides a psychological floor that encourages continued risk-taking.

The denial phase is particularly dangerous for a specific type of investor: the sophisticated amateur who has read enough to understand that crashes happen, but not enough to grasp how they actually unfold. These investors see the increased volatility and start trying to time their exit. They sell after a sharp down day, only to watch the market rip higher in the next session. They buy back in near a local peak, then panic sell again at the next low. This whipsaw action bleeds away capital and, more importantly, emotional resilience. By the time the real crash comes, these investors are exhausted, confused, and often entirely in the wrong position.

Professional investors face their own challenges during this phase. Those who positioned defensively during the warning phase have already suffered career damage from underperformance. Now, as volatility increases, their clients or bosses are questioning their decisions even more intensely. The pressure to "get back in" before missing the next rally becomes immense. Many capitulate during this phase, abandoning their defensive positioning just as the market enters its most dangerous period.

The denial phase ends with what technical analysts call a "breakdown", a decisive move below a major support level that triggers a cascade of additional selling. This might be a violation of the 200-day moving average for the major indices, or a break of the lows from a previous correction. What matters isn't the specific technical level, but the psychological impact. Something that was supposed to hold didn't hold. The buyers who consistently stepped in to "buy the dip" are suddenly absent, or worse, they're joining the sellers.

Phase Three: The Acceleration Phase

When denial breaks, acceleration begins. This is the phase that defines a crash as distinct from a mere correction. The selling becomes self-reinforcing, feeding on itself in a vicious cycle that overwhelms all attempts to stem the tide.

The acceleration phase typically unfolds with stunning speed, compressing what would normally be months of price movement into days or even hours. In 1929, the market lost 23 percent in just two days, Black Thursday and Black Tuesday. In 1987, the Dow Jones Industrial Average fell 22.6 percent in a single day. During the 2008 crisis, the market lost 18 percent in a single week in October. The COVID crash saw the S&P 500 plunge 34 percent in just 23 trading days, the fastest drawdown of that magnitude in history.

Several mechanisms drive this acceleration. First and most important is forced liquidation. Investors who bought on margin receive margin calls from their brokers, demanding they either add cash or sell securities to bring their account back into compliance. Since most don't have additional cash on hand during a market crash, they're forced to sell into a declining market, pushing prices lower and triggering additional margin calls for other investors. This cascade effect was the primary driver of the 1929 crash and played a significant role in 2008 as well.

Modern markets have additional acceleration mechanisms. Algorithmic trading and quantitative strategies often incorporate stop-loss orders or risk management rules that force selling when certain thresholds are breached. When many algorithms incorporate similar rules, they can all hit their triggers simultaneously, creating waves of coordinated selling that have nothing to do with fundamental value. The "flash crash" of May 2010, when the market dropped nearly ten percent in minutes before largely recovering, illustrated this dynamic on a small scale.

Exchange-traded funds (ETFs), particularly leveraged ones, introduce another acceleration mechanism. As ETF prices fall, their managers must sell the underlying securities to maintain their target exposure ratios. This selling pressures the underlying stocks, which lowers the ETF price further, creating a feedback loop. During periods of extreme stress, the arbitrage mechanism that normally keeps ETF prices in line with their net asset value can break down, leading to severe dislocations.

Options markets amplify the acceleration through dealer hedging. Market makers who sold put options to investors must hedge their exposure by selling the underlying stocks or futures as prices fall, a practice called "delta hedging." The lower prices fall, the more they must sell to remain hedged.

This dynamic, known as a "gamma squeeze" in reverse, can add tremendous selling pressure at precisely the wrong moment.

The psychology during the acceleration phase is one of pure panic. The careful analyses and thoughtful considerations of the earlier phases evaporate. Investors stop thinking about value, about buying opportunities, about long-term horizons. The only thought is: get out. The pain of watching positions lose value by the minute becomes unbearable. The fear of total loss, that irrational but overwhelming dread that the market might go to zero takes hold.

Financial news during this phase shifts from denial to alarm. Anchors struggle to maintain composure as they report cascading losses. Market observers who were bullish days earlier suddenly discover deep concerns they hadn't mentioned previously. The talking heads who promised that "this is a buying opportunity" during the denial phase are either absent or scrambling to explain why their analysis didn't account for what's happening.

Credit markets, which had been flashing warning signs during earlier phases, now seize up entirely. Corporate bond spreads explode wider as investors flee anything with even a hint of risk. High-yield bonds, junk bonds become nearly impossible to trade at any price. Liquidity vanishes as dealers widen their bid-ask spreads or simply stop making markets altogether. Companies that need to roll over maturing debt find themselves unable to do so at any reasonable rate, if at all.

Banks, which had been tightening lending standards gradually during the warning and denial phases, now slam the credit window shut. Lending standards that seemed prudent weeks earlier suddenly appear suicidally lax. The easy credit that fueled the asset bubble reverses violently, becoming a credit contraction that amplifies the downturn.

Real economic effects manifest quickly. Consumers, watching their 401(k) statements crater, immediately pull back spending. The "wealth effect" that helped drive growth during the boom years now works in reverse. Business confidence collapses, leading to hiring freezes, layoffs, and canceled investments. The purely financial crisis starts infecting the real economy, creating a negative feedback loop that validates and intensifies the market's decline.

The acceleration phase typically ends with some form of intervention or with sheer exhaustion. In 1929, there was no meaningful intervention, and the acceleration burned itself out only after the most leveraged and fragile participants had been completely wiped out. In 2008, the Federal Reserve and global central banks intervened with unprecedented monetary policy, while governments deployed massive fiscal stimulus. These interventions didn't prevent the crash, but they eventually helped establish a floor.

The end of the acceleration phase doesn't mark the end of the bear market, however. What follows is typically a period of grinding lower punctuated by sharp rallies that trap the hopeful and exhaust the patient.

The Role of Catalysts vs. Underlying Fragility

One of the most persistent misconceptions about market crashes is that the catalyst, the event that seems to trigger the selling, is the cause. This confusion is understandable but dangerous because it leads investors to worry about the wrong things and miss the real risks.

A catalyst is merely the spark. The underlying fragility is the dynamite. You can throw a match onto concrete all day and nothing will happen. But throw that same match onto a pile of dynamite, and the results are catastrophic. Markets work the same way. When markets are healthy, well-balanced, and reasonably valued, even major shocks are absorbed without systemic breakdown. When markets are fragile, overleveraged, overvalued, and psychologically extended the tiniest spark can ignite a conflagration.

Consider the 1929 crash. The conventional narrative often points to the Babson Break on September 5, 1929, when economist Roger Babson gave a speech predicting a crash, causing a one-day mini-panic. Or it points to the Hatry scandal in Britain, where Clarence Hatry's fraud was exposed in late September, causing British markets to decline sharply. These events seem like plausible triggers, but they weren't the cause.

The cause was years of excessive leverage, overvaluation, and speculative excess. Investment trusts were leveraged three or four times over. Margin requirements were absurdly low, allowing investors to control ten dollars of stock with just one dollar of actual money. Valuations had reached extremes that bore no relationship to earnings or dividends. The entire structure was precarious, balanced on a knife's edge. The specific event that finally tipped it over, whether Babson's speech or the Hatry scandal or simple profit-taking in early October was almost irrelevant. Something was going to tip it over eventually because the structure itself was unstable.

The 2000 dot-com crash provides another clear example. Many accounts point to Microsoft's antitrust case or to Y2K fears or to various other potential catalysts. But the real cause was simple: internet stocks were trading at infinite price-to-earnings ratios because they had no earnings. Companies with no revenue were valued at billions of dollars based purely on projected future dominance of markets that might not even exist. This couldn't continue indefinitely. When it ended, the specific trigger mattered far less than the underlying absurdity of the valuations.

The 2008 crisis illustrates the distinction even more clearly. Some accounts point to Bear Stearns' collapse in March 2008 as the catalyst. Others point to Lehman Brothers' bankruptcy in September. But again, these were symptoms rather than causes. The cause was a decade of increasingly reckless lending, securitization of subprime mortgages into complex derivatives that disguised their risk, excessive leverage throughout the financial system, and a housing bubble that had pushed home prices to unsustainable levels. Bear Stearns and Lehman didn't cause the crisis; they were casualties of an already existing fragility that had built up over years.

This distinction between catalysts and underlying fragility has profound implications for investors trying to protect themselves. Many investors spend enormous energy trying to predict what specific event might trigger the next crash. Will it be a geopolitical crisis? A corporate bankruptcy? A policy mistake by the Federal Reserve? A pandemic? A terrorist attack? An election result?

This approach is fundamentally misguided because the specific trigger is unpredictable and, more importantly, irrelevant. What matters is the underlying fragility. If markets are healthy, well-capitalized, reasonably valued, and not over-leveraged, then even major shocks will cause corrections but not crashes. The September 11 attacks, horrific as they were, caused only a relatively brief market decline because the underlying financial system in 2001, while struggling with the aftermath of the dot-com bust, was not systemically fragile. The pandemic of 2020 caused the fastest crash in history, but the subsequent recovery was equally rapid because central banks and governments intervened immediately and massively.

Investors should focus their attention not on predicting triggers but on assessing fragility. Is leverage at extremes? Are valuations disconnected from fundamentals? Is speculative activity rampant? Are credit standards deteriorating? Are new investors piling into markets they don't understand? Are previously uncorrelated assets all moving together, suggesting a common factor of excessive liquidity? Are risk premia compressed to minimal levels, implying investors are being paid almost nothing for taking risk?

These are the questions that matter. If the answers suggest high fragility, then the prudent approach is defensive positioning regardless of whether you can identify a specific catalyst on the horizon. If the answers suggest low fragility, then even obvious risks on the horizon, a looming recession, political uncertainty, geopolitical tensions may be manageable.

The problem, of course, is that assessing fragility is more art than science. The indicators don't all move in lockstep, and thresholds aren't clearly defined. Markets can remain fragile but stable for extended periods, frustrating those positioned defensively. This is why the warning phase can persist for so long, the underlying fragility is building, but without a catalyst, the structure remains standing.

Why Timing Is Nearly Impossible

If crashes follow predictable patterns, why can't we time them? This question torments every serious investor who has studied market history. The answer is both simple and frustrating: knowing that something will happen is very different from knowing when it will happen.

The core problem is that markets can remain irrational longer than most investors can remain solvent or employed. This observation, attributed to John Maynard Keynes, captures the essential challenge of crash timing. Even if you correctly identify that markets are in a bubble destined to burst, positioning for that burst too early can be financially and professionally devastating.

Consider the case of Michael Burry, who became famous for his prescient bet against subprime mortgages before the 2008 crisis. Burry identified the housing bubble and the fraudulent underwriting of mortgages as early as 2005. He convinced his investors to let him buy credit default swaps, essentially insurance policies that would pay off when mortgage-backed securities failed.

For more than two years, Burry watched his positions lose money as he paid premiums on his insurance while the securities he was betting against continued to perform. His investors revolted, demanding he close the positions and threatening lawsuits. His personal stress was immense. If the crisis had delayed another year, he might have been forced to exit his positions just before they became hugely profitable. As it happened, his timing was just barely good enough, he was vindicated in 2007 and 2008 but it came perilously close to disaster despite being fundamentally correct about the biggest financial crisis in generations.

If Burry, with his detailed analysis and specific insights into mortgage fraud, struggled with timing, what hope do ordinary investors have? The challenge is that bubble dynamics include a reflexive element that makes them self-reinforcing until they suddenly aren't. Rising prices create wealth effects that fuel more buying, which drives prices higher, creating more wealth effects. This feedback loop can persist far longer than rational analysis suggests is possible.

Moreover, the longer a bubble inflates, the more social and institutional pressure builds to participate. Portfolio managers who stay defensive watch their competitors post huge gains and win new client mandates. Their own clients become restless, questioning why they're missing out. The institutional imperative to track or beat benchmarks becomes overwhelming. Even if you're certain a crash is coming, losing clients and your job before it arrives is poor consolation for being eventually proven right.

Technical analysts sometimes believe they can time crashes through chart patterns, momentum indicators, or other technical tools. These methods occasionally work, but more often they generate false signals that lead to premature exits from rallies that have much further to run. The problem is that late-stage bubbles often feature the most powerful price appreciation, what traders call "the blow-off top." Exiting too early means missing enormous gains, while waiting for confirmation of the top often means holding through the initial crash.

Some investors try to use valuation metrics for timing. When the market's price-to-earnings ratio or price-to-sales ratio or other valuation measures reach extreme levels, they assume a crash is imminent. But valuation metrics can remain extreme for years. The CAPE ratio, the cyclically adjusted price-to-earnings ratio popularized by Robert Shiller, reached high levels in 1997 three years before the market peaked in 2000. Investors who went defensive in 1997 missed extraordinary gains.

Waiting for policy shifts is equally unreliable for timing. Many investors assumed the 2008 crisis would begin when the Federal Reserve started raising interest rates after years of easy money. In fact, the Fed began raising rates in 2004, and the market continued rising until 2007, well after the tightening cycle had ended. The 2022 bear market, by contrast, began almost immediately after the Fed started raising rates, but that market decline was a correction rather than a crash, and markets recovered quickly.

Sentiment indicators suffer from similar limitations. Surveys showing excessive bullishness or extreme leverage can persist at elevated levels for months or years. The AAII Investor Sentiment Survey, which tracks whether individual investors are bullish or bearish, regularly shows extreme readings that aren't followed by crashes. Margin debt can remain at record levels relative to GDP for extended periods during strong bull markets.

The fundamental problem is that market tops are a process, not a point. They form gradually, through stages, with false alarms and temporary recoveries. The final top is only identifiable in hindsight, after the decline has already begun. This means that attempting to time an exit near the top is essentially impossible with any consistency.

What about timing the bottom? Surely once a crash has begun, investors can time their re-entry? This proves equally challenging. Bear markets typically feature powerful counter-trend rallies that feel like the beginning of a new bull market. In 2008, the market rallied sharply in spring and again in summer, each time convincing many investors that the worst was over. Both times, the market subsequently fell to new lows. The ultimate bottom in March 2009 felt like financial apocalypse, it was the moment of maximum pessimism, when buying seemed insane. Those who waited for "confirmation" that the bottom was in ended up buying much higher.

The sequence is consistent across crashes: an initial decline that feels scary but manageable, a rally that convinces many the crisis is over, a resumption of selling that breaks to new lows, another rally that fails, then finally either a capitulation crash (like the final washout in 1932 or 2009) or a slow grinding bottom (like 2002). Calling the exact bottom requires either extraordinary luck or positioning that accepts significant uncertainty and short-term paper losses.

The Difference Between Corrections and Crashes

Not every decline is a crash, and recognizing the difference is crucial for maintaining sanity and making rational decisions during market volatility. Corrections are normal, healthy, and inevitable features of bull markets. Crashes are different in kind, not just degree.

A correction is generally defined as a decline of 10 to 20 percent from recent highs. The stock market experiences corrections relatively frequently, on average every year or two. These declines serve an important purpose: they shake out weak hands, reset valuations to more reasonable levels, and reduce excessive leverage and speculation. After a correction, the market typically resumes its upward trend without major systemic damage.

Corrections unfold relatively slowly, usually taking weeks or months to play out. They're characterized by orderly selling, with plenty of buyers willing to step in at lower levels. The financial system continues functioning normally. Credit markets remain open. Companies can still borrow money to fund operations. Economic growth might slow but doesn't typically turn sharply negative. Most importantly, corrections don't trigger cascading failures or feedback loops that spiral out of control.

Crashes, by contrast, typically involve declines of 30 percent or more and unfold with stunning speed. They're characterized by panic selling, dysfunctional markets, and systemic breakdowns. Liquidity vanishes as buyers disappear and selling becomes forced rather than voluntary. The financial system comes under severe stress, with credit markets freezing and major institutions failing or requiring bailouts. The real economy contracts sharply as the financial crisis spills over into business operations and consumer behavior.

The key distinction lies in the presence or absence of fragility and leverage. Corrections happen when markets are fundamentally healthy but somewhat extended. Crashes happen when underlying fragility has built up to critical levels and the system is vulnerable to cascading failures. A healthy person might stumble and fall, suffering bruises that heal quickly. A person with brittle bones might fall and shatter, requiring months or years of recovery. The fall looks similar, but the underlying condition determines the outcome.

Several characteristics help distinguish a developing crash from a correction:

Speed matters. Corrections typically take weeks or months to reach their lows. Crashes compress major declines into days. In 2020, the COVID crash dropped 34 percent in 23 trading days, that speed indicates panic rather than orderly repricing. By contrast, the 2011 correction dropped 19 percent over four months fast enough to be painful but slow enough to remain controlled.

Breadth matters. In corrections, the decline is typically focused on overvalued or overextended sectors while other areas hold up reasonably well. In crashes, everything goes down together as investors sell whatever they can, not what they want to. Correlations spike toward 1.0, meaning all assets move together. This indiscriminate selling indicates liquidity issues and forced liquidation rather than thoughtful reallocation.

Credit market behavior matters. In corrections, credit markets might wobble but they continue functioning. Corporate bonds trade at reasonable bid-ask spreads. Commercial paper markets remain open. Bank lending continues. In crashes, credit markets seize up. Spreads explode. Lending stops. The plumbing of the financial system clogs or breaks entirely.

Volatility matters. Corrections feature elevated but manageable volatility. The VIX, a measure of expected volatility, might rise from its typical level around 15 to perhaps 25 or 30. In crashes, the VIX spikes to 40, 50, or even higher, indicating extreme fear and uncertainty. These volatility spikes reflect not just price declines but breakdowns in normal market functioning.

Policy response matters. Corrections typically don't trigger aggressive policy responses. Central banks might pause interest rate increases or make dovish statements, but they don't deploy emergency measures. In crashes, policymakers panic along with markets, implementing emergency rate cuts, asset purchases, lending facilities, and fiscal stimulus. The scale and urgency of the policy response signals whether authorities believe the system is in danger.

Understanding these distinctions helps investors maintain perspective during market turmoil. When a correction begins, the natural human tendency is to catastrophize, to assume this is the beginning of a major crash. This fear often leads to panic selling at the worst possible moment. Conversely, when a crash begins, the tendency is initially to dismiss it as just another correction, leading to complacency and failure to take defensive action.

The challenge is that early in a decline, it's genuinely difficult to know which type you're experiencing. The first 10 percent down looks similar whether it's the start of a 15 percent correction or a 50 percent crash. By the time the distinction becomes clear, much of the damage has already occurred.

This is why the earlier sections of this chapter emphasize watching for underlying fragility rather than trying to identify crashes in real-time. If you've positioned appropriately based on the level of systemic fragility, you're prepared for a crash without overreacting to every correction. If fragility is low and you're experiencing a correction, your broadly diversified portfolio will recover. If fragility is high and you're experiencing the beginning of a crash, your defensive positioning will protect you.

The most dangerous moment is when a correction in a fragile market gets dismissed as routine volatility. Investors who have lived through multiple corrections without major consequences become conditioned to "buy the dip." This conditioning works beautifully until it doesn't, until the correction is actually the opening phase of a crash. Then the habit of buying dips becomes a costly mistake.

Conversely, investors who have lived through crashes often become permanently scarred, seeing every correction as the beginning of another disaster. This leads to perpetual defensive positioning that misses enormous gains during healthy bull markets. Finding the balance of being prepared for crashes without living in constant fear of them is the essential challenge of long-term investing.

The critical sequence outlined in this chapter of warning, denial and acceleration provides a framework for understanding where you are in the cycle. Corrections typically don't progress through all three phases. They might include a brief warning phase and a quick acceleration, but they lack the extended denial phase where markets become increasingly choppy and dysfunctional while participants refuse to acknowledge the deterioration. That denial phase, where hope fights reality for weeks or months, is the characteristic signature of a developing crash rather than a routine correction.

Ultimately, the difference between corrections and crashes isn't just quantitative but qualitative. It's the difference between a temporary repricing and a systemic breakdown. It's the difference between a healthy body fighting off an infection and an immune system collapse. The symptoms might look similar initially, but the underlying dynamics and ultimate outcomes are entirely different. Learning to recognize these differences, while acknowledging that certainty is impossible until after the fact, is part of the wisdom that separates successful long-term investors from those who are repeatedly caught on the wrong side of major market moves.

Chapter 16

Your Personal Early Warning System

The most valuable early warning system you can build isn't a collection of market indicators or economic data, it's a deep understanding of how your specific portfolio would behave under various stress scenarios. Most investors have only a vague sense of their actual risk exposure, operating under comfortable assumptions that evaporate during real crises. Rigorous stress testing transforms vague worry into concrete knowledge, allowing you to make rational adjustments before markets force your hand.

Portfolio stress testing means asking hard questions about your holdings and answering them honestly. What happens to your portfolio if the stock market drops 30 percent? What if it drops 50 percent? What if that decline happens over three days rather than three months? What if your bonds, which you own for "safety," also decline because interest rates spike or credit spreads blow out? What if the decline happens when you're on the verge of retirement and need to start drawing income? What if it happens when you've just lost your job and might need to liquidate holdings?

These aren't pleasant questions, but they're essential. The time to discover your portfolio can't withstand a serious downturn isn't when that downturn is actually occurring and you're making decisions in a state of panic. It's now, when markets are calm and you can think clearly.

Start with the simplest stress test: calculate your portfolio's maximum drawdown tolerance. This is the largest percentage decline you can endure without either selling at the bottom or suffering serious lifestyle consequences. For most people, this number is somewhere between 20 and 40 percent, though it varies enormously based on age, income stability, expenses, temperament, and time horizon.

Be brutally honest about this number. Many investors believe they can tolerate large declines because they've never experienced one with serious money at stake. They watched their small portfolio drop 30 percent in 2008 or 2020 and convinced themselves they're comfortable with volatility.

But experiencing a 30 percent decline on a $50,000 portfolio when you're thirty years old and employed is completely different from experiencing it on a $2 million portfolio when you're sixty-five and recently retired. The dollar magnitude of the loss changes everything about the psychological experience.

Once you know your maximum drawdown tolerance, calculate your portfolio's expected maximum drawdown based on its actual allocation. A portfolio of 100 percent stocks has historically experienced drawdowns of 50 percent or more in major bear markets. A 60/40 portfolio (60 percent stocks, 40 percent bonds) typically sees maximum drawdowns around 30 percent, though this assumes bonds perform their traditional role as diversifiers, which isn't guaranteed. A 40/60 portfolio might see 20 percent maximum drawdowns.

If your expected maximum drawdown exceeds your tolerance, you have a fundamental mismatch that needs correction before a crisis arrives. This might mean reducing equity exposure, increasing cash holdings, or adding alternative assets with different risk characteristics. The specific solution matters less than recognizing and fixing the mismatch.

Beyond simple drawdown analysis, construct specific scenarios based on historical crashes and imagine how your portfolio would have performed. The 2008 financial crisis provides an excellent template because it stressed multiple asset classes simultaneously. In that crisis, U.S. stocks fell 57 percent from peak to trough. Investment-grade corporate bonds fell 13 percent. High-yield bonds collapsed 36 percent. Real estate investment trusts dropped 68 percent. Even supposedly safe assets like FDIC-insured bank CDs became problematic when banks failed and depositors faced delays accessing their money above the insurance limits.

Take your current allocation and apply those historical drawdowns. A portfolio of 70 percent stocks (40 percent down during a lesser crisis), 20 percent corporate bonds (10 percent down), and 10 percent cash (0 percent down) would decline roughly 30 percent in a 2008-style event. Can you tolerate that? More importantly, can you tolerate it without selling? If your answer is uncertain, your portfolio is too aggressive for your risk tolerance.

Run multiple scenarios with different assumptions. What if stocks fall 40 percent but bonds actually rise because the Federal Reserve slashes rates? What if stocks fall 30 percent and bonds also fall 15 percent because inflation spikes and rates rise? What if your portfolio's international holdings get hit even harder than U.S. stocks due to currency collapses or geopolitical crises? What if the alternative investments you bought for diversification turn out to be illiquid and you can't access that capital when you need it?

These scenario analyses reveal hidden concentrations and unexpected correlations in your portfolio. You might discover that your supposedly diversified portfolio is actually making a massive bet on a single factor, perhaps continued low interest rates, or stable credit markets, or U.S. economic outperformance. Once you identify these hidden bets, you can decide whether you're comfortable making them or whether you need to adjust your portfolio to reduce concentration.

Pay particular attention to liquidity mismatches in your scenario planning. Liquidity, the ability to sell an asset quickly at a fair price is the most underappreciated risk factor in portfolio construction. During calm markets, almost everything seems liquid. During crises, liquidity vanishes precisely when you most need it. Real estate, private equity, hedge funds, structured products, thinly traded bonds, and even some ETFs can become effectively illiquid during stress periods.

Ask yourself: if you needed to raise cash quickly during a market crisis, which holdings would you sell? If your answer is "my most liquid holdings," recognize that you'll be selling what's easiest to sell rather than what makes the most strategic sense. This often means selling your highest-quality assets at depressed prices while being stuck holding your riskiest, most illiquid positions. A portfolio that looks well-balanced on paper can become dangerously unbalanced when liquidity constraints force suboptimal decisions.

The solution is maintaining adequate liquidity buffers, cash and highly liquid securities that you can access quickly without significant price concessions. How much liquidity you need depends on your specific circumstances, but a useful framework is covering at least one to two years of expenses in highly liquid assets if you're retired, or six to twelve months of expenses if you're working. This buffer allows you to avoid forced selling during market dislocations.

Diversification Beyond Traditional 60/40

The traditional 60/40 portfolio, 60 percent stocks, 40 percent bonds has served investors reasonably well for decades, but it faces unprecedented challenges in the current environment. Understanding these challenges and how to diversify beyond the traditional approach is essential for building an effective early warning system and resilient portfolio.

The 60/40 portfolio worked because stocks and bonds were negatively correlated for most of recent history. When stocks fell, investors fled to the safety of government bonds, pushing bond prices up and offsetting some of the equity losses. This negative correlation provided natural risk reduction. During the 2008 financial crisis, for example, the S&P 500 fell 37 percent but the Bloomberg Aggregate Bond Index rose 5.2 percent, cushioning the blow for balanced portfolios.

However, this relationship isn't a law of nature, it's a historical artifact that can and does break down. In the 1970s, stocks and bonds fell together as inflation surged. In 2022, the 60/40 portfolio experienced one of its worst years in history, with both stocks and bonds declining simultaneously as the Federal Reserve rapidly raised interest rates to combat inflation. The traditional diversification benefit disappeared precisely when investors needed it most.

Several structural factors suggest the traditional stock-bond correlation could remain challenged going forward. Bond yields started the 2020s near historic lows, limiting bonds' ability to rally further during equity crises. Government debt levels have exploded globally, raising questions about sovereign creditworthiness and potentially limiting governments' willingness to let central banks suppress yields indefinitely. Inflation has returned after decades of dormancy, and if it becomes persistently elevated, both stocks and bonds could struggle simultaneously.

This doesn't mean abandoning the 60/40 framework entirely, but it does mean thinking more carefully about what you're trying to achieve with the "40" portion of your portfolio and whether traditional bonds still accomplish those goals. The purpose of the bond allocation is threefold: providing income, preserving capital, and diversifying equity risk. You need to evaluate whether your current bond holdings actually serve these purposes under various scenarios.

Short-term, high-quality bonds such as Treasury bills and investment-grade corporate bonds with maturities under three years provide minimal income in most environments but offer strong capital preservation and liquidity. They won't drop much even if interest rates rise, and they're easily sold if you need cash. The downside is that their returns barely exceed cash in normal times, making them feel like "dead weight" during bull markets.

Longer-term bonds such as ten-year Treasuries or longer offer more income but carry significant interest rate risk. If rates rise, these bonds will decline substantially in value. However, they also offer the most powerful diversification benefit when that traditional negative correlation with stocks reasserts itself. During a deflationary crisis or severe recession, long-term government bonds can rally spectacularly while stocks crash.

Investment-grade corporate bonds sit somewhere in between, offering more yield than government bonds but introducing credit risk. During financial crises, corporate bond spreads widen dramatically as investors worry about defaults, causing these bonds to decline even as government bonds rally. High-yield corporate bonds such as junk bonds offer even higher yields but behave more like stocks during crises, falling sharply when equity markets tumble.

Given these tradeoffs, a more robust approach to the bond allocation might include a barbell strategy: holding both very short-term bonds (for liquidity and capital preservation) and longer-term government bonds (for diversification and deflation protection), while minimizing exposure to the middle maturities that offer neither strong safety nor strong diversification benefits.

Beyond traditional bonds, investors should consider alternative diversifiers that might maintain or increase value during equity market crashes. Gold has a long history of preserving wealth during financial crises, though it's volatile and produces no income. During the 2008 crisis, gold rose 5 percent while stocks collapsed. During the 2020 COVID crash, gold initially fell with everything else but quickly recovered and went on to new highs. Gold's behavior is unpredictable in the short term, but over longer periods it tends to maintain purchasing power and provides a hedge against both inflation and financial system stress.

Treasury Inflation-Protected Securities (TIPS) adjust their principal value based on inflation, protecting purchasing power if inflation accelerates. However, TIPS can decline in value if interest rates rise faster than inflation, and they offer minimal yield in low-inflation environments.

They're most valuable as insurance against unexpected inflation spikes rather than as total return investments.

Commodities broadly, not just gold but oil, agricultural products, industrial metals tend to perform well during inflationary periods when stocks and traditional bonds struggle. However, commodity investments are complex, volatile, and can experience prolonged periods of poor performance. They're best used as a modest allocation (perhaps 5-10 percent of a portfolio) for diversification rather than as core holdings.

Real estate, typically accessed through REITs, provides income and some inflation protection but tends to correlate with stocks more than investors expect. During the 2008 crisis, REITs fell even more than the broader stock market. Real estate works best as an equity diversifier during normal times but shouldn't be counted on as a safe haven during financial crises.

Cash itself is an underappreciated diversifier. While inflation erodes cash's purchasing power over time, cash provides perfect liquidity and eliminates volatility entirely. During market crashes, cash is the only asset that doesn't decline, its value relative to all other assets actually increases. The optionality that cash provides the ability to opportunistically buy assets when they're discounted can be more valuable than the modest returns you'd earn staying fully invested.

Alternative investments like hedge funds, private equity, and managed futures promise diversification but come with significant caveats. Many supposedly uncorrelated alternative strategies are actually leveraged bets on traditional assets with hidden correlations that appear during stress. Liquidity is often severely limited. Fees are high. Transparency is low. For most individual investors, alternatives introduce more complexity and cost than benefit.

The key insight is that diversification isn't about owning different things, it's about owning things that behave differently. A portfolio containing U.S. large-cap stocks, U.S. small-cap stocks, international developed market stocks, and emerging market stocks is diversified across geographies and market capitalizations, but all those assets are stocks and will largely move together during global equity selloffs. True diversification requires assets with genuinely different risk characteristics and return drivers.

Liquidity Considerations and Redemption Gates

Liquidity is the silent killer of investment portfolios. During calm markets, it's invisible and seemingly unimportant. During crises, it becomes the difference between surviving and being wiped out. Building liquidity awareness into your early warning system is absolutely critical.

Liquidity exists on a spectrum. At one end, Treasury bills and large-cap stocks can be sold almost instantly at transparent prices with minimal transaction costs. At the other end, real estate, private equity, and collectibles might take months or years to sell and might require steep discounts to attract buyers in distressed markets. Most investments fall somewhere in between, with their liquidity varying dramatically based on market conditions.

The problem is that investors typically assess liquidity based on normal market conditions. A corporate bond that trades easily with tight bid-ask spreads during calm periods might become nearly impossible to sell at any reasonable price during a crisis. ETFs that track illiquid underlying assets, like high-yield bonds or emerging market stocks can trade at substantial discounts to their net asset value during stress, effectively trapping investors. Even mutual funds investing in liquid securities can impose redemption fees or outright redemption gates if too many investors try to withdraw simultaneously.

Redemption gates are particularly insidious because they turn apparently liquid investments into illiquid ones at the worst possible moment. A mutual fund or hedge fund facing a surge of redemption requests can invoke provisions in its prospectus to limit or halt withdrawals, trapping investors in declining assets. This happened repeatedly during the 2008 crisis, when various funds froze redemptions to prevent a death spiral where redemptions forced asset sales at fire-sale prices, causing the fund's value to decline further, triggering more redemptions.

Even more concerning, some investment vehicles have tiered liquidity structures. You might be able to withdraw 10 percent of your investment quarterly, or 5 percent monthly, but not access the full amount. This is common in hedge funds, private equity, and some alternative investment vehicles. During a personal financial emergency or market crisis, discovering you can only access a fraction of what you thought was available can be devastating.

Real estate deserves special attention in liquidity analysis. Home equity represents a huge portion of net worth for most Americans, but it's deeply illiquid. You can't sell your house quickly without accepting a potentially significant discount, and even then the process takes weeks or months. Home equity lines of credit seem to solve this problem, but banks can and do freeze these credit lines during financial crises when they're worried about property values declining. In 2008, many homeowners who had counted on HELOCs as emergency liquidity discovered those lines had been revoked just when they needed them most.

Commercial real estate is even less liquid. Private real estate investments, whether through syndications, funds, or direct ownership, can become completely illiquid during market stress. The real estate funds that allowed quarterly redemptions might suddenly impose gates. The syndication you invested in might have no mechanism for early withdrawal at all. Real estate crowdfunding platforms, while offering smaller minimums and seeming more accessible, typically lock up capital for years with no secondary market to speak of.

The question every investor must answer is: how much of my portfolio might become illiquid simultaneously during a crisis? This isn't just about which assets are inherently illiquid, but about which assets might become effectively illiquid due to market dislocations. A sobering exercise is categorizing your holdings into liquidity tiers:

Tier 1 - Immediate liquidity (accessible within days at fair prices): Cash, money market funds, Treasury bills, large-cap stocks, large-cap stock ETFs, short-term Treasury bond funds.

Tier 2 - High liquidity (accessible within weeks at reasonable prices): Investment-grade corporate bonds, municipal bonds, mid-cap and small-cap stocks, developed international market stocks, total stock market index funds.

Tier 3 - Moderate liquidity (accessible within months, potentially at discounted prices): High-yield bonds, emerging market stocks, sector-specific equity funds, actively managed mutual funds with diverse holdings, TIPS, commodities ETFs.

Tier 4 - Low liquidity (might take many months and could require significant discounts): Individual municipal bonds, private credit investments, leveraged loan funds, certain alternative ETFs, closed-end funds trading at substantial discounts.

Tier 5 - Illiquid (months to years, significant uncertainty on pricing): Real estate (excluding REITs), private equity, hedge funds with gates, unlisted investments, collectibles, structured products.

Now ask yourself: if I needed to raise 20 percent of my portfolio value within a week, could I do it from Tier 1 and Tier 2 holdings? If the answer is no, you have a liquidity mismatch. During a personal emergency such as a job loss, medical crisis or family need you might be forced to liquidate Tier 3 or lower holdings at exactly the wrong time, crystallizing losses that would have recovered given time.

The solution is maintaining liquidity buffers appropriate to your life circumstances. A young professional with stable employment and no dependents can tolerate more illiquidity than a retiree depending on their portfolio for living expenses. A business owner with irregular income needs more liquidity than a tenured professor with a guaranteed salary. Someone with substantial home equity and a HELOC has more backup liquidity than someone who rents (though as noted, that HELOC can disappear in a crisis).

A reasonable guideline is keeping at least 10-20 percent of your portfolio in Tier 1 and Tier 2 combined, with the specific percentage higher for retirees or anyone whose employment stability is uncertain. This liquidity buffer serves multiple purposes: providing emergency reserves, enabling opportunistic purchases when assets are cheap, and reducing the psychological pressure that leads to panic selling during market crashes.

The Importance of Uncorrelated Assets

Correlation measures how assets move together. A correlation of +1.0 means two assets move in perfect lockstep, when one goes up, the other always goes up by a proportional amount. A correlation of -1.0 means they move in perfect opposition. A correlation of 0 means their movements are independent. Real-world correlations are rarely at these extremes, instead falling somewhere in between.

The mathematical reality is that combining assets with low or negative correlations dramatically reduces portfolio volatility without necessarily reducing returns. This is the only free lunch in investing, the diversification benefit that comes from holding assets that zig when others zag. However, capturing this benefit requires understanding that correlations are unstable and that apparent diversification can vanish during crises.

During normal markets, correlations between various asset classes remain relatively stable and moderate. U.S. and international stocks might have a correlation of 0.85, highly correlated but not perfectly so. Stocks and bonds might have a correlation of 0.2 or even slightly negative. Gold and stocks might show minimal correlation, somewhere around 0. These moderate correlations provide meaningful diversification benefits during normal market volatility.

During crises, something dangerous happens: correlations spike toward 1.0. When markets are in free fall, investors sell everything, making all risky assets move together regardless of their fundamental characteristics. In October 2008, almost every asset class declined simultaneously, U.S. stocks, international stocks, commodities, real estate, high-yield bonds, even some investment-grade corporate bonds. The diversification benefit largely disappeared when investors needed it most.

This correlation breakdown is driven by several factors. First, leverage forces indiscriminate selling, investors receiving margin calls must sell whatever they can, not what they want to. Second, risk-off sentiment drives investors toward the safest assets (Treasury bills, gold) and away from everything else, regardless of specific merits. Third, fund redemptions force portfolio managers to sell their most liquid holdings first, which often means their highest-quality assets, creating selling pressure across different asset classes simultaneously.

The implication is that traditional diversification across stocks, bonds, and real estate, while valuable, provides less protection during severe market stress than most investors expect. You need to think harder about uncorrelated assets that might maintain their value or even appreciate during crisis periods.

True uncorrelated assets are rare, but they exist. Cash, as mentioned earlier, has zero correlation with everything, it neither rises nor falls with markets. Government bonds, particularly long-term Treasuries, have historically shown negative correlation with stocks during crises as investors flee to safety. This negative correlation is the theoretical foundation of the 60/40 portfolio, though as noted, it can break down during inflationary periods.

Gold's correlation with stocks is low but variable. During deflationary financial crises like 2008, gold tends to perform well as a store of value and hedge against financial system risk. During inflationary crises, gold typically performs very well as a hedge against currency debasement. During normal periods, gold can languish for years or even decades, providing no return while stocks climb. Gold is thus most valuable not as a return generator but as crisis insurance.

Managed futures strategies, systematic trading strategies that go long or short various futures contracts based on trend-following or other quantitative signals have historically shown low or negative correlation with traditional assets. During major equity bear markets (2000-2002, 2008), managed futures indices posted positive returns while stocks collapsed. However, individual managed futures funds vary enormously in quality, fees are often high, and the strategy can experience prolonged drawdowns during trendless markets.

Truly alternative assets such as farmland, timberland, infrastructure and certain types of insurance-linked securities can provide genuine diversification, but they're difficult for individual investors to access efficiently. Most require substantial minimums, long lockup periods, and sophisticated due diligence. For most investors, the complexity and costs outweigh the benefits.

A more practical approach to achieving uncorrelated exposure is understanding and managing your factor exposures. Factor investing recognizes that returns come from exposure to various risk factors such as equity risk, interest rate risk, credit risk, momentum, value, size, quality, volatility, and others. By consciously balancing exposure across different factors, you can build a portfolio that's more resilient to any single factor experiencing stress.

For example, a portfolio heavily weighted toward high-momentum growth stocks is making a concentrated bet on the momentum and growth factors. If those factors reverse as they did dramatically in 2022 when high-growth tech stocks collapsed the portfolio will suffer severe losses. Adding value stocks, which have negative correlation with growth stocks over long periods, provides diversification at the factor level even though both are equities.

Similarly, a portfolio entirely invested in domestic U.S. assets is making a concentrated bet on U.S. economic and political stability, dollar strength, and U.S. market valuations. Adding international exposure, particularly to markets with different economic cycles or currency regimes, provides genuine diversification even though both are stock investments.

The key is recognizing that asset class labels can be misleading. Two investments labeled "stocks" or "bonds" might have very different factor exposures and risk characteristics. Conversely, investments in different asset classes might have more similar exposures than you'd expect. The only way to build a truly diversified portfolio is understanding what factors drive returns for each of your holdings and ensuring you're not overly concentrated in any single factor.

When to Trust Your Instincts vs. Stay the Course

The final component of your personal early warning system is the most difficult to calibrate: your own instincts and emotional responses to market conditions. Every investor faces a tension between trusting their gut feelings that something is wrong and maintaining discipline through the inevitable volatility of long-term investing. Getting this balance right separates successful investors from failed ones.

The conventional wisdom in investing emphasizes discipline and emotional control. "Stay the course." "Don't try to time the market." "Ignore short-term noise." This advice is generally sound because most investors are their own worst enemy, buying high out of greed and selling low out of fear. Study after study shows that the average investor significantly underperforms the market precisely because they can't control their emotions and make poor timing decisions.

However, this doesn't mean your instincts are always wrong. Sometimes that growing sense of unease, that feeling that markets have become unmoored from reality, that intuition that everyone around you has lost their minds, sometimes those instincts are correct and valuable. The challenge is distinguishing legitimate warning signals from mere anxiety or risk aversion that would cause you to miss major gains.

Trust your instincts when they're based on observable facts rather than emotional reactions to price movements. If you notice that everyone you talk to is discussing their stock market gains, that previously conservative friends are trading options, that valuations have reached levels that have historically preceded major declines, that leverage indicators are flashing red, these fact-based observations should inform your positioning. This isn't market timing based on fear; it's risk management based on evidence.

Trust your instincts when you notice yourself rationalizing away concerns. If you find yourself making arguments like "this time is different" or "valuations don't matter anymore" or "the Fed will never let markets fall", pause and examine whether you're rationalizing because you've become emotionally attached to your positions or because you're afraid of missing out. These rationalizations are often signs that you've lost objectivity and need to reassess.

Trust your instincts when you're uncomfortable with your portfolio's risk level. If you lie awake worrying about a potential market decline, if you check your portfolio balance compulsively, if market volatility is affecting your mood and relationships your portfolio is too aggressive regardless of what any calculator or advisor says. The "right" asset allocation isn't determined purely by mathematics; it's the allocation you can maintain through a full market cycle without panicking.

However, distrust your instincts when they're purely reactions to recent price movements. If markets drop 10 percent and you suddenly want to sell everything, that's probably panic rather than prudent risk assessment. If markets have risen 30 percent in a year and you feel compelled to pile in now, that's probably greed rather than opportunity recognition. Price movements alone absent any change in fundamentals or risk indicators should not drive major portfolio changes.

Distrust your instincts when they conflict with your long-term plan. If you've done careful analysis, established appropriate asset allocation targets, and created a rebalancing discipline, don't abandon that plan based on passing emotions. The plan exists precisely to guide you through periods when your emotions might lead you astray. Trust the process over the impulse.

Distrust your instincts when they're based on anecdotes or media narratives rather than data. The financial media thrives on emotional narratives, either euphoric bullishness or apocalyptic bearishness because those narratives capture attention. Stories about people who got rich or got wiped out make for compelling television but terrible investment guidance.

Your instincts filtered through the lens of media sensationalism are worse than useless.

A practical framework for navigating this tension is the "trust but verify" approach. When you feel strongly that markets are becoming dangerously extended or that a crash is imminent, don't immediately act on that feeling. Instead, verify it against objective indicators. Check valuation metrics. Examine credit spreads. Review sentiment surveys. Look at margin debt levels. If your instincts align with multiple objective warning signs, taking defensive action is prudent. If your instincts are contradicted by the data, if you're fearful but indicators suggest markets are reasonably valued and not overly leveraged then staying the course is appropriate.

Similarly, when you feel comfortable and confident about markets, challenge that comfort. Ask yourself whether you're truly seeing clear sailing ahead or whether you've simply become complacent. Check the same objective indicators. If they confirm your positive outlook, maintain your positioning. If they suggest more risk than you're acknowledging, let the data override your comfort.

The ultimate goal is achieving what could be called "informed instinct", where your gut feelings and your analytical assessment align because you've trained your instincts through study, experience, and continuous reality-testing. Investors who survive multiple market cycles develop this informed instinct. They've seen enough patterns that their subconscious recognizes warning signs before their conscious mind fully articulates them. But that instinct is only reliable because it's built on a foundation of knowledge, data, and honest self-assessment.

Your personal early warning system, then, is not a collection of indicators or a mechanical formula. It's an integrated framework combining rigorous stress testing, genuine diversification, careful liquidity management, and calibrated instincts. It requires ongoing maintenance, regularly updating your scenario analyses as your circumstances change, rebalancing to maintain diversification as market movements alter your allocation, periodically reassessing your risk tolerance, and continuously testing your instincts against objective reality.

The investors who navigate crashes successfully aren't those who predict them with precision, such prediction is impossible. They're the investors who build robust systems that can withstand various scenarios, who maintain discipline without rigidity, and who trust themselves enough to act on warning signs while remaining humble enough to acknowledge uncertainty. That balance, more than any specific indicator or allocation, is what transforms market knowledge into investment survival.

Chapter 17

Policy Exhaustion Signals

For the past four decades, central banks have been the ultimate backstop for financial markets. The implicit promise that monetary authorities would step in to prevent serious market dislocations has become so embedded in investor psychology that it's known simply as "the Fed put." Investors believe that if markets fall too far or too fast, the Federal Reserve (and other central banks) will ease monetary policy, inject liquidity, or take other measures to support asset prices. This belief has been validated repeatedly since the 1987 crash, creating a powerful positive feedback loop: central bank interventions prevent crashes, which reinforces belief in central bank power, which encourages greater risk-taking, which eventually requires even larger interventions.

But what happens when this cycle breaks? When central banks lose credibility or exhaust their toolkit, the consequences for financial markets are profound. Recognizing the warning signs of central bank policy exhaustion is perhaps the most critical element of any early warning system for market crashes.

Central bank credibility rests on two pillars: the belief that they have the tools to influence economic and financial conditions, and the belief that they will use those tools effectively. When either pillar cracks, markets become fundamentally more fragile.

The first signs of credibility loss often appear in the divergence between central bank actions and market responses. In a healthy relationship, when the Fed cuts interest rates, markets rally in anticipation of easier financial conditions and stronger economic growth ahead. When the Fed raises rates, markets initially decline but then stabilize as investors accept that the central bank is successfully managing inflation. The policy transmission mechanism works smoothly: central bank actions produce predictable market and economic responses.

Credibility erosion shows up when this transmission mechanism breaks down. Markets might fail to rally after rate cuts, suggesting investors believe the cuts are insufficient or that monetary policy has lost its effectiveness. Alternatively, markets might rally excessively after minor policy shifts, suggesting investors are so desperate for support that they're overinterpreting dovish signals. Both responses indicate loss of confidence in the central bank's control.

The European Central Bank's experience from 2014 through 2019 provides a clear example. Despite implementing negative interest rates, massive quantitative easing programs, and targeted lending facilities, the ECB struggled to generate the inflation and growth it sought. Each new policy announcement produced diminishing market impact. Investors began questioning whether the ECB had any remaining tools or whether monetary policy had simply reached its limits. While this didn't immediately trigger a crash, other factors provided support, it illustrated how central bank credibility can erode gradually as policy effectiveness wanes.

The Bank of Japan offers an even more extreme case study. After more than two decades of zero or negative interest rates, aggressive bond purchases, and direct equity market intervention through ETF purchases, the BOJ has failed to achieve its inflation target or generate sustained economic growth. Japanese investors have learned through bitter experience that central bank intervention cannot conjure prosperity from monetary policy alone. The BOJ has become a cautionary tale of policy exhaustion, demonstrating that even unlimited determination cannot overcome fundamental economic constraints.

For U.S. investors, signs of Federal Reserve credibility loss would be particularly ominous because so much market confidence rests on faith in Fed omnipotence. Key warning signs include:

Policy reversals or inconsistency: If the Fed shifts course repeatedly within short timeframes, it signals either that they don't understand economic conditions or that they're being buffeted by political pressure or market reactions rather than following a coherent strategy. The worst-case scenario is a Fed that tightens to fight inflation, then quickly reverses to support markets, then tightens again, creating whipsaw volatility and demonstrating they're trapped between conflicting mandates.

Speeches that contradict actions: When Fed officials' verbal guidance diverges from their actual policy decisions, it suggests internal disagreement or external constraints limiting their options. Markets depend on forward guidance as a policy tool itself. When that guidance becomes unreliable, an important pillar of policy transmission crumbles.

Unusual or desperate measures: If the Fed resorts to policies it previously dismissed or avoided, it signals they're running out of conventional tools. Examples might include yield curve control (which they rejected as unnecessary), direct equity purchases (which the BOJ pioneered but the Fed has avoided), or explicit coordination with fiscal authorities that compromises central bank independence.

Market behavior that ignores Fed signals: Perhaps the clearest sign of credibility loss is when markets simply stop responding to Fed communications. If a dovish speech fails to boost stocks or a rate cut produces minimal reaction, it suggests investors no longer believe the Fed can materially impact outcomes.

The deeper issue underlying central bank credibility is the question of whether monetary policy has fundamental limits. The traditional view held that central banks could always stimulate demand by making money sufficiently cheap and abundant. Cut rates low enough, print enough money, and economic activity would inevitably increase. This view has been challenged by the post-2008 experience in Japan, Europe, and even the United States, where aggressive monetary stimulus produced disappointing growth and persistent below-target inflation, at least until the massive fiscal stimulus of 2020-2021 combined with supply disruptions to finally generate significant inflation.

The modern challenge is that central banks face a trilemma: they cannot simultaneously maintain price stability (their core mandate), support financial markets (which they've implicitly promised to do), and preserve their independence from political pressure. When inflation rises, fighting it requires tightening that will hurt asset prices and potentially trigger a recession. Markets that have become dependent on easy money will demand the Fed choose market support over inflation fighting. Politicians facing voter anger about inflation or recession will pressure the Fed to prioritize their preferred outcome.

If the Fed is perceived as prioritizing market support over price stability, essentially sacrificing the real economy to protect financial asset prices, its credibility as an independent, credible inflation fighter evaporates. If it prioritizes inflation fighting regardless of market consequences, the Fed put disappears and markets must price risk without that backstop. Either outcome represents a fundamental regime change with profound implications for market stability.

Fiscal Stimulus Limits and Political Gridlock

While central banks have dominated economic policy responses to crises over recent decades, fiscal policy, government spending and taxation often matters more for real economic outcomes. The 2008 financial crisis was ultimately contained not just by monetary policy but by massive fiscal interventions: bank bailouts, stimulus spending, and automatic stabilizers like unemployment insurance. The 2020 COVID crisis response was even more heavily fiscal, with trillions in direct payments, enhanced unemployment benefits, and business support programs.

But fiscal capacity is not unlimited, and political willingness to deploy it is even more constrained. Recognizing when governments approach fiscal limits is crucial for assessing systemic fragility because once both monetary and fiscal policy are exhausted, no policy response remains to arrest a crisis.

Government debt levels provide the most obvious indicator of fiscal capacity. When debt-to-GDP ratios are low, governments have substantial room to borrow and spend during crises. When debt levels are already elevated, additional borrowing becomes more problematic. High debt levels constrain policy in several ways:

Interest costs crowd out other spending: As debt levels rise, a larger portion of government budgets must go toward interest payments rather than programs that might support growth or provide social benefits. When interest rates are near zero, this constraint is minimal. When rates rise to normal levels, interest costs can explode, consuming resources that might otherwise fund stimulus.

Bond market vigilantes emerge: At some threshold of debt accumulation, bond investors begin demanding higher yields to compensate for perceived sovereign credit risk. This was the dynamic that created the European sovereign debt crisis in 2010-2012, when yields on Italian, Spanish, and Greek government bonds spiked as investors worried about default risk. If the U.S. Treasury market experienced a similar loss of confidence with buyers demanding significantly higher yields, the resulting spike in interest costs could create a fiscal death spiral where more borrowing is required to finance the interest on existing debt.

Political opposition intensifies: As debt levels rise, political opposition to additional borrowing increases, even during crises when stimulus is most needed. Deficit hawks emerge to block spending, creating political gridlock precisely when aggressive fiscal response is most necessary. The U.S. debt ceiling fights—where Congress battles over authorizing the Treasury to borrow money to pay obligations Congress already incurred illustrate how high debt levels create political dysfunction that constrains policy flexibility.

Intergenerational conflict: High government debt represents a transfer from future taxpayers to current beneficiaries. As debt accumulates, younger generations increasingly resist bearing the costs of past borrowing, creating political tensions that make additional debt-financed stimulus harder to pass.

The United States entered the 2020s with federal debt around 100 percent of GDP, roughly double the level before the 2008 crisis. The COVID response pushed it even higher. While these levels aren't necessarily catastrophic, Japan has sustained debt above 200 percent of GDP for years, they represent a significant constraint on future fiscal capacity. More importantly, the rapid accumulation created political resistance that will make future stimulus efforts more difficult.

Political gridlock poses an independent constraint on fiscal policy effectiveness. Even when fiscal capacity exists in principle, political dysfunction can prevent its deployment. The U.S. political system, with its multiple veto points and increasingly polarized parties, is particularly vulnerable to gridlock. Key warning signs include:

Extended debt ceiling standoffs: When Congress approaches debt ceiling deadlines without clear resolution paths, it signals deep political dysfunction. While these crises have always been resolved eventually, each episode chips away at global confidence in U.S. governance. A genuine default, even a brief technical default would shatter Treasury markets and eliminate the risk-free asset on which the entire global financial system is built.

Inability to pass stimulus during downturns: If the economy weakens or markets crash and Congress cannot quickly agree on stimulus measures, it signals that political gridlock has reached crisis levels. The relatively quick passage of COVID relief bills in 2020, despite election-year politics, was reassuring. But the subsequent inability to agree on infrastructure spending or other measures suggested the political system's capacity for coordinated action was limited.

Federal Reserve politicization: When politicians of either party routinely attack the Federal Reserve for its policy decisions, it threatens central bank independence. A Fed that feels political pressure to ease monetary policy when tightening is warranted, or vice versa, cannot effectively manage the economy. The political attacks on Fed Chair Jerome Powell from both political parties at various points suggested growing threats to Fed independence.

State-level fiscal stress without federal support: If individual states face fiscal crises, unable to fund basic services or meet pension obligations and the federal government doesn't provide support due to political considerations, it signals that the fiscal union is weakening. This dynamic was visible during the COVID crisis when some politicians opposed aid to states based on their political alignment.

The combination of fiscal limits and political gridlock creates a dangerous scenario where markets crash but policy response is insufficient or delayed. The 2008 crisis response worked in part because both monetary and fiscal authorities acted aggressively and in coordination. The Fed slashed rates to zero, implemented quantitative easing, and created emergency lending facilities. Congress passed stimulus packages and authorized bank bailouts (however controversial). This coordinated response eventually stabilized markets and the economy.

If a future crisis finds fiscal policy constrained by debt levels and political gridlock while monetary policy is already at or near its limits, the policy response could be too little, too late. Markets that have come to depend on aggressive policy support would face a terrifying reality: this time, nobody's coming to the rescue.

Currency Market Stress and Dollar Strength

Currency markets are often the canary in the coal mine for broader financial stress. Exchange rates reflect global capital flows, trade balances, relative monetary policies, and confidence in sovereign creditworthiness. Disruptions in currency markets can both signal underlying problems and trigger cascading crises through their effects on trade, debt servicing, and capital flows.

The U.S. dollar holds a unique position in the global financial system as the world's reserve currency. Most international trade is denominated in dollars. Most central banks hold dollars as reserves. Most emerging market debt is denominated in dollars. This creates complex dynamics where dollar strength or weakness has far-reaching implications beyond simple exchange rate movements.

Extreme dollar strength can signal several types of stress. During financial crises, global investors often flee to the safety of dollar-denominated assets, particularly U.S. Treasury securities. This "flight to safety" pushes the dollar higher even as it reflects deep pessimism about global economic conditions. The dollar strengthened sharply during the worst phases of the 2008 crisis and again during the acute stress of March 2020. A rapidly strengthening dollar, particularly if accompanied by weakness in most other major currencies often signals that global investors are panicking and seeking safety.

However, dollar strength also creates its own problems. For the many countries and companies that borrowed in dollars, a stronger dollar makes their debt more expensive to service. Emerging market economies are particularly vulnerable to this dynamic. If a Brazilian company borrowed dollars when the exchange rate was 3 reals per dollar, but the rate moves to 5 reals per dollar, the company's debt burden increases by 67 percent in local currency terms even though the dollar amount hasn't changed. This can trigger default cascades in emerging markets, which in turn creates losses for global banks and investors exposed to those markets.

Dollar strength also pressures commodities, which are typically priced in dollars globally. As the dollar rises, commodities become more expensive for buyers using other currencies, reducing demand and pushing prices lower. This creates headwinds for commodity-producing nations and companies, potentially triggering crises in resource-dependent economies.

The opposite scenario, extreme dollar weakness also signals problems, though of a different nature. A collapsing dollar suggests loss of confidence in U.S. fiscal sustainability, Federal Reserve policy, or American political stability. While the U.S. benefits from dollar weakness in some ways (making exports more competitive, reducing the real value of dollar-denominated debt), a rapid decline would be highly disruptive. It would spike inflation by making imports more expensive, potentially force the Fed to raise rates even during economic weakness to defend the currency, and raise questions about the dollar's role as reserve currency.

The most dangerous currency market signal is a loss of confidence in the Treasury market itself. Treasury securities are considered the world's risk-free asset, the benchmark against which all other assets are priced. If major foreign holders of Treasuries (China, Japan, oil-exporting nations) began selling in significant quantities, it would trigger a crisis in the foundation of the global financial system. Warning signs might include:

Auction failures: If Treasury auctions fail to attract sufficient demand at reasonable yields, it signals loss of confidence in U.S. creditworthiness. While this has never happened for standard Treasury securities, it would represent a catastrophic breakdown of global finance.

Yield spikes disconnected from fundamentals: If Treasury yields surge not because of growth and inflation expectations but because of credit concerns or supply/demand imbalances, it signals fundamental problems. The difference matters: yields rising because the economy is strong and the Fed is normalizing policy is healthy; yields rising because buyers are disappearing is catastrophic.

Dollar swap line usage: During extreme stress, the Federal Reserve provides dollar liquidity to other central banks through swap lines. When foreign central banks draw heavily on these facilities, as they did in March 2020 it signals acute dollar funding stress in global markets. While the Fed's willingness to provide this liquidity is stabilizing, the need for it indicates serious problems.

Emerging market currency crises: When multiple emerging market currencies collapse simultaneously, it often precedes broader financial stress. The 1997 Asian Financial Crisis began with the Thai baht but spread throughout the region and eventually contributed to the Russian default and Long-Term Capital Management collapse in 1998. Similarly, the 2013 "taper tantrum", when emerging market currencies plunged after the Fed suggested slowing its bond purchases, previewed vulnerabilities that surfaced again in subsequent years.

Currency stress can interact with other policy exhaustion signals in dangerous ways. If the Federal Reserve needs to raise rates to defend the dollar, but the domestic economy needs lower rates for stimulus, the Fed faces an impossible tradeoff. If foreign central banks are forced to raise rates to prevent currency collapse, it can trigger recessions that reduce demand for U.S. exports and create losses for U.S. companies and banks with international exposure.

The Plaza Accord of 1985 and the Louvre Accord of 1987 demonstrated that currency coordination among major economies is possible when problems are recognized and political will exists. However, these agreements came during a period of stronger international cooperation and less political polarization than exists today. The question is whether such coordination could be achieved in a future crisis, or whether nationalist politics would prevent the collective action needed to stabilize currency markets.

International Coordination Breakdown

Global financial crises require global policy responses. The 2008 crisis was contained in part because central banks and governments around the world acted in coordination, implementing stimulus measures simultaneously and agreeing on bank capital standards through the Basel III framework. The COVID crisis response was similarly coordinated, with unprecedented monetary and fiscal stimulus deployed globally.

But international coordination cannot be taken for granted. It requires shared analysis of problems, trust among leaders, functional international institutions, and willingness to subordinate narrow national interests to collective stability. All of these prerequisites have weakened over the past decade.

Warning signs of coordination breakdown include:

Trade wars and protectionism: When major economies engage in tit-for-tat tariff escalations, it signals broader breakdown in international cooperation. Trade wars not only damage growth directly but create an environment where coordinated crisis response becomes politically difficult. If countries are fighting over trade policy, they're unlikely to cooperate effectively on financial stability.

Central bank policy divergence: While some policy divergence is natural given different economic conditions, extreme divergence can create destabilizing capital flows and currency volatility. If the Federal Reserve is tightening while the ECB and BOJ are easing aggressively, it can create massive distortions in global financial markets.

Institutional weakening: International institutions like the International Monetary Fund, World Bank, and Bank for International Settlements provide forums for coordination and expertise for crisis response. When these institutions are weakened, through reduced funding, political attacks, or great power competition the infrastructure for coordination deteriorates.

Failure of G7/G20 cooperation: When summits of major economies produce only vague communiques rather than concrete coordinated actions, it signals political leaders cannot agree on responses to shared challenges. The increasingly contentious nature of these summits, with leaders unable to agree even on joint statements, is troubling.

Bilateral breakdowns: The U.S.-China relationship is particularly critical given their roles as the world's two largest economies. If that relationship deteriorates into genuine conflict, through financial decoupling, technology restrictions, or geopolitical confrontation coordinated crisis response becomes nearly impossible. Similarly, EU unity is essential; if the eurozone fragments or EU institutions collapse, global coordination suffers.

Competing currency systems: The development of alternative payment systems that bypass dollar-based infrastructure such as China's Cross-Border Interbank Payment System or cryptocurrency-based settlement could fragment the global financial system. While diversification away from dollar dominance has some benefits, a disorderly fragmentation could create coordination challenges during crises.

The fundamental problem is that financial globalization has created a tightly integrated global financial system where shocks propagate rapidly across borders, but political systems remain nationally focused and increasingly nationalist. This creates an architecture mismatch: we have a global financial system but only national policy tools and limited international coordination mechanisms.

History suggests this mismatch ends badly. The 1930s saw a similar dynamic where financial globalization under the gold standard required international cooperation, but nationalist politics prevented it. Competitive devaluations, trade wars, and beggar-thy-neighbor policies deepened the Depression. Only after World War II, with new international institutions and renewed commitment to cooperation, was stable globalization restored.

If international coordination breaks down during the next crisis, policy responses will be uncoordinated and potentially contradictory. One country's stimulus might leak abroad through imports, reducing its effectiveness. Currency interventions might trigger retaliation. Bank bailouts might face nationalistic opposition ("why are we saving foreign banks?"). Credit provision might stop at borders just when global trade finance is most needed.

The "Pushing on a String" Phenomenon

The metaphor of "pushing on a string" captures a fundamental limit of monetary policy: a central bank can make credit available, but it cannot force banks to lend or borrowers to borrow. When the economy is overheating, the central bank can raise rates and tighten credit, pulling on the string to slow things down. But when the economy is in recession or crisis, cutting rates and providing liquidity might not stimulate activity, the string goes slack.

This phenomenon represents perhaps the ultimate form of policy exhaustion: when central banks do everything technically within their power and it simply doesn't work. Markets that have come to depend on central bank omnipotence face an existential crisis when that power proves illusory.

Several conditions make the pushing-on-a-string problem more likely:

Zero lower bound: When interest rates are already at or near zero, further rate cuts are impossible (unless negative rates are implemented, which create their own problems). Monetary policy loses its most direct tool for stimulus.

Liquidity trap: If households and businesses are so pessimistic or indebted that they won't borrow regardless of how cheap credit becomes, monetary stimulus fails to generate growth. This was the situation Japan faced for decades and that concerned policymakers after 2008.

Broken credit transmission: If banks are unwilling to lend despite abundant reserves, either because they're worried about their own capital positions or because they view all potential borrowers as too risky, easy money doesn't reach the real economy. The credit channel through which monetary policy normally works gets blocked.

Debt deflation dynamics: If falling prices increase the real burden of existing debt, borrowers focus on deleveraging rather than taking on new debt regardless of interest rates. This was the dynamic Irving Fisher identified in the Great Depression and that Japan experienced in the 1990s.

Lack of productive investment opportunities: If businesses don't see profitable opportunities, either because of overcapacity, technological stagnation, or structural problems they won't borrow to invest regardless of low rates. Easy money might inflate asset prices but not create real economic growth.

Evidence of the pushing-on-a-string phenomenon includes:

Reserves piling up: If banks accumulate massive excess reserves rather than lending them out, it indicates credit transmission is broken. This was visible after 2008 when bank reserves exploded due to quantitative easing but lending growth remained tepid.

Declining money velocity: Velocity of money measures how many times a dollar circulates through the economy. Declining velocity indicates money is sitting idle rather than being spent or invested. Velocity has declined dramatically since 2008, suggesting much of the monetary stimulus never reached the real economy.

Asset price inflation without growth: If monetary stimulus inflates stock and real estate prices but doesn't generate robust GDP growth or wage increases, it suggests the money is stuck in financial markets rather than flowing to productive uses. This creates dangerous inequality and asset bubbles without solving underlying economic problems.

Ineffective forward guidance: Central banks increasingly rely on forward guidance, promises about future policy as a tool. If markets stop believing or responding to this guidance, the tool loses effectiveness. This might show up as markets pricing in rate hikes despite the Fed promising to keep rates low, or vice versa.

Negative rates failing: Several central banks have experimented with negative interest rates, essentially charging banks to hold reserves in hopes of forcing them to lend. The results have been disappointing, with limited credit growth and potential perverse effects like banks being reluctant to pass negative rates to depositors, compressing their margins.

The pushing-on-a-string problem is particularly dangerous because it represents true policy impotence. When central banks pull out every tool and nothing works, when they've cut rates to zero, implemented unlimited QE, provided forward guidance, and still can't generate growth or inflation, what's left? Markets that have built their entire risk models on the assumption of central bank support face the terrifying realization that the support might be ineffective.

This was the specter that haunted policymakers in 2009 and 2010: what if massive monetary and fiscal stimulus wasn't enough? What if the economy remained mired in depression despite unprecedented intervention? While the recovery eventually came, it was slow and uneven, raising legitimate questions about policy effectiveness.

The combination of policy exhaustion signals, central bank credibility loss, fiscal limits, political gridlock, currency stress, coordination breakdown, and pushing-on-a-string ineffectiveness creates maximum financial market fragility. When all policy tools are exhausted or ineffective, markets have no safety net. The Fed put expires. Fiscal cavalry isn't coming. International coordination fails. Currency markets spiral. And nothing policymakers do makes any difference.

This is the nightmare scenario that should concern investors most: not simply a crash caused by economic weakness or valuation excess, but a crash that occurs when policy authorities are powerless to arrest it. The 1930s provides the historical template, when governments and central banks tried various policies but couldn't break the deflationary spiral until World War II spending finally provided sufficient stimulus.

Recognizing policy exhaustion signals doesn't mean you can predict exactly when a crisis will occur or precisely how it will unfold. But it does mean you can assess whether the policy safety net that has supported markets for decades remains intact or whether it's becoming unreliable. If multiple policy exhaustion signals are flashing, if central bank credibility is eroding, fiscal space is limited, politics are gridlocked, currency markets are stressed, international coordination is breaking down, and monetary policy seems ineffective then markets are vulnerable in a way they haven't been during any crisis since at least the 1970s and perhaps since the 1930s.

In such an environment, traditional assumptions about buying the dip, the Fed put, or inevitable recovery become dangerously unreliable. The normal playbook, stay invested because authorities will support markets no longer applies. This doesn't necessarily mean investors should panic or go to cash entirely, but it does mean risk management becomes paramount. Defensive positioning, diversification, liquidity buffers, and psychological preparation for a different type of crisis than those experienced over the past forty years all become essential.

The hardest part is that policy exhaustion tends to build gradually over years or even decades, making it easy to ignore until a crisis reveals the weakness. Markets can remain elevated even as policy space shrinks, creating a false sense of security. The warning signs are there for those who look carefully, but they rarely trigger immediate consequences. Until they do. And by then, it's too late for adjustment, you can only endure the storm with whatever preparation you've made in advance.

Part VI: Preparing for the Inevitable

Chapter 18

Investment Strategies for Uncertain Times

The hardest part of investing isn't recognizing that markets will crash, it's figuring out what to do about it. Those who liquidate everything and move to cash at the first sign of trouble often watch from the sidelines as markets continue climbing for years. Meanwhile, those who ignore all warning signs ride the elevator all the way down, clutching their portfolios as they evaporate. The challenge is finding the middle path: maintaining enough exposure to participate in continued growth while building resilience for the inevitable downturn.

This chapter isn't about predicting the next crash or timing your exit perfectly. Instead, it's about constructing a portfolio that can weather extreme turbulence while still allowing you to sleep at night and meet your long-term goals. Think of it as financial architecture designed for an earthquake country, you're not trying to predict when the big one will hit but you're sure as hell making sure your foundation can handle it.

The Fallacy of Perfect Positioning

Before we dive into specific strategies, we need to address a dangerous fantasy that haunts investors during uncertain times: the belief that you can position yourself to profit from a crash while risking nothing if you're wrong. This is the siren song that has wrecked countless portfolios.

Consider the investor who, convinced a crash is imminent, buys put options on the S&P 500. If markets rise another twenty percent over the next year, those puts expire worthless, a total loss. If markets trade sideways, the puts still decay to zero due to time premium. Only if markets crash quickly enough and severely enough does the strategy pay off. This investor hasn't eliminated uncertainty; they've made a leveraged directional bet that requires precise timing.

Or take the person who moves entirely to cash in 2020 at the first sign of pandemic trouble. They avoided a thirty percent drawdown in March, true but they also missed the sixty percent rally that followed by year's end. Worse, with inflation running hot, their "safe" cash position lost purchasing power every day it sat idle.

The uncomfortable truth is that there is no free lunch in portfolio construction. Every defensive move you make carries an opportunity cost. Every aggressive position increases your vulnerability. The goal isn't to eliminate these tradeoffs but to manage them intelligently based on your specific circumstances, risk tolerance, and time horizon.

Defensive Positioning Without Missing Growth

The first principle of uncertain-times investing is maintaining exposure to assets that can grow while reducing vulnerability to severe drawdowns. This isn't about going to cash, it's about quality over quantity, about owning businesses that can survive and thrive through economic stress.

The Quality Bias

During market manias, quality becomes boring. When speculative garbage is doubling monthly, blue-chip companies grinding out steady earnings growth feel like watching paint dry. But this dynamic reverses violently when markets crash. The companies with strong balance sheets, consistent cash flows, pricing power, and proven management teams don't just survive, they often use crises to gain market share as weaker competitors fail.

What defines quality? Start with return on invested capital (ROIC). Companies that consistently generate high returns on the capital they deploy have something valuable, a competitive moat, a strong brand, operational excellence, or a combination of all three. Look for businesses that have maintained high ROIC through previous economic cycles, not just during good times.

Next, examine the balance sheet. Companies carrying excessive debt relative to earnings become distressed when credit markets freeze or revenue stumbles. A simple metric: look for debt-to-EBITDA ratios below three, and prefer companies that could service their debt even if earnings fell thirty percent. During the 2008 crisis, heavily leveraged companies saw their stocks crater even when their underlying businesses remained viable, simply because markets feared bankruptcy.

Free cash flow generation matters enormously. Companies that convert earnings into actual cash can weather storms, invest opportunistically, and return capital to shareholders through buybacks and dividends even when markets panic. Beware of businesses that report impressive accounting earnings but never seem to generate cash, these are often concealing deteriorating fundamentals behind aggressive accounting.

Sector Rotation and Defensive Anchors

Not all sectors are created equal when markets get choppy. Consumer staples, healthcare, and utilities have historically provided ballast during crashes. People still need to eat, take medications, and keep the lights on regardless of market sentiment. These sectors won't make you rich overnight, but they can prevent portfolio devastation.

This doesn't mean loading up entirely on defensive sectors, that would sacrifice too much upside. Instead, consider them as portfolio anchors. If your portfolio normally allocates sixty percent to equities, perhaps shift that allocation during uncertain times: reduce high-beta technology and discretionary spending plays to forty percent of the equity allocation, and position twenty percent in defensive sectors. You're still participating in equity markets, but you've reduced volatility and drawdown risk.

Within technology, a sector many investors have no desire to abandon given its long-term growth trajectory favor established profitable companies over unprofitable growth stories. The companies generating billions in free cash flow and trading at reasonable valuations will fare far better than those trading on dreams and narratives when sentiment shifts.

The Role of Cash in a Portfolio

Cash gets a bad rap among aggressive investors. "Cash is trash," they proclaim, pointing to guaranteed purchasing power erosion from inflation. During bull markets, holding cash feels like volunteering to lose money. Yet cash serves critical functions that transcend its return profile.

Cash as Optionality

The most powerful aspect of cash isn't its safety, it's the optionality it provides. When markets crash, cash becomes enormously valuable because it allows you to buy assets at distressed prices. This optionality has real value even if you never use it, much like insurance has value even if you never file a claim.

Think back to March 2020. Investors with substantial cash positions could buy high-quality stocks at forty percent discounts. Those fully invested not only lacked buying power but often faced the opposite problem: needing to raise cash by selling into the crash to meet expenses or margin calls. The psychology of this is devastating, watching opportunities fly by because you're tapped out or, worse, forced to sell at the bottom.

How much cash should you hold during uncertain times? This depends entirely on your personal situation. For someone with stable income, adequate emergency reserves, and a long time horizon, keeping five to ten percent of your portfolio in cash provides meaningful dry powder without sacrificing too much market exposure. For someone nearing retirement or with lumpy income, twenty to thirty percent might be appropriate.

Tiering Your Cash

Not all cash is created equal in terms of purpose. Consider structuring your cash in tiers:

Tier One - Emergency Reserves: This is your six-to-twelve-month living expense buffer, held in FDIC-insured accounts. This cash is never invested, never touched except for genuine emergencies. It's not part of your investment portfolio, it's financial bedrock.

Tier Two - Tactical Reserves: This is the dry powder for opportunities, typically five to twenty percent of your investment portfolio. It sits in money market funds or short-term Treasury bills, earning some yield while remaining instantly accessible. This is the cash that buys the crash.

Tier Three - Strategic Cash: This represents deliberate underweighting of risk assets based on valuation concerns. If you normally maintain eighty percent equity exposure but valuations are extreme, you might drop to sixty percent, with that twenty percent difference sitting in cash-like instruments until opportunities improve. This isn't market timing per se, it's valuation-aware allocation adjustment.

The critical point: never feel pressure to deploy cash just because you have it. One of the most expensive mistakes investors make is forcing capital into mediocre opportunities because holding cash feels uncomfortable. Better to hold cash earning two percent and wait for exceptional opportunities than to chase yield into increasingly risky assets.

Gold, TIPS, and Inflation Protection

Inflation has returned to the conversation after decades of dormancy, and with it, renewed interest in inflation-hedging assets. But not all inflation hedges are created equal, and their effectiveness depends on the type of economic stress you're hedging against.

The Case for Gold

Gold occupies a strange place in modern portfolios. It generates no cash flows, has limited industrial use, and its price seems to fluctuate based on collective sentiment rather than fundamental valuation. Yet throughout human history, gold has maintained purchasing power through wars, currency collapses, and financial crises.

Gold's value in a portfolio comes from its negative correlation to traditional assets during stress events. When stocks crash and bonds fail to provide sufficient offset (particularly if inflation is high), gold often rallies as investors seek safety and inflation protection. During the 2008 crisis, gold rose while stocks collapsed. During the inflation surge of the 1970s, gold increased twenty-five fold while stocks went nowhere for a decade.

The research on optimal gold allocation suggests five to ten percent of a portfolio provides meaningful diversification benefits without excessive drag during periods when gold underperforms. This is enough to matter when you need it, not so much that it becomes a speculative position.

One critical consideration: gold performs best during crises that involve currency debasement or loss of confidence in central banks. During deflationary crashes where the concern is economic collapse rather than inflation (like 1929-1933), gold's performance has been more mixed. Know what you're hedging against.

Treasury Inflation-Protected Securities (TIPS)

TIPS offer a more straightforward inflation hedge than gold: their principal adjusts with the Consumer Price Index, ensuring you maintain purchasing power. When inflation runs hot, TIPS outperform nominal bonds. When inflation stays low, they lag.

The challenge with TIPS is their negative real yields in recent years. You might preserve purchasing power, but you're not growing wealth. Still, for the portion of your portfolio allocated to bonds, TIPS provide better inflation protection than nominal Treasuries when inflation expectations are rising.

A reasonable approach: allocate twenty to thirty percent of your fixed-income exposure to TIPS, with the remainder in nominal Treasuries of varying maturities. This provides some inflation protection without fully committing to negative real yields.

Real Assets and Commodities

Beyond gold and TIPS, consider broader commodity exposure through funds that invest in energy, agriculture, and industrial metals. Commodities tend to perform well during inflationary periods and poorly during deflations. They're volatile, cyclical, and timing-dependent but a small allocation (perhaps five percent of a portfolio) can provide valuable diversification.

Real estate, whether through REITs or direct ownership, offers another inflation hedge with the added benefit of income generation. Property values and rents typically rise with inflation over long periods. However, real estate also carries substantial leverage risk and illiquidity, so treat it as a distinct allocation rather than a substitute for other inflation hedges.

Short Volatility Risks Hidden in Portfolios

One of the most insidious risks facing investors today is hidden short volatility exposure, strategies that collect small premiums consistently but occasionally suffer catastrophic losses. Many investors have this exposure without realizing it.

The Volatility-Selling Epidemic

Selling options has become democratized. Retail investors now routinely sell covered calls on their holdings to "generate income," not recognizing that they're capping their upside for small premiums. Investment funds employ complex option strategies marketed as "low volatility" or "enhanced yield" that systematically sell insurance against market crashes.

This works beautifully until it doesn't. Selling volatility is like picking up pennies in front of a steamroller, you collect small consistent profits until the day you get crushed. The 2018 "Volmageddon" event saw several volatility-targeting funds collapse overnight, with investors losing everything.

Audit your portfolio for short volatility exposure. Are you in funds that employ option overlay strategies? Do you sell covered calls or cash-secured puts regularly? Have you invested in "low volatility" strategies that may actually be implicitly short volatility? These positions amplify risk precisely when you most need protection.

Leverage by Another Name

Many modern investment products embed leverage in ways that aren't immediately obvious. Leveraged and inverse ETFs, structured notes with participation rates and caps, and certain private credit investments all use leverage or derivatives to amplify returns (and risks).

The problem isn't leverage itself but hidden or misunderstood leverage. If you're going to use leverage, do so explicitly and with full understanding of the risks. Better yet, avoid it entirely during periods of market uncertainty. Leverage transforms corrections into catastrophes.

Quality Over Momentum

Market momentum, the tendency of winning stocks to keep winning is one of the most persistent factors in finance. During bull markets, momentum strategies crush value-focused approaches. But momentum has an Achilles heel: it performs horribly during trend reversals and high volatility regimes.

When markets crash, momentum strategies suffer twice, first from owning the most overvalued, overbought names, and second from the forced deleveraging as momentum signals reverse. The stocks that were working magnificently last month become the biggest losers this month.

Quality, by contrast, shows its worth during dislocations. High-quality businesses may lag momentum during manias, but they provide ballast during crashes. They're boring and that's exactly the point.

A practical approach: during normal market conditions, maintain a balanced allocation between momentum and quality factors. As warning signs accumulate and valuations stretch, rotate toward quality. You'll give up some upside if the party continues, but you'll preserve capital when the music stops.

This doesn't mean abandoning growth entirely. Some high-quality companies also offer strong growth prospects. The key is avoiding low-quality momentum plays, unprofitable companies trading on narratives, stocks with deteriorating fundamentals held up by technical buying, and sectors where valuations have detached entirely from reality.

Portfolio Construction: Putting It All Together

Theory is useless without implementation. Here's how to construct a portfolio for uncertain times based on different investor profiles:

Conservative Portfolio (Low Risk Tolerance, Short Time Horizon)

- 30% High-quality large-cap stocks (focus on dividend aristocrats, low debt)

- 15% Defensive sector equity (healthcare, consumer staples, utilities)
- 30% Investment-grade bonds (mix of TIPS and nominal Treasuries)
- 15% Cash and short-term fixed income
- 5% Gold
- 5% Real estate or commodities

This portfolio prioritizes capital preservation while maintaining some growth potential. The substantial cash and fixed-income allocation provides stability, while equity exposure is focused on quality and defense.

Moderate Portfolio (Balanced Risk Tolerance, Medium Time Horizon)

- 35% High-quality large-cap stocks
- 15% International developed market stocks (quality-focused)
- 10% Defensive sectors
- 20% Fixed income (blend of investment-grade bonds, TIPS)
- 10% Cash
- 5% Gold
- 5% Alternative diversifiers (commodities, real assets)

This maintains meaningful equity exposure for growth but with quality bias and diversification. The cash allocation provides optionality without excessive defensiveness.

Aggressive Portfolio (High Risk Tolerance, Long Time Horizon)

- 40% Diversified equity (quality tilt but maintaining growth exposure)
- 15% International markets (developed and emerging)
- 15% Small/mid-cap stocks (quality-focused)
- 10% Fixed income (primarily TIPS for inflation protection)
- 10% Cash (tactical reserves)

- 5% Gold
- 5% Alternatives

Even aggressive investors benefit from quality focus and modest defensive positioning during uncertain times. This portfolio maintains substantial equity exposure but with enough quality bias and diversification to survive a major drawdown without forced liquidation.

Dynamic Rebalancing and Risk Management

Static portfolios are fine during calm markets, but uncertain times demand more active risk management. This doesn't mean day trading or constant tinkering, it means systematic rebalancing based on risk metrics rather than calendar dates.

Volatility-Based Rebalancing

Instead of rebalancing quarterly regardless of market conditions, consider rebalancing when portfolio volatility exceeds certain thresholds. If your target equity allocation is sixty percent but market turbulence has pushed your actual exposure to seventy percent through appreciation, rebalance back to target. Similarly, if a crash drops you to fifty percent exposure, add to equities systematically.

This approach naturally buys low and sells high without requiring market timing. You're simply maintaining your target risk level, which automatically means taking profits during manias and deploying capital during crashes.

Drawdown Limits

Establish hard limits on portfolio drawdowns that trigger defensive action. For example, if your portfolio declines twenty percent from its peak, you might reduce equity exposure by ten percentage points. If it falls thirty percent, reduce another ten percentage points. These rules prevent the paralysis that often afflicts investors during crashes, when you have a predetermined plan execution becomes mechanical rather than emotional.

Equally important: establish rules for re-risking when markets recover. If your portfolio regains lost ground and reaches new highs, gradually restore equity exposure to target levels. This ensures you don't stay permanently defensive after a crash passes.

Correlation Monitoring

During crashes, correlations surge toward one diversification fails precisely when you need it most. Monitor the correlation structure of your portfolio regularly. If assets that normally provide diversification begin moving in lockstep with equities, that's a warning sign that systemic risk is rising.

When correlations surge, consider moving toward truly uncorrelated or negatively correlated assets: cash, gold, long-dated Treasuries. These are the only reliable diversifiers during market panics.

The Psychology of Defensive Positioning

The hardest part of implementing these strategies isn't intellectual, it's emotional. You will feel stupid holding substantial cash while markets continue rising. You will question your quality bias when speculative junk triples. You will be tempted to abandon defensive positioning after watching others get rich while you lag.

This is where discipline separates investors who survive crashes from those who don't. Remember: the goal isn't maximizing returns in all environments. The goal is achieving satisfactory returns while avoiding catastrophic losses. Taleb's advice is apt: "Never do anything that might result in your ruin, even if the probability is low."

Consider the opportunity cost of catastrophic loss. If your portfolio drops sixty percent, it must gain one hundred fifty percent just to break even. That's years of compounding lost. Meanwhile, if you sacrifice some upside to avoid that sixty percent drawdown, you may compound steadily through the crisis and emerge far ahead of those who rode the elevator down and up.

The Power of Staying in the Game

The most successful long-term investors aren't those who hit home runs, they're those who avoid striking out. They maintain consistency, protect capital during crashes, and compound steadily over decades. They're boring, but they're wealthy.

Your job during uncertain times isn't to predict the future or position for maximum returns. It's to construct a portfolio that keeps you in the game regardless of what happens. If markets continue rising, you participate. If they crash, you survive and have capital to deploy. Either way, you're still standing, still compounding, still building wealth.

This is the essence of antifragility in investing: building systems that may not optimize for every scenario but can handle almost any scenario without breaking. It's the difference between being right and staying solvent, between paper gains and realized wealth, between investing and gambling.

When to Adjust and When to Stay the Course

The final critical skill is knowing when your defensive positioning has served its purpose and when to maintain discipline despite discomfort.

Stay the course when markets rise and you feel left behind. This is precisely when defensive positioning feels most painful and when it's most important to maintain. Bull markets can continue far longer than seems rational. Your cash and quality bias may underperform for years. That's the price of insurance, and it's worth paying.

Adjust when fundamental conditions change meaningfully. If extreme valuations normalize, if credit markets show health, if policy tools are replenished, these might justify gradually reducing defensive positioning. The key word is gradually. Never rush from defensive to aggressive in a single move. Scale into risk as conditions warrant.

Be especially alert to false signals. Markets often rally sharply early in crashes before resuming their decline. Economic data lags market action. Sentiment can shift from panic to euphoria in days. Don't abandon your defensive strategy because of short-term moves or superficial improvements in conditions.

Trust your framework, not your feelings. If your indicators suggest continuing caution, maintain your defensive positioning regardless of how you feel about it. If your framework suggests conditions have genuinely improved, adjust accordingly. The framework should be mechanical enough to remove emotion from decision-making while flexible enough to respond to changing conditions.

Remember that investment strategy isn't about being perfectly positioned for one outcome, it's about being adequately positioned for a range of outcomes. Your defensive strategy should work well enough if markets crash, acceptably if they muddle through, and tolerably even if they continue rising. It won't be optimal for any single scenario, but it will be robust across scenarios.

That robustness more than any specific prediction or positioning is what allows you to navigate uncertain times successfully and build lasting wealth regardless of when the next crash arrives.

Chapter 19

Lessons from Those Who Saw It Coming

History remembers the prophets who correctly predicted crashes, but it often forgets the complicated truths of their stories. Being right about a market crash sounds like a ticket to wealth and vindication, yet the reality is far more nuanced and often darker. This chapter examines those rare individuals who saw catastrophe coming, acted on their convictions, and lived to tell the tale, along with those who saw it coming but couldn't survive being early, or who let their success destroy them.

The lessons here aren't just about identifying market tops. They're about the psychological, professional, and practical challenges of acting on bearish convictions in a world designed to punish skeptics. They're about the razor's edge between genius and ruin, between vindication and bankruptcy, between wealth and self-destruction.

Jesse Livermore: The Man Who Made Millions Twice and Lost Everything

Jesse Livermore's story is perhaps the most instructive and tragic in the history of market speculation. In 1907, he shorted the market during a financial panic and made three million dollars, a fortune worth hundreds of millions today. Then, in 1929, he did it again, shorting at the peak and extracting another hundred million from the crash. He was vindicated twice, wealthy beyond imagination twice, and dead broke twice. He eventually took his own life in 1940, penniless and forgotten.

The 1929 Vindication

In the summer of 1929, Livermore recognized the signs he'd seen before. The fevered speculation, the margin buying, the taxi drivers giving stock tips, the new paradigm thinking it all reminded him of previous manias. While the rest of Wall Street celebrated the "New Era," Livermore quietly accumulated short positions.

The conventional wisdom says he shorted the very top and rode it down, but the reality was messier. He built his position over months, enduring painful paper losses as the market continued rising through September. His brokers grew nervous. His wife questioned his judgment. Friends who knew about his positions thought he'd lost his mind.

When Black Thursday arrived on October 24, 1929, Livermore's positions exploded in value. As panic sellers overwhelmed the market, every point the market fell added millions to his fortune. By the time the dust settled, he'd extracted roughly one hundred million dollars from the crash making him one of the wealthiest men in America.

The Psychology of Shorting

What made Livermore successful wasn't just recognizing the bubble, it was having the psychological fortitude to maintain short positions while losing money and facing ridicule. Shorting requires a unique mindset. You're fighting human optimism, institutional momentum, and the natural upward bias of markets. You're paying carrying costs daily while waiting for vindication that may never come.

Livermore understood something crucial: markets can remain irrational far longer than you can remain solvent. He sized his positions to withstand the pain of being early. He used his own capital rather than leverage that could force liquidation. He accepted that he might look like a fool for months or even years.

But here's the darker truth: the psychological traits that allowed Livermore to short the 1929 top were the same traits that eventually destroyed him. His willingness to stand against the crowd became contrarianism for its own sake. His confidence in his market timing became arrogance. His discipline in risk-taking eventually gave way to gambling.

The Unraveling

Within a few years of his 1929 triumph, Livermore had lost everything again. He tried to time the bottom and went long too early. He overtraded. He became convinced he could predict every market move. The man who had shown discipline in building short positions over months began taking impulsive gambles on daily wiggles.

The lesson isn't that being right about crashes doesn't matter, it's that one successful trade, no matter how spectacular, doesn't ensure lasting wealth. Livermore's genius was episodic, not systematic. He could read market psychology brilliantly, but he couldn't build a sustainable approach to wealth management. Every triumph planted the seeds of his next defeat.

For modern investors, Livermore's story offers a warning: even perfect market timing can't save you from yourself. If you're fortunate enough to sidestep a crash or profit from it, what you do next matters far more than the trade that got you there. Preservation of capital and sustainable strategy trump any single moment of brilliance.

Michael Burry and the Subprime Short: The Cost of Being Early

Michael Burry's story, immortalized in "The Big Short," represents a more modern example of profitable crash prediction but one that nearly destroyed him in the process. His experience illuminates how the institutional investment world punishes those who position for crashes, even when they're ultimately proven right.

The Lonely Analysis

In 2005, Burry began analyzing subprime mortgage bonds and recognized what should have been obvious: they were fundamentally mispriced. Lenders were making loans to borrowers who couldn't possibly repay. These loans were being packaged into securities that ratings agencies stamped with AAA ratings. The whole structure depended on home prices never declining.

Burry's analysis was meticulous. He didn't rely on gut feelings or vague concerns, he read hundreds of mortgage prospectuses, examined default data, and constructed models showing the inevitable collapse. His conclusion was clear: this was the big short opportunity of a lifetime.

The problem? He reached this conclusion in 2005. The housing market didn't peak until 2006. Subprime securities didn't collapse until 2007. The real devastation didn't hit until 2008. In the investment world, being two to three years early is indistinguishable from being wrong.

The Professional Cost

Burry managed money for outside investors through his fund, Scion Capital. When he began buying credit default swaps on subprime mortgage bonds, essentially insurance that paid off if the bonds failed, he was using his investors' capital to bet against the entire financial system.

For months, then years, these positions bled money. Credit default swaps have carrying costs; you pay premiums monthly for your insurance. Meanwhile, the housing market kept rising. His investors watched their statements each month showing losses on these esoteric positions they didn't understand.

The phone calls started. Polite at first, then angry. What was he doing? Why was he betting against the American economy? When would he close these losing positions? Several investors demanded their money back. Some threatened legal action. His largest investor insisted he halt the strategy entirely.

Burry had to make an excruciating decision: close the positions and admit defeat, or restrict redemptions and force his investors to stay while he waited for vindication. He chose the latter, effectively locking investors in while their portfolios showed losses. Legally, he had the right. Professionally, it was near-suicidal.

The Vindication and Its Aftermath

When the subprime market finally collapsed in 2007-2008, Burry's positions exploded in value. Investors who'd demanded redemptions watched from the sidelines as those who remained made returns exceeding four hundred percent. Burry had been spectacularly, undeniably right.

Yet he closed his fund shortly after. The psychological toll of those years, the investor anger, the professional isolation, the constant doubt had exhausted him. He'd made generational wealth for his investors and himself, but at an enormous personal cost.

More importantly, several investors who'd been forced to wait years for vindication sued him anyway. They argued that regardless of the ultimate outcome, restricting redemptions was improper. Some who'd stayed and made enormous returns still resented the years of uncertainty and paper losses.

The Career Risk of Contrarianism

Burry's experience exposes a fundamental problem with institutional money management: the incentive structures punish those who position for crashes, even if they're right.

Consider the math from a portfolio manager's perspective. If you position defensively and are wrong, markets continue rising, you underperform peers, lose assets under management, and potentially lose your job. If you position defensively and are right but early, you underperform for years, face redemptions, and may go out of business before vindication arrives. Only if you're right and well-timed do you benefit, a narrow range of outcomes.

Meanwhile, if you stay fully invested and optimistic, you perform well during bull markets (which represent most of the time), keep clients happy, gather assets, and earn fees. If a crash comes, you lose money but so does everyone else. You have company in misery, and clients typically don't redeem during market crashes because there's nowhere better to go.

This explains why so few professional investors position defensively even when they privately harbor concerns. The career risk of being a lonely bear is simply too high. Better to be wrong with the crowd than right alone.

For individual investors, this creates opportunity. You don't face redemptions. You don't have quarterly performance rankings. You can afford to be early, to underperform during late-stage bubbles, to position defensively without career risk. This is one of the few structural advantages individual investors have over professionals, use it.

Paul Tudor Jones: Predicting the 1987 Crash

Paul Tudor Jones offers a different model: a trader who called a crash, profited enormously, and built a sustainable career afterward. His approach and the lessons he drew from his success provide a healthier template than Livermore's tragedy.

The Setup

By 1987, Jones was already a successful trader, but the October crash made his reputation. Throughout 1987, he became increasingly concerned about market valuations and technical patterns that reminded him of 1929. He began positioning his fund for a major decline.

What distinguished Jones from many crash prophets was his methodology. He didn't just express a bearish view, he constructed a portfolio designed to profit from volatility and decline while limiting losses if he was wrong. He used options to create asymmetric payoffs: positions that would lose limited amounts if markets continued rising but would explode in value during a crash.

When October 19, 1987 arrived, Black Monday, when markets fell twenty-two percent in a single day Jones's fund reportedly gained close to sixty percent. He'd positioned for catastrophe and been vindicated with precise timing.

The Sustainable Approach

What happened next separates Jones from Livermore. Rather than seeing his 1987 success as proof of his prophetic abilities, Jones viewed it as one good trade. He didn't assume he could repeat it at will. He didn't lever up and try to predict the next crash.

Instead, he built a systematic approach to risk management that assumed he didn't know the future. He became famous for the phrase "defense wins championships," emphasizing capital preservation over home-run swinging. His fund focused on managing downside risk in all environments, not just positioning for crashes.

Jones also recognized that crashes are rare events. You can't build a career solely on predicting discontinuities. Between crashes, you need strategies that perform acceptably during normal markets. His approach evolved into a global macro strategy that could adapt to various environments rather than a one-note bearish positioning.

The Lesson of Adaptability

Jones's story teaches that successful crash prediction isn't about your one great call, it's about what you do before and after. Before the crash, you need a framework for risk management that doesn't depend on perfect timing. After vindication, you need the humility to recognize that you got lucky on timing even if your analysis was sound.

The traders and investors who build lasting success don't predict crashes, they build robust portfolios that can handle crashes whenever they arrive.

They use position sizing, options, diversification, and dynamic risk management to ensure that no single market call determines their fate.

This approach lacks the drama of Livermore's story. It won't make you a legend by extracting a fortune from a single crash. But it will let you survive and compound over decades, which matters far more than any single spectacular trade.

Jeremy Grantham: The Professional Permabear

Jeremy Grantham represents yet another archetype: the institutional investor who has built a career on skepticism and bubble-calling. His firm, GMO, has called several major market peaks, including the 2000 tech bubble and the 2008 housing bubble. Yet Grantham's experience shows both the value and the limitations of perennial bearishness.

The Value of Historical Perspective

Grantham's approach is rooted in historical analysis. He studies how asset valuations revert to mean over long periods. When valuations reach extremes, he sounds alarms. When they normalize, he becomes more constructive. This framework has served him well in identifying major bubbles.

In the late 1990s, GMO's analysis showed that technology stocks were trading at unprecedented valuations relative to earnings, sales, and assets. Grantham warned that a crash was inevitable. For this, he endured years of mockery as tech stocks continued soaring. GMO lost clients who couldn't tolerate underperformance.

When the tech bubble burst in 2000-2002, Grantham was vindicated. Technology stocks fell eighty percent. GMO's defensive positioning preserved capital. Vindication felt sweet after years of ridicule.

Similarly, in 2006-2007, Grantham warned that housing prices and associated securities were in a bubble. Again, the warnings seemed premature. Again, he was eventually proven right by the 2008 crisis.

The Cost of Constant Warnings

Yet here's the complication: Grantham has also warned about bubbles that didn't burst, at least not on expected timescales. He's called the post-2009 bull market a bubble multiple times. He's warned that U.S. stocks are overvalued for most of the past fifteen years. Some of these warnings may eventually prove correct, but the timing has been off by years or even a decade.

For GMO's clients, this creates a dilemma. The firm's long-term track record is strong, and its major crash calls have been accurate. But spending years underinvested waiting for crashes that don't come exacts an opportunity cost. Clients who joined GMO in 2010 expecting the next crash waited over a decade while markets tripled.

This exposes a challenge with crash-focused investing: markets spend far more time rising than falling. If you're perpetually defensive, you'll occasionally look brilliant but often lag. Your long-term returns may be acceptable but not spectacular.

Finding the Right Bear

Grantham's value isn't in perfect timing, it's in providing a skeptical counterweight to prevailing optimism. In a world where most institutions are structurally bullish (they need markets to rise to justify fees and grow assets), having voices warning about overvaluation serves a purpose.

For individual investors, the lesson is to listen to the Granthams of the world without letting them dominate your strategy. When serious, thoughtful analysts warn that valuations are extreme, take it seriously.

Adjust your positioning, reduce risk, build in protection. But don't go to cash entirely and wait years for vindication that may not come on your timeline.

Think of bears like Grantham as providing valuable signals about risk levels, not timing signals for when to exit markets entirely. When they're warning loudly, that's a sign to be cautious, quality-focused, and defensive. It's not necessarily a signal to liquidate everything.

John Paulson: One Great Trade

John Paulson's story combines elements of Burry's analysis with Livermore's ultimate lesson. Paulson made one of the most successful trades in history by betting against subprime mortgages, personally making billions. Yet his post-crisis track record has been mixed at best, illustrating how even spectacular crash predictions don't guarantee sustained investment excellence.

The Subprime Score

Like Burry, Paulson recognized the housing bubble and positioned his funds to profit from its collapse. His approach was even more aggressive: he raised dedicated funds specifically to bet against subprime mortgages, telling investors explicitly that this was a one-time opportunity to profit from an obvious mispricing.

The results were historic. His main credit fund returned nearly six hundred percent in 2007. Personally, Paulson made roughly four billion dollars, perhaps the largest single-year payday in investment history. He became a legend overnight.

The Aftermath

What's less celebrated is what happened next. Paulson expected severe inflation to follow the Fed's crisis response, so he positioned heavily in gold and gold mining stocks. Gold did rally for several years, but then collapsed. His gold funds lost enormous amounts.

He made other macro bets that failed to pan out. His performance in the 2010s was poor enough that he returned outside capital and converted his firm to a family office. The man who'd made one of history's great trades couldn't translate that success into sustained performance.

The Danger of Single-Trade Thinking

Paulson's experience reinforces a critical lesson: one successful crash prediction doesn't make you an oracle. The specific conditions that made the subprime short obvious, fraudulent lending, mispriced securities and inevitable defaults don't repeat precisely. Fighting the last war rarely works.

Moreover, the mindset required to make a massive, high-conviction bet on a crash can become a liability. If you've made billions betting against conventional wisdom once, you may be tempted to try it again even when the setup isn't as clear. Contrarianism becomes a hammer, and every market looks like a nail.

For investors drawing lessons from Paulson's story, the takeaway is humility. Even if you successfully navigate a crash and sidestep losses or profit from them don't assume you've gained supernatural market insight. One correct call doesn't mean the next ten will be correct. Stay humble, stay systematic, and never bet so much on a single view that you can't recover from being wrong.

Robert Shiller: The Academic Prophet

Robert Shiller offers a different model entirely: the academic who built valuation frameworks that identified bubbles but who never personally managed money to profit from them. His story shows that you can be right about market overvaluation without needing to trade on it aggressively.

The Frameworks

Shiller developed the cyclically-adjusted price-to-earnings ratio (CAPE ratio, also called the Shiller P/E), which compares stock prices to ten-year average earnings adjusted for inflation. This framework showed that stocks were overvalued in 1996-2000 and again in 2006-2007. Both times, he wrote about it publicly. Both times, markets eventually crashed.

What Shiller didn't do was short the market or position aggressively for crashes. Instead, he provided frameworks for understanding valuation and risk. He wrote books, gave interviews, and educated investors about historical patterns. He let others decide how to act on his analysis.

The Luxury of Academia

Shiller could afford this approach because he wasn't managing money. He faced no redemptions, no quarterly performance reviews, no clients demanding action. He could be early by years without professional consequences.

This actually made his warnings more valuable. Unlike fund managers who might have conflicts of interest (talking their book) or career pressures (needing to time the market precisely), Shiller could be objective and patient. His analysis was about what was likely to happen eventually, not what would happen next quarter.

The Lesson of Separation

Shiller's approach suggests a useful separation: analysis and action can be distinct activities. You can recognize that markets are overvalued without making aggressive bets on imminent collapse. You can use frameworks like the CAPE ratio to inform your positioning, perhaps reducing equity exposure from eighty percent to sixty percent when valuations are extreme without trying to call the exact top.

This measured approach sacrifices the possibility of Livermore-like profits from perfect market timing. But it also avoids the career and psychological risks of aggressive bearish positioning. You participate in late-cycle gains (though with reduced exposure), preserve capital better during crashes, and avoid the pain of being extremely early.

Common Threads and Critical Lessons

Examining these varied experiences reveals several common lessons about crash prediction and successful navigation:

Being Right Isn't Enough

Every person discussed here was fundamentally correct about major market overvaluation. Yet their outcomes varied wildly, from Livermore's suicide to Shiller's successful academic career. Being right about the analysis is merely the beginning. Position sizing, timing, psychological resilience, and what you do after vindication matter as much or more.

Early Equals Wrong in the Short Term

Nearly everyone who successfully predicted crashes suffered through periods of looking foolish. Burry faced redemption demands. Grantham lost clients. Even Livermore endured paper losses before his 1929 vindication. The market's ability to stay irrational exceeds most investors' ability to maintain contrarian positions.

This means that if you position for a crash, you must size positions to survive being early. You need psychological fortitude to endure ridicule.

You need financial resources to withstand carrying costs and opportunity costs. Most investors lack one or more of these requirements.

One Great Trade Doesn't Make a Career

Livermore and Paulson both made spectacular profits from single trades, yet neither sustained long-term success. Meanwhile, Jones and Shiller built frameworks for risk management that worked across multiple cycles. The lesson: process trumps outcomes. One successful crash trade might be luck; a repeatable framework for risk management is skill.

Career Risk Is Real

For professional investors, positioning aggressively for crashes is career suicide unless you're exactly right on timing. Burry nearly lost his fund despite being correct. This creates a systematic bias toward underestimating crash risk in the institutional investment world, a bias individual investors can exploit by being more patient and independent.

Humility After Vindication

The most successful crash prophets shared one trait: they didn't let vindication inflate their egos. Jones emphasized defense over prediction. Shiller continued focusing on frameworks rather than market calls. Grantham acknowledged his timing misses alongside his successes.

The least successful let vindication convince them they could predict everything. Livermore became increasingly reckless after his 1929 score. Paulson made increasingly aggressive macro bets after his subprime success. Pride, not ignorance, preceded their falls.

Applying These Lessons

What should modern investors take from these stories?

First, recognize that successfully navigating crashes isn't about calling the top perfectly. It's about building portfolios that can handle crashes whenever they arrive. Think like Jones building robust risk management, not like Livermore trying to time the perfect short.

Second, accept that defensive positioning will feel wrong most of the time. If you build in protection when valuations are extreme, you'll underperform during the final manic phase of the bubble. That's the cost of insurance. Pay it willingly if you want protection.

Third, don't let one successful crash navigation convince you that you've unlocked market secrets. Humility and systematic approaches beat hubris every time. Even if you're fortunate enough to sidestep or profit from a crash, return to your disciplined framework rather than making increasingly aggressive bets.

Fourth, separate analysis from action. You can believe markets are overvalued without making career-ending bets on imminent collapse. Adjust your positioning gradually based on valuation frameworks. Reduce risk when appropriate, increase it when valuations normalize, but never go all-in on any single view.

Finally, remember that the goal isn't to be the next Livermore making a legendary fortune from one trade. The goal is to be the investor still standing decades from now, having navigated multiple cycles, preserved capital during crashes, and compounded steadily through recoveries. That's the real success, boring, methodical, and wealthy.

Chapter 20

The Crash After the Crash

The initial crash is terrifying. Watching your portfolio hemorrhage value, seeing wealth evaporate in hours or days, enduring the psychological trauma of a market in freefall, it's the stuff of nightmares. But here's what most investors don't realize until they've lived through it: the first crash is rarely the end of the story. In fact, the period after the initial plunge is often more treacherous, more psychologically devastating, and more wealth-destructive than the crash itself.

This chapter examines what happens after markets crater, the false rallies, the second and third legs down and the grinding bear markets that destroy hope more thoroughly than any single day of panic. Understanding these patterns won't let you time the bottom perfectly, but it will help you avoid the classic mistakes that turn survivable losses into permanent capital destruction.

The Myth of V-Shaped Recovery

Modern investors have been conditioned by recent history to expect V-shaped recoveries. The 1987 crash recovered within two years. The 2020 pandemic crash recovered within five months. Even the 2008-2009 crisis saw markets bottom within eighteen months and recover to new highs within five years. This has created a dangerous assumption: crashes are buying opportunities, bottoms are quick and obvious, and patient investors who buy the dip are rewarded promptly.

But this pattern is the exception, not the rule. Throughout history, major market crashes have typically been followed by extended bear markets with multiple false bottoms, grinding declines, and years of sideways trading before genuine recovery begins.

The 1929-1932 Experience

The 1929 crash is instructive precisely because it defies the V-shaped recovery narrative. The initial crash in October 1929 saw the Dow Jones fall from 381 to 198, a forty-eight percent decline in just a few weeks. Devastating, but not unprecedented.

What happened next was the real destroyer of wealth. The market rallied back to 294 by April 1930, a forty-eight percent gain from the lows. Investors who bought the crash felt vindicated. Newspapers declared the worst was over. The recovery seemed underway.

Then the real bear market began. From that April 1930 high, the market ground lower for another two and a half years. By July 1932, the Dow bottomed at 41, an eighty-six percent decline from the 1929 peak, and an eighty-six percent decline from that false recovery high in 1930. Investors who thought they'd bought the bottom in late 1929 or early 1930 lost everything anyway.

The Dow didn't regain its 1929 peak until 1954, twenty-five years later. Anyone who bought the initial crash and held on needed more than two decades just to break even in nominal terms. Adjusted for deflation during the Great Depression, the real break-even came sooner, but the nominal psychological impact was devastating.

The 2000-2002 Tech Wreck

The tech bubble offers a more recent example. The Nasdaq peaked in March 2000 at 5,048. It then crashed forty-three percent to 2,853 by December 2000. Many investors saw this as a buying opportunity, the correction everyone had been waiting for. Tech stocks were finally reasonably priced, or so it seemed.

But the decline had barely started. Over the next eighteen months, the Nasdaq fell another sixty percent from that December 2000 level, bottoming at 1,114 in October 2002, a seventy-eight percent decline from the peak overall. Investors who bought what they thought was the bottom in late 2000 still lost sixty percent.

The Nasdaq didn't regain its March 2000 peak until 2015, fifteen years later. For individual tech stocks, the picture was even grimmer. Cisco, which peaked at $80 in 2000, traded below $15 in 2002 and still hasn't regained its 2000 peak more than two decades later. Countless other tech darlings went to zero entirely.

Why Crashes Have Crashes

The pattern repeats because crashes unfold in phases, each driven by different dynamics:

Phase One - The Panic: This is the initial crash that makes headlines. It's driven by fear, forced liquidations, margin calls, and the sudden recognition that valuations were absurd. This phase is dramatic but often relatively brief, days to weeks.

Phase Two - The Relief Rally: After the panic subsides, markets rally sharply. Bargain hunters emerge. Shorts cover. Headlines declare the worst is over. This rally can be substantial, forty percent or more is common. It feels like the recovery has begun.

Phase Three - The Grind: Reality sets in. The underlying economic problems that caused the crash aren't resolved. Corporate earnings decline. Unemployment rises. Credit markets remain frozen. The market enters a grinding decline or sideways churn that slowly destroys hope. This phase can last years.

Phase Four - The Capitulation: Eventually, after months or years of grinding losses and false rallies, investors give up entirely. The final holders throw in the towel. Sentiment reaches maximum pessimism. This is often the actual bottom, but it's nearly impossible to identify in real-time because it looks like a rational response to terrible conditions.

Dead Cat Bounces and Bull Traps

The relief rally after the initial crash is so reliable that it has its own terminology: the dead cat bounce. The phrase, morbid as it is, captures the essence even a dead cat will bounce if it falls far enough. The rally isn't driven by improving fundamentals but by the mechanical dynamics of oversold conditions and short covering.

These rallies are dangerous precisely because they look and feel like genuine recoveries. Volume increases. Breadth improves. Technical analysts point to bullish chart patterns. Media sentiment shifts from panic to cautious optimism. Every indicator suggests the worst is over.

Characteristics of False Rallies

How can you distinguish a false rally from a genuine recovery bottom? There are no perfect indicators, but certain patterns repeat:

Duration and Magnitude: False rallies tend to be sharp but brief. They unfold over days or weeks rather than months. They recover thirty to fifty percent of the initial decline but rarely more. When the rally stalls, it rolls over quickly rather than consolidating.

Leadership Quality: False rallies are often led by the most damaged stocks, the speculative garbage that fell hardest initially. Quality names lag. This makes sense mechanically: the worst stocks have the most short interest to cover and attract the most aggressive bottom-fishing. But it's a warning sign that the rally is technical rather than fundamental.

Economic Disconnect: During false rallies, economic data continues deteriorating even as markets rise. Unemployment keeps climbing. Corporate earnings keep missing. Credit spreads remain elevated. The market is rallying despite the fundamentals, not because of them.

Low Conviction: False rallies tend to occur on declining volume or erratic volume patterns. They lack the steady accumulation that characterizes genuine bottoms. Professional investors remain skeptical even as retail investors pile in.

Sentiment Extremes: Paradoxically, false rallies often generate extreme bullish sentiment very quickly. After weeks of panic, investors are desperate for good news. A rally of any magnitude triggers FOMO and declarations that the bottom is in. Genuine bottoms, by contrast, tend to occur when sentiment is thoroughly destroyed and skepticism persists even as markets rise.

The Second Leg Down: When Hope Dies

The second major decline, the one that follows the relief rally is often more psychologically devastating than the initial crash. The initial crash, while scary, happens quickly enough that many investors don't fully process the losses. They're in shock, somewhat paralyzed, waiting to see what happens next.

The relief rally then provides false comfort. Investors tell themselves they were smart to hold on. They didn't sell at the bottom. The recovery has begun. Some even add to positions, confident the worst is behind them.

When the second leg down begins, these psychological supports crumble. Investors realize the rally was a trap. They watched their portfolios recover somewhat, only to see those gains evaporate and losses mount beyond the initial crash lows. The hope that sustained them through the first decline dies.

The 2008-2009 Pattern

The financial crisis demonstrates this pattern clearly. Bear Stearns collapsed in March 2008, and markets fell through the summer. But the truly catastrophic phase didn't begin until September 2008 with Lehman Brothers' bankruptcy.

After the initial panic in September-October 2008, markets rallied into early January 2009. The S&P 500 climbed from around 800 to 940, a seventeen percent gain. Many investors saw this as the recovery beginning.

Then the second leg hit. From January through March 2009, markets fell another twenty-seven percent, ultimately bottoming at 666 on March 6, 2009. This leg down was slower but more demoralizing than the initial panic. It ground away hope day by day, week by week.

Investors who'd held through the initial crash often sold during this phase. Having survived the panic and waited through the rally, they couldn't endure watching their portfolios hit new lows. The psychological impact of hope deferred and then destroyed proved too much.

Ironically, of course, March 2009 was the actual bottom. Those who sold in the final capitulation missed the entire subsequent bull market. This is the cruel irony of bear markets: the actual bottom tends to occur when conditions look darkest and hope is most thoroughly extinguished.

Secular Bear Markets: The Long Grind

Not all crashes are followed by grinding bear markets, but the worst ones are. A secular bear market is a prolonged period, typically lasting a decade or more during which markets make little to no progress in nominal terms and lose ground in real (inflation-adjusted) terms.

1966-1982: The Forgotten Bear

The Dow Jones peaked at 995 in February 1966. Sixteen years later, in August 1982, it closed at 777, a twenty-two percent decline in nominal terms. During that period, inflation ran rampant, with prices roughly tripling. In real terms, investors lost about seventy percent of their wealth.

This wasn't a single crash followed by recovery. It was a series of brutal declines interrupted by rallies that failed to reach new highs. Markets crashed in 1970, rallied, crashed again in 1973-1974, rallied, crashed again in 1980-1982. Each time, investors who bought the rally hoping for recovery to new highs were disappointed.

The psychological toll was immense. Investors who'd experienced the 1950s bull market entered the late 1960s with high confidence. By the late 1970s, that confidence was utterly destroyed. Magazine covers declared the "death of equities." Pension funds abandoned stocks for bonds and real estate. The average investor wanted nothing to do with markets.

Of course, 1982 marked the beginning of an eighteen-year bull market but only those with fortitude to buy when pessimism was universal benefited.

2000-2013: The Lost Decade-Plus

The S&P 500 peaked in March 2000 at 1,527. It didn't meaningfully exceed that level until 2013, thirteen years later. During that period, it experienced two fifty-percent-plus crashes (2000-2002 and 2007-2009) and a few weak rallies that failed to reach new highs.

Investors who dollar-cost-averaged through this period came out fine. Those who bought the highs in 2000 and held, endured more than a decade of going nowhere. This period destroyed confidence in buy-and-hold strategies and generated an entire industry of tactical allocation approaches designed to avoid such prolonged stagnation.

The Characteristics of Secular Bears

Secular bear markets share certain characteristics:

Multiple Cyclical Swings: Rather than a single decline and recovery, secular bears feature multiple boom-bust cycles, each reaching lower real highs. You might see forty percent rallies followed by fifty percent declines, repeated multiple times.

Valuation Normalization: Secular bears typically begin from extreme overvaluation and don't end until valuations compress to below-average levels. This process can take years or decades as earnings slowly grow into excessive prices.

Economic Stagnation: Secular bears coincide with periods of economic stress, high inflation, productivity slowdowns, geopolitical instability, or financial system dysfunction. The economic problems take years to resolve.

Sentiment Destruction: Perhaps most importantly, secular bears thoroughly destroy investor confidence in equities. They don't end until the average investor views stocks as dangerous speculation rather than viable long-term investments.

Recognizing Real Bottoms: The Signs of Genuine Recovery

If crashes have multiple phases and false rallies are common, how do you recognize when the actual bottom has arrived and genuine recovery is beginning?

The honest answer is: you usually can't in real-time. Bottoms are most obvious in hindsight. However, certain conditions tend to be present at major market bottoms that can help assess probability.

Valuation Normalization

Real bottoms tend to occur when valuations have compressed to below historical averages. If markets crash from extreme overvaluation but only fall to average valuations, there's room for further decline. But when valuations reach historically cheap levels, Shiller P/E below 15, price-to-book under one, dividend yields above average the probability of a durable bottom increases.

This doesn't mean markets can't get cheaper still. In 2009, with the Shiller P/E around 13, markets were cheap but they'd been cheaper in previous major bottoms. Still, valuation provides a useful framework. It's hard to make the case that stocks are in a bubble when they're priced below historical norms.

Sentiment Capitulation

Major bottoms coincide with universal pessimism. This isn't the fear you see during initial crashes, that's panic which is different. Capitulation is the quiet giving up after months or years of hoping for recovery. It's when your brother-in-law who's always talking about stocks says he's done with them forever. It's when pension consultants recommend shifting from sixty percent equity to forty percent. It's when magazine covers declare stocks dead.

Contrarian indicators reach extremes. The American Association of Individual Investors bull-bear spread turns deeply negative. Put-call ratios spike. Investors Intelligence survey shows bears outnumbering bulls by wide margins. These extreme readings don't guarantee an immediate bottom, but they suggest much of the selling pressure has been exhausted.

Leadership Transition

At major bottoms, market leadership shifts from speculation to quality. The stocks that lead the recovery are typically those with strong balance sheets, consistent earnings, and reasonable valuations, not the speculative garbage that briefly rallied during the dead cat bounce.

You'll also see sector rotation into cyclicals and financials, which tend to lead recoveries. Defensive sectors, which outperformed during the decline, start lagging. This breadth improvement and leadership transition signal that smart money is positioning for recovery.

Economic Stabilization

Bottoms tend to coincide with stabilization (not improvement) in economic data. The key is the rate of change: when deterioration slows or stops, markets often bottom even though conditions remain poor. You're looking for unemployment claims to peak, manufacturing surveys to stop plunging, credit spreads to stop widening.

Markets are forward-looking mechanisms. They don't bottom when conditions are good, they bottom when conditions stop getting worse at an accelerating rate. Learning to distinguish between "bad but stable" and "bad and deteriorating" is crucial.

Policy Response Effectiveness

Major bottoms often require effective policy intervention. Not just any intervention, markets have usually ignored multiple policy attempts before the bottom but intervention that demonstrably addresses the underlying problem.

In 2009, the bottom coincided with stress tests proving banks were adequately capitalized and the Fed's aggressive asset purchases providing liquidity. In 2020, the bottom came when fiscal stimulus and Fed intervention made clear that the government would provide unlimited support.

The signal isn't policy action per se, there's plenty of ineffective policy intervention during bear markets but policy that markets judge adequate to address the core problem.

Building Wealth in the Aftermath

The period after a major crash bottom, once genuine recovery begins, offers the best wealth-building opportunity most investors will see in their lifetimes. Assets are cheap, sentiment is pessimistic, and the next bull market is just beginning. Yet most investors can't capitalize on these opportunities because they're traumatized, skeptical, or tapped out from losses.

The Recovery Trade

The first leg of recovery from major bottoms is typically violent and fast. Markets might gain fifty percent or more in the first year off the bottom. This initial surge recaptures the easiest gains, the panic premium that drove valuations to irrational lows.

Investors who buy during the final capitulation phase capture this entire move. Those who wait for confirmation miss much of it by the time recovery is obvious, markets have already rallied substantially. This creates the paradox: buying feels least comfortable precisely when it's most profitable.

Quality and Cyclicals

The stocks that perform best in the early recovery phase are typically quality cyclicals, companies with strong fundamentals that are highly sensitive to economic growth. Think industrials, materials, financials, consumer discretionary. These got hammered during the downturn despite solid balance sheets, creating opportunities.

Avoid the temptation to buy the most damaged speculative names. While these might bounce initially, many will ultimately fail or become permanently impaired. The goal is capturing recovery upside in companies that will not only survive but thrive.

Dollar-Cost Averaging After Crashes

If you can't identify the exact bottom and you probably can't systematic buying during the post-crash period works well. Once valuations are compressed and sentiment is negative, begin deploying capital systematically over months. You'll buy some too early and some too late, but you'll capture the average price during the bottoming process.

This requires having capital available to deploy, which brings us back to the importance of defensive positioning discussed in previous chapters. If you preserve capital during the crash, you have ammunition for the recovery. If you're fully invested and need to sell to raise cash, you've likely missed the opportunity.

The Long-Term Perspective

Major crashes and subsequent recoveries separate investors into two groups: those who use the opportunity to build lasting wealth, and those whose psychological scars prevent them from participating in the next bull market.

The investors who build wealth aren't necessarily those who timed the bottom perfectly. They're those who maintained perspective, preserved capital during the crash, and had the courage to buy when conditions looked darkest. They recognized that extreme pessimism and cheap valuations create opportunity, even when it feels terrifying to act.

The Importance of Learning from Each Cycle

Every crash and recovery teaches lessons, but only if you're paying attention. The investors who navigate future crashes successfully are often those who lived through previous ones and internalized the patterns.

What to Remember

First, the initial crash is rarely the end. Don't assume that because markets have fallen forty percent, they can't fall another forty percent from there. Preserve capital for the possibility of further decline.

Second, sharp rallies after crashes are usually false starts. Don't let a thirty or forty percent bounce convince you the recovery has begun. Wait for the signs of genuine bottoming, valuation normalization, sentiment capitulation and leadership transition.

Third, the period after major bottoms offers exceptional opportunities. When valuations are compressed and sentiment is destroyed, that's when to be greedy while others are fearful.

Fourth, every crash is different in details but similar in structure. The sequence of panic, relief rally, grinding decline, and final capitulation repeats. The catalysts change, housing bubbles, tech speculation, pandemic shocks, inflation spirals but the patterns persist.

Avoiding the Permanent Scar

The greatest danger in the aftermath of crashes isn't financial, it's psychological. Investors who lose substantial wealth often develop a permanent fearfulness that prevents them from participating in subsequent bull markets. They're so scarred by losses that they can't bring themselves to own equities even when valuations are attractive and recovery is underway.

This permanent scar turns temporary losses into permanent wealth destruction. The portfolio losses from the crash were bad; missing the entire subsequent bull market compounds the damage. You lose twice, once in the crash, and again by sitting out the recovery.

The way to avoid this trap is accepting that crashes are inherent features of markets, not aberrations. They will happen. You will experience multiple major drawdowns during an investing lifetime. Building a mindset that views crashes as inevitable and even opportunistic, rather than as proof that markets are rigged or hopeless allows you to maintain equilibrium through the cycle.

Conclusion: The Cycle Continues

The crash after the crash, whether it's a false rally that rolls over into new lows or a grinding bear market that destroys hope over years, is when many investors make their worst mistakes. They sell near actual bottoms after surviving the initial crash. They buy false rallies and then panic during the second leg down. They become so traumatized that they miss the recovery entirely.

Understanding these patterns won't let you time the market perfectly. You'll still feel fear during the second leg down. You'll still be tempted by false rallies. You'll still doubt yourself when buying during the final capitulation.

But knowledge of historical patterns provides a framework for decision-making that transcends emotion. When you understand that relief rallies are normal, you're less likely to view them as signals that the worst is over. When you know that second legs down are common, you're less surprised and more prepared psychologically. When you recognize the signs of genuine bottoming, you're more likely to act when opportunity presents itself.

The investors who build lasting wealth don't avoid crashes, they navigate them with enough skill and discipline to emerge with capital and confidence intact, ready to deploy during the recovery. They understand that the crash after the crash, terrifying as it is, represents the final hurdle before the next great opportunity.

This is the cycle that repeats throughout market history. Mania, crash, false recovery, grinding decline, capitulation, genuine bottom, recovery. Learning these patterns doesn't eliminate the pain of living through them, but it provides a map through the wilderness and maps, while imperfect, are far better than wandering blind.

Conclusion

If you've reached this point expecting a definitive prediction about when the next crash will occur, I have disappointing news: I don't know. Nobody does. Anyone claiming otherwise is either selling something or deluding themselves.

But here's what I do know with certainty: markets will crash again. Perhaps next month, perhaps next decade, but inevitably. The precise catalyst is unknowable, it might be something we're currently worried about, or it might be something that hasn't even registered as a possibility yet. The timing is unpredictable, every warning sign could flash red for years before anything happens, or everything could look fine until the day it isn't.

This book hasn't been about predicting the future. It's been about preparing for the inevitable while living fully in the present. It's about understanding that market crashes aren't aberrations or failures of the system, they're features not bugs. They're the price we pay for the extraordinary wealth-building capacity of market-based capitalism.

Markets Will Crash Again, It's a Feature, Not a Bug

Throughout this book, we've examined the parallels between the 1920s and today, the warning signs that precede crashes, the experiences of those who saw crashes coming, and the treacherous aftermath of market collapses. A pattern emerges from all this analysis: crashes are inevitable consequences of human psychology meeting financial markets.

Markets crash because humans are optimistic creatures who periodically convince ourselves that this time is different. We create narratives to justify ever-higher prices. We point to new technologies, new paradigms, new eras of prosperity. We leverage ourselves to amplify returns. We dismiss warnings as outdated thinking from people who don't understand the modern world.

And then, eventually, reality reasserts itself. Valuations matter. Fundamentals matter. Leverage cuts both ways. The new paradigm reveals itself as the old delusion repackaged. Markets crash, wealth evaporates, and we swear we'll never be so foolish again.

Until the next time.

This pattern has repeated for as long as markets have existed. The South Sea Bubble of 1720. The Panic of 1907. The Crash of 1929. The Nifty Fifty collapse of 1973-1974. The tech bubble of 2000. The housing crisis of 2008. Each time, we tell ourselves we've learned our lesson and installed safeguards to prevent future crashes. Each time, we find new ways to repeat the same mistakes.

This isn't a flaw in markets, it's a feature of human nature interacting with financial systems. Trying to create markets that never crash would require eliminating the very dynamism that makes them wealth-creating engines in the first place. The boom-bust cycle, painful as it is, serves a function: it reallocates capital from misguided ventures to productive uses, punishes excessive risk-taking, and creates opportunities for new growth.

The question isn't whether crashes will happen, they will. The question is whether you'll be prepared when they do.

The Impossibility of Precise Prediction

One of the most dangerous temptations in investing is believing that enough analysis, enough study of history, enough attention to warning signs will allow you to predict crashes with precision. This book has provided frameworks for understanding when risk is elevated, but that's fundamentally different from predicting when a crash will occur.

Consider the challenges:

Valuations can remain extreme for years. The tech bubble was obviously overvalued by 1997 standards, yet it inflated for another three years. Anyone who positioned defensively in 1997 missed enormous gains and looked foolish for years before vindication arrived. Being early is expensive.

Warning signs can persist indefinitely without resolution. Margin debt can stay elevated, credit spreads can remain compressed, sentiment can register extreme bullishness for extended periods. These conditions tell you that risk is high, not that a crash is imminent.

Catalysts are unpredictable. The subprime mortgage crisis was identifiable to careful observers years before it exploded. Yet the specific catalyst, Lehman Brothers' bankruptcy in September 2008 wasn't predictable. Markets might have continued if Bear Stearns had been allowed to fail instead, or if Lehman had been rescued, or if any number of other contingencies had played out differently.

Market psychology is non-linear. Small pieces of news can trigger crashes when markets are fragile, while major shocks might be absorbed when sentiment is resilient. The specific trigger matters less than the underlying fragility, but that fragility can persist without consequence until it suddenly can't.

This isn't an argument for ignoring warning signs, it's an argument for intellectual humility. Use frameworks to assess risk levels. Adjust your positioning based on valuations, sentiment, and economic fundamentals. Build resilience into your portfolio. But don't convince yourself that you can time the market with precision.

The investors who navigate crashes successfully aren't those who predict them perfectly. They're those who build portfolios that can handle crashes whenever they arrive and who maintain enough exposure to benefit when crashes don't materialize as quickly as feared.

Balancing Preparation with Participation

This brings us to perhaps the most difficult challenge in investing: how do you prepare for inevitable crashes while still participating in markets that spend most of their time rising?

Go entirely to cash, and you avoid crashes but miss the compounding that builds wealth. Stay fully invested in aggressive assets, and you capture all the upside but expose yourself to catastrophic drawdowns. Neither extreme works.

The answer lies in balance, a word that sounds simple but requires constant calibration. Balance means maintaining enough defensive positioning to survive crashes without sacrificing so much growth potential that you fall behind your goals. It means adjusting your exposure based on changing conditions without trying to time markets perfectly. It means building resilience while staying in the game.

This balance is personal. A thirty-year-old with stable employment, decades until retirement, and the psychological fortitude to endure volatility can maintain higher equity exposure and recover from crashes through time and additional contributions. A sixty-five-year-old entering retirement with limited flexibility to earn more and a need for portfolio stability requires more conservative positioning.

But beyond age and circumstances, balance also depends on your honest assessment of your own psychological resilience. How did you feel in March 2020 when markets fell thirty percent in weeks? Did you feel calm or panicked? Did you see an opportunity or catastrophe? Your visceral response to volatility tells you something important about your true risk tolerance, which often differs from your theoretical risk tolerance.

Build a portfolio that lets you sleep at night. If market volatility causes genuine distress, that's data suggesting you should position more conservatively than standard age-based advice might recommend. Better to sacrifice some upside and maintain psychological equilibrium than to optimize for maximum returns and panic-sell during the next crash.

Conversely, if you genuinely can maintain discipline during crashes and this is rarer than people think you can afford more aggressive positioning because you'll have the fortitude to hold through downturns or even add during them.

The key is honesty with yourself about who you are as an investor, not who you wish you were or who you think you should be.

The Danger of Permabears and Perennial Pessimism

Throughout this book, we've focused heavily on warning signs, crash dynamics, and defensive positioning. This creates a risk: that readers will conclude the appropriate stance is permanent bearishness.

That would be a mistake as costly as ignoring risks entirely.

Permabears, investors who are perpetually pessimistic about markets are always predicting the next crash. And they're always right... eventually. But they're also wrong for years or decades at a time, missing extraordinary bull markets while waiting for crashes that don't materialize on their predicted timeline.

Consider someone who went bearish in 2010, convinced that the post-crisis recovery was artificial and unsustainable. They would have been wrong for over a decade while markets more than tripled. Even being right about crashes in 2018 and 2020 wouldn't have compensated for missing the entire bull market between.

The problem with permanent bearishness is that markets have a long-term upward bias. Over extended periods, economies grow, companies create value, productivity improves, and innovation generates wealth. Markets crash periodically, but they spend far more time rising than falling. A strategy optimized for avoiding crashes necessarily underperforms over long horizons.

More insidiously, permabears often suffer from confirmation bias. Every piece of data gets interpreted as evidence of impending doom. Good economic news is dismissed as artificial or manipulated. Market rises are viewed as bubbles getting bigger rather than potentially justified gains. This mindset prevents objective assessment of conditions and traps investors in permanent defensiveness.

The goal isn't to become a permabear, it's to be a discerning participant. Stay engaged with markets. Maintain exposure appropriate to your circumstances and risk tolerance. Adjust positioning based on valuation frameworks and warning signs. But don't let caution curdle into pessimism that keeps you sidelined during the vast majority of time when markets are building wealth.

Think of it this way: you buy insurance for your house, but you don't refuse to buy a house because houses sometimes burn down. You wear seatbelts, but you don't refuse to drive because accidents happen. Similarly, you build defensive elements into your portfolio, but you don't abandon investing because crashes occur.

The investors who build lasting wealth are neither permabulls who ignore all risks nor permabears who see crashes everywhere. They're pragmatic participants who recognize both the wealth-building potential of markets and their cyclical nature. They prepare for crashes while hoping they don't happen soon. They maintain exposure while building resilience.

Building Resilience in Your Financial Life

Ultimately, preparing for market crashes is just one component of building a resilient financial life. Resilience means constructing a situation where market crashes, while painful, don't derail your plans or force desperate actions.

Multiple Sources of Security

Resilience starts with not depending entirely on your portfolio. Maintain emergency reserves in cash that can cover six to twelve months of expenses. This ensures that a market crash doesn't force you to sell investments at the worst possible time to pay bills.

Develop income sources beyond your portfolio when possible. Skills that remain valuable across economic cycles. Side income that diversifies beyond a single employer. Social capital and relationships that provide opportunities and support. The more sources of financial security you have, the less any single source including your portfolio can devastate you if it falters.

Appropriate Debt Levels

High debt loads transform market volatility into existential threats. If you're highly leveraged and markets crash, you may face margin calls, forced liquidations, or the inability to service debt from income alone. This forces sale of assets at precisely the wrong time.

Keep debt levels manageable relative to income and assets. Avoid using leverage in investment portfolios unless you're truly sophisticated and can withstand the consequences of being wrong. Remember that leverage amplifies both gains and losses and in crashes the losses come fast while the gains build slowly.

Long-Term Perspective

Resilience requires maintaining perspective across time horizons measured in decades, not days or months. If your investment horizon is twenty or thirty years, a crash that takes three years to recover from represents less than fifteen percent of your timeframe. It's a blip, not a catastrophe.

This long-term perspective allows you to make rational decisions during crashes rather than emotional ones. When everyone else is panicking about short-term portfolio declines, you can focus on whether your long-term strategy remains sound. Usually it does, which means crashes represent opportunities to buy more of what you already wanted to own, just at better prices.

Psychological Preparation

Perhaps most importantly, resilience requires psychological preparation for the inevitability of crashes. If you expect crashes, understand they're normal, and have a plan for navigating them, you're far less likely to panic when they arrive.

Run scenarios in your mind now, while markets are calm. How would you feel if your portfolio fell thirty percent? Fifty percent? What would you do? Would you sell, hold, or buy more? Walking through these scenarios mentally creates a form of exposure therapy that can reduce panic during actual events.

Understand that watching your portfolio decline will feel terrible regardless of intellectual preparation. But there's a difference between feeling terrible while maintaining discipline and feeling terrible while making destructive decisions. The former is the price of investing; the latter is avoidable.

The Path Forward

So where does this leave us? You've spent twenty chapters learning about crashes, warning signs, defensive strategies, and the psychology of market collapses. You understand the parallels between the 1920s and today. You know that crashes follow predictable patterns even when their timing remains unknowable. You've learned from those who successfully navigated previous crashes and from those who failed despite being right.

What should you actually do with this knowledge?

Start with Assessment

Begin by honestly assessing your current situation. What's your portfolio allocation? How much risk are you carrying? Do you have adequate cash reserves? Are you positioned appropriately for your age, circumstances, and psychological tolerance for volatility?

Use the warning signs discussed in this book to evaluate current market conditions. Where are valuations relative to history? What are sentiment indicators showing? How are credit markets behaving? This assessment provides context for decisions without requiring precise predictions.

Build Your Framework

Develop a systematic approach to portfolio management that doesn't depend on predicting crashes. This might include:

- Target allocations that balance growth and defense
- Rebalancing rules based on volatility or drawdown levels
- Valuation thresholds that trigger shifts toward more conservative positioning
- Cash buffers that provide optionality during dislocations
- Quality biases that emphasize resilient companies over speculative plays

Write down your framework. When emotions run high during crashes or bubbles, having a written plan helps maintain discipline.

Take Incremental Action

If your assessment reveals excessive risk or inadequate preparation, don't try to fix everything immediately. Dramatic portfolio shifts are usually mistakes. Instead, take incremental steps toward better positioning.

If you're overexposed, reduce equity positions by five or ten percentage points rather than liquidating everything. If you lack cash reserves, start building them systematically rather than selling half your portfolio at once. Gradual adjustments allow you to course-correct without making huge bets on timing.

Maintain Perspective

Remember that the goal isn't avoiding all losses or capturing every gain. The goal is achieving satisfactory long-term results while avoiding catastrophic mistakes. You will experience crashes during your investing lifetime. Your portfolio will decline, sometimes substantially. That's not failure, that's participation in markets.

What matters is whether those declines derail your long-term plans. If a thirty or fifty percent drawdown doesn't force you to sell, doesn't prevent you from meeting obligations, and doesn't destroy your psychological equilibrium, then you're positioned appropriately. The losses are temporary; your ability to recover is what matters.

Stay Engaged

Finally, don't let preparation for crashes become an excuse to disengage from markets entirely. The permabear path is as destructive as the permabull path. Markets will crash, yes but they'll also continue creating wealth, rewarding innovation, and compounding over time.

Stay engaged. Keep learning. Adjust your positioning as conditions warrant. But maintain exposure appropriate to your circumstances and goals. The worst outcome isn't experiencing a crash, it's being so fearful of crashes that you miss the wealth creation that occurs between them.

The Final Truth

We began this book by examining the 1929 crash and tracing parallels to today's markets. We've explored warning signs, studied those who successfully navigated previous crashes, and examined the treacherous aftermath of market collapses. The cumulative message might seem dire.

But here's the final truth: investors who stay disciplined, who build resilient portfolios, who maintain appropriate exposure while preparing for volatility, and who keep perspective across decades rather than days, these investors build lasting wealth regardless of crashes.

Yes, crashes will come. They'll be scary. You'll watch wealth evaporate, perhaps for months or years. You'll question your decisions and doubt your strategies. That's normal, it's the psychological price of participation in markets.

But if you've built resilience, if you have cash reserves, appropriate diversification, quality holdings, and the psychological fortitude to maintain discipline you'll survive. More than survive you'll position yourself to capitalize on the extraordinary opportunities that crashes create.

The next crash isn't a question of if, but when. You can't control the timing or the catalyst. You can't predict it with precision. But you can prepare for it, survive it, and emerge positioned for the recovery that inevitably follows.

That's not a guarantee of easy profits or painless investing. It's something better: a framework for navigating uncertainty while still building wealth over time. It's the knowledge that crashes, terrifying as they are, represent temporary disruptions in the long-term wealth-creation capacity of markets.

The investors who compound wealth across lifetimes aren't those who avoid all crashes, that's impossible. They're those who position themselves to survive crashes without permanent impairment, who maintain discipline when others panic, and who recognize that the goal isn't perfection but adequacy over long horizons.

Build your resilience. Trust your framework. Maintain your discipline. And remember that uncertainty isn't something to eliminate, it's something to live with skillfully while continuing to move forward.

The next crash is coming. You'll be ready.

www.ingramcontent.com/pod-product-compliance
Lightning Source LLC
LaVergne TN
LVHW052032200926
848481LV00005B/1650
9798232103323